Vision Critical Studies

General Editor: Anne Smith

The Art of Emily Brontë

THE ART OF EMILY BRONTË

edited by
Anne Smith

VISION

Vision Press Limited
11–14 Stanhope Mews West
London SW7 5RD

ISBN 0 85478 483 7

76·19859 (B+N)

→ 76-381542

Printed in Great Britain
by Clarke, Doble & Brendon Ltd., Plymouth
MCMLXXVI

Contents

Introduction: Towards a New Assessment

by ANNE SMITH

> Never in all her life had she lingered over any task that lay
> before her, and she did not linger now. She sank rapidly. She
> made haste to leave us. Yet, while physically she perished, men-
> tally, she grew stronger than we had yet known her.[1]

At the age of thirty, just eighteen months after the publication
of *Wuthering Heights*, Emily Brontë died. But her death was only
a beginning; and the manner of it placed her more quickly and
absolutely in that other world to which she and her works, even
in her lifetime, belonged: the enigmatic world of myth, of

> ... Undying Life ...
> So surely anchored on
> The steadfast rock of Immortality.[2]

More than a hundred years of idolatrous literature have swelled
the myth; more than a hundred years of critical interpretation,
carried out almost universally in that tone "of personal tenderness, even of passionate homage",[3] have deepened the enigma—
for Emily Brontë is still several steps ahead of her critics. Even
the iconoclasts, those who come to mock, stay to praise, and the
tenderness and homage are the result rather than the cause of
close critical reading.

In his introduction to an earlier collection of critical essays,
Ian Gregor distinguished three critical approaches to *Wuthering
Heights*: the metaphysical, which focuses on the relationship of
Cathy and Heathcliff, and seeks to find echoes of their polarity
in the novel's structure; in reaction to this, the sociological

7

approach, which is a notorious failure; and, also in reaction to the metaphysical approach, the reading of the novel as a reflection of the growth of its author's creative imagination, from Gothic fantasy to mature reconciliation.[4] None of these approaches, as Ian Gregor says, accounts for the whole novel, and when we place them side by side, their somewhat mutually exclusive interpretations only emphasize the fact that the novel seems to fall into two parts, with a rough seam binding the story of Cathy and Heathcliff to that of young Cathy and Hareton. Yet if that were all the enigma, it might be easily solved: we could call *Wuthering Heights*, like *Sons and Lovers*, an immature—or premature—production, analyse the parts, pick at the seam, and set it all down pat, leaving it to others to add the footnotes.

We don't do this – or we do it, but it leaves us unsatisfied – because, fortunately, after we have subjected *Wuthering Heights* to the wise scepticism of our critical minds, our whole selves, the human beings who have experienced the book, are still left with a sense that *Wuthering Heights* was a whole experience, the effect of an art

> Which without passing through the judgement gains
> The heart, and all its end at once attains.

It is this saving sixth sense that sends us perplexed and not a little humbled, back to the book. We all, as critics, play Heathcliff to Emily Brontë's Cathy: like Cathy, "her presence evokes maddening sensations". Somewhere, we feel, just on the edge of consciousness, there is a critical interpretation which will fit the whole novel, and lay it open at last.

Yet this, as any critic of less than tender years knows, while it is the most exciting challenge his profession has to offer, is also the most dangerous. We begin by looking for "keys" to *Wuthering Heights*, and we end up, like amateur clockmenders, with something partial, strange, and useless, while the left-over bits lie scattered around, alien but inexorable. Or we discover in our own imaginations something that Emily Brontë, the laconic beginner, left out: some further hint about Nelly's treachery, perhaps, or of an incestuous relationship between Cathy and Heathcliff, or something of the Madame Bovary, of the immature selfish commonplace bitch, about Cathy. Above all, we look for the villain who brought about this tragedy, and before it begins to function, the critical mind is already disabled by some Gothic disease. At their best such approaches have enriched our appreciation of the parts, but they never can account for the whole. And critics who have sought to interpret the whole novel have not yet succeeded in accounting for all the parts. The biggest step forward criticism of *Wuthering Heights* has taken in the past twenty years is in recognizing this; in at last acknowledging the complexity of what for too long we had allowed ourselves to be misled into thinking was "a rude and strange production".

But having gone so far, it seems we stuck. *Wuthering Heights* does not only test the maturity of its critics, it tests the maturity of our critical practice. The next step we must take, if we are ever to get to the heart of the enigma, is to recognize that Emily Brontë has something to teach us which, if we can learn it, will make us better critics. Charlotte Brontë was not entirely wrong: in its own way *Wuthering Heights* is as strange a production as *Tristram Shandy*. Comparisons with other novels have taught us very little; comparisons with poetry or plays are misleading intellectual abstractions, and criticism of this kind merely relishes the enigma, explores it but does not explain it: what appeared to be main roads have turned out to be fascinating by-ways. Indeed, one suspects, after all those years of earnest endeavour, that there is no main road in to the heart of this novel. Yet there may be a rough track somewhere which, in our comfort-loving sophistication, we have overlooked: some route to the centre which will let us experience all its variety on the way. The time has come, surely, to take a fresh look at *Wuthering Heights*, to see it steady and to see it whole.

Perhaps we should begin again at the beginning, with Lockwood. We may ask why he is in the novel at all, since he would seem to have nothing to do with the development of the narrative itself. It may be that living at the Grange he should to some extent be identified with the "civilized" life there: the man who sets out "to devastate the moors" may not be so far removed from the child who is capable of engaging in a tug of war over a puppy. And, like Isabella, Lockwood is being satirized in the novel. Yet there is a basic difference in the treatment of these two artificial characters: Lockwood is satirized by Emily Brontë herself, while Isabella is satirized by Cathy and Heathcliff, from within the novel. And in the end we are moved to pity her in a distant, perhaps even condescending way, although we cannot sympathize with her. She is the victim of her own false passion, and of Heathcliff's passion for revenge. Lockwood is invariably a complete outsider, a figure of scornful fun for the reader, who, contrary to our expectation, provides no gloss, no objective perspective, on the world he observes.

He observes the world of the novel, but he does not see it. His comment to Heathcliff, "it is strange how custom can mould our tastes and ideas" (II, 20), is ironic to the point of high comedy, considering how palpably he himself is the product of an effete culture. He brings his "busy world" to Yorkshire with him, and looks on the new scenes with his mind's eye turned inward to his memory of the old. One of the funniest incidents in the early part of his narrative is also the most revealing. It comes when he is doing his social best to engage young Cathy in conversation:

'Ah, your favourites are among these!' I continued, turning to an obscure cushion full of something like cats.
'A strange choice of favourites,' she observed scornfully. Unluckily, it was a heap of dead rabbits (II, 19).

His perceptions of reality in any form, physical or metaphysical, are invariably perverse. Emily Brontë surely knew what she was doing when she made Cathy's ghost manifest itself so tangibly to him of all people, at the end of a nightmare: ambivalence is the essence of the supernatural mode.

Lockwood's language also often postulates a degenerate reality, in phrases like "shameless boys", referring to the cupids carved above the door of the Heights; or his description of the woman with whom he flirted at the seaside as a "real goddess"; or his talk of his "susceptible heart" (I, 15), or of going "to devastate the moors" (XXXII, 241)—a phrase which both echoes the eighteenth-century "finny darters of the deep" euphuistic extremes, and looks forward to the sinister twentieth-century euphemisms of war. The artificiality of his language is clearly a means of cushioning himself from emotional reality, with which he cannot cope. Yet this becomes a positive virtue when he passes

10

on Nelly's tale, for we can be sure that any interpolation of his would be instantly detectable.

Since the language he uses is so stylized that it can only express the ready-made stereotypes of feeling, when he believes he wishes to communicate he resorts to the language of looks. But here again, he gives himself away. When he recalls his mute overtures to "the most fascinating creature" he describes her as "a real goddess in my eyes, *as long as she took no notice of me*" (my italics), then goes on

> I "never told my love" vocally; still, if looks have language, the merest idiot might have guessed I was over head and ears: she understood me at last. . . . (I, 15).

The half-conscious juxtaposition of these two thoughts, "the merest idiot might have guessed" and "she understood me at last", comically undermines Lockwood's whole pretence at having "a susceptible heart". He has either an adolescent or a homosexual fear of women—most probably the latter, if we are to judge by the next sentence, in which he confesses that as soon as the "goddess" responded in kind, he "shrunk icily back into" himself, "like a snail". There is a faint hint of woman as predator there, and, set down so close to the casual "my dear mother used to say" a few sentences back (I, 15), it provides us with a clear picture of the whole frozen emotional condition of the man. He wants no response: the language of looks, like the language of words, is a mere mirror to him, in which he can with satisfaction view himself act out the whole hollow charade of "the busy world". Lockwood most certainly is a misanthropist, with a schizoid fear of human feelings in any form, in himself or others. In the scene which immediately follows these intimate revelations of his private life, when he teases the dogs—"Not anxious to come in contact with their fangs, I sat still; but, imagining they would scarcely understand tacit insults, I unfortunately indulged in winking and making faces at the trio" (I, 16)—we have this comically underlined for us.

It is as much because of his emotional sterility as because of his distinctive language that we accept Lockwood as a reliable scribe for Nelly's tale. He takes no imaginative part in the emotions she chronicles; he cannot involve himself in the love of Heathcliff and Cathy until he has reduced it to some kind of Mudie's Library romance. This is made plain in his casual aside about Heathcliff's visit to his sickbed, when Nelly is well into her tale of his and Cathy's love: "how could I offend a man who was charitable enough to sit at my bedside a good hour, and talk of some other subject than pills and draughts. . . .?" (X, 80). Four sentences later, about to ask Nelly to resume her tale, he refers to its "hero" as if that hero were a piece of fiction, nothing to do with the man who has just visited him, with no comment at all on the strange contrast between the demonic misanthrope of Nelly's account and the man who sends grouse, and enquires after the invalid. Then, as he is about to leave the Grange for the first time, he remarks:

> What a realization of something more romantic than a fairy tale it would have been for Mrs Linton Heathcliff, had she and I struck up an attachment, as her good nurse desired, and migrated together into this stirring atmosphere of the town (XXXI, 240–1).

He has accepted Nelly's story as if it were an old nurse's fairy-tale, told during an interlude in his life when he lay like a child, ill in bed, wanting "amusement".

Yet he is not in the novel simply to provide the light relief of a Malvolio-figure, or as an excuse to have Nelly tell her tale in such a way as to make it intelligible to outsiders. He has another function, at least equally important, which can be shown by an examination of his intrusions into the narrative. When he first appears we learn of Cathy's ghost and Heathcliff's broken heart:

> "Come in! come in!" he sobbed. "Cathy, do come. Oh, do— *once* more! Oh! my heart's darling, hear me *this* time—Catherine, at last!"
>
> The spectre showed a spectre's ordinary caprice; it gave no sign of being. . . . (III, 33).

Even as Lockwood's insensitivity amuses us, it shifts our sympathies, which had up to this point been hovering around him as the hero of his own narrative, dramatically and unequivocally to Heathcliff. With the unconscious contradiction of the next lines—". . . but the snow and wind whirled wildly through, even reaching my station, and blowing out the light"—he pushes us even further towards accepting the ghost, and with it, the notion of a love that persists after death, on both sides.

Once Nelly has begun her tale, the first interruption comes just after Heathcliff has vowed his revenge on Hindley for flogging him:

> "I'm trying to settle how I shall pay Hindley back. I don't care how long I wait, if I can only do it, at last . . . while I'm thinking of that, I don't feel pain" (VII, 57).

When Nelly interrupts herself, Lockwood entreats her to go on, with "I am interested in every character you have mentioned, *more or less*" (VII, 58; my italics), then comments

> I perceive that people in these regions acquire over people in towns the value that a spider in a dungeon does over a spider in a cottage, to their various occupants; and yet the deepened attraction is not entirely owing to the situation of the looker on. They *do* live more in earnest, more in themselves, and less in surface change, and frivolous external things. I could fancy a love for life here almost possible; and I was a fixed unbeliever in any love of a year's standing (VII, 58).

This is the grudging, half-sarcastic admission of a cynic who is only partly convinced. We cannot miss the implication that where there is a wider range of potential lovers from which to choose, a lifelong love may well be *unnecessary*. In his contrast between what to him seem merely to be two extremes of love, we feel the ice of Lockwood's nature seriously for the first time, and turn away from it with a shudder to the fire of Heathcliff's passion for Cathy. It also goes a long way, by association, to reconciling us to the notion of Heathcliff's need to have revenge, no matter how long it takes. Emily Brontë promotes this reaction with many a subtle touch: for example, in having Nelly interrupt her tale of how Cathy could not eat for sympathy after Heathcliff has been flogged and banished to the attic, and of Heathcliff's two fasts, with: "I'm annoyed how I should dream of chattering on . . . and your gruel cold" (VII, 57).

When Lockwood takes his attempt at analysis further, his remarks, with their formal Johnsonian antithesis, drive the reader even deeper into a romantic reaction:

> One state resembles setting a hungry man down to a single dish on which he may concentrate his entire appetite, and do it justice;

the other, introducing him to a table laid out by French cooks. (VII, 58).

We rebel in disgust from the idea of a lover as food, and, no matter how well disguised it may be, from the Thersitic idea of the need to love as a physical appetite rather than as a quest for the fulfilment of the whole self—the kind of quest that brings Heathcliff back from the "busy world" to Cathy, and leaves him wholly unsatisfied with the more than willing Isabella.

Nelly's narrative is broken again just after Heathcliff vanishes and Cathy suffers her first illness: "I thought she was going mad . . . Mr. Kenneth, as soon as he saw her, pronounced her dangerously ill; she had a fever" (IX, 78). Lockwood, always self-conscious but never self-aware, complains during his interruption of his own "Four weeks' torture, tossing and sickness!" (X, 80). Immediately after, when he mentions Heathcliff's visit to him, the reader is obliquely reminded of Heathcliff's tormented soul, and ironically, of the comparison Lockwood made between himself and Heathcliff at first. There is always, the further we go into the novel, lurking at the back of our consciousness the suspicion that Lockwood is a comic parody of Heathcliff. Heathcliff, like Lockwood, could not speak his love at the appropriate moment; like Lockwood, Heathcliff worships a real goddess, and, for the second half of the book, the Gothic exaggeration of what Heathcliff has to say seems almost to join the rococo artificiality of Lockwood's language, at the point where extremes meet, having swerved away from reality. Both make it plain—Lockwood by the decorated formality of his speech, Heathcliff in the aggressive tone of everything he says—that they do not wish to communicate with their auditors on even faintly intimate terms. Both speak more for an invisible audience than to that which is physically present: Lockwood has "the busy world" in mind, and Heathcliff, no doubt, "whatever gods may be". But there the similarity ends, and it ends in an apparent paradox, for the invisible world to which Heathcliff addresses himself is more real in terms of the novel, has more human relevance, than Lockwood's assumed audience of fashionable society, those tin gods who devastate moors.

It is through Lockwood that we are alerted to the problem of language which Emily Brontë had to face in writing of the love of Heathcliff and Cathy: the problem of expressing a great tragic passion in nineteenth century prose. In seeing the problem, and tackling it, she showed herself to be far ahead of her time, for not until D. H. Lawrence did another novelist even attempt to find a language—a prose language—for passion. Yet her solution was one appropriate to her own time, an oblique solution, one of silences and stark contrasts. When the current language of love was so debased—by Byron's faithless reputation, by the prevailing sentimentality of the era, with its relentless socialising pressure squeezing the individuality out of people—she had to resort, like Wordsworth, to "language such as men do use", language which must inevitably offend her readers.[5] Or at least, offend their public selves, while affecting their private selves as deeply and directly as she intended it would. For anyone who has ever loved has experienced the struggle to express the uniqueness of his feeling— in the first throes, at least, as passionate as Cathy's and Heathcliff's—in the debased register of love-talk, has attempted that

> ... raid on the inarticulate
> With shabby equipment always deteriorating
> In the general mess of imprecision of feeling,
> Undisciplined squads of emotion.

Having experienced this, and seeing the process of debasement in action in Lockwood's speech, we are prepared to read *Wuthering Heights* with our sensibilities more vulnerable than they would normally be.

Lockwood's next interruption, which is brief, comes just after we learn of Isabella's "moral teething", and there is some hint that Nelly's tale has been a moral teething of a kind for him too, in a way not dissimilar to that which Isabella is undergoing. He remarks "I'll extract wholesome medicine from Mrs Dean's bitter herbs" (XIV, 130), then, after telling us that he has heard all his "neighbour's history", says, "I am so many days nearer health" (XV, 130). The lesson he has learned is expressed in his own self-centred way: "I should be in a curious taking if I surrendered my heart to [young Cathy], and the daughter turned out a second edition of the mother!" (XIV, 130): but is nonetheless something of a step forward for him. Like Isabella, if less painfully, he is learning the difference between fancy and love:

15

Tell me where is fancy bred . . .?

. . . .

It is engender'd in the eyes,
With gazing fed, and fancy dies
In the cradle where it lies.

Significantly, in her next interruption to her tale, Nelly comments: "I some way fancy no one could see Catherine Linton, and not love her . . . why have you asked me to hang her picture over your fireplace?" (XXV, 204–5). Here, Nelly's hints about Lockwood's fancy for Cathy draw from him the cautious "It may be very possible that I should love her; *but would she love me?*" (XXV, 205; my italics); which plainly shows that he has come a long way from the man he was at the beginning of the book, where he compared himself to Heathcliff with: "He'll love and hate, equally under cover, and esteem it a species of impertinence to be loved or hated again" (I, 15). This scene is the last in which Lockwood has any interest for us in himself. We can see that he is not completely "cured", but when he appears again it is only to further the narrative, and to put the finishing touch to the whole story in a voice which is suspiciously unlike his own.

Our attention shifts to Nelly, whose character is made more clear to us in this scene than it has been from what goes before. Her heavy humour—"Yet who knows how long you'll be a stranger? You're too young to rest always contented, living by yourself" (XXV, 204)—must be taken as at least a half-serious hope that Lockwood will pursue his fancy. We could guess that she is teasing Lockwood here for her own amusement, but there is nothing in the rest of the book to confirm that, and more than enough to show that she likes him. To Linton, whom she dismisses as "a pale, delicate, effeminate boy" (XIX, 163), she is quite pitiless: "Happily . . . he'll not win twenty! . . . and small loss to his family, whenever he drops off" (XXIII, 195). To Lockwood, who resembles Linton in many respects, and whose teasing of the dogs is brought back to us by Heathcliff's comment on Linton, "He'll undertake to torture any number of cats if their teeth be drawn, and their claws pared" (XXVII, 219), she is pleasantly companionable:

16

"Are you feeling better this morning?"
"Much."
"That's good news" (X, 81).

Up to this point it was possible to take Nelly's friendliness to Lockwood as a matter of manners, or of enjoying the novelty of so exotic a stranger. Here we see that she is sincere, and it comes as something of a shock. Until this scene, Nelly's role in the novel could have been interpreted as normative, both in terms of the whole novel and of her own story. She has tried to operate as an emotional thermostat—as well as being the reed that bends —cheering up the despondent, or toning down flights of fanciful conceit; constantly striving for the even tenor of existence which seems to be the summit of her desires:

> The twelve years, continued Mrs Dean, following that dismal period, were the happiest of my life: my greatest troubles . . . rose from our little lady's trifling illnesses (XVIII, 155).

In her longing for peace and order, Nelly has provided the most effective counterpoise to the passion of Cathy and Heathcliff. She has seemed to represent an equally active life, but one that rests on the instinctive, soothing rituals of domesticity, as opposed to their dangerous struggle for individual freedom and fulfilment. The fact that she herself has no children stresses all the more that hers is an alternative way of life, rather than a female necessity. Part of the power of *Wuthering Heights* springs from Emily Brontë's ability to contain and dramatize this most basic of human dilemmas, between the yearning for a love that will fulfil and transcend our mere humanity, and the instinct to merge into the simple, thoughtless rhythm of existence, to be part of a greater whole.

We have more or less from the beginning of Nelly's tale taken her at her own word, and believed that she is "a steady, reasonable kind of body" who has been "taught wisdom" through "sharp discipline" (VII, 59). From that point, where she presents her credentials as a narrator, we are inclined to believe that her character is as clear-cut, and statically conceived as Lockwood's. Doubts about this creep in gradually as the story progresses, until they are finally confirmed when we see her so misjudging Cathy, or Lockwood, or both, as to encourage a match between them.

17

This scene sends us back through the whole novel, to revise our estimate of her. Lockwood is not quite the throw-away narrative device he at first appears to be: Emily Brontë has used him to great effect throughout the novel.

The choice of Nelly Dean as a narrator was a master-stroke: only such a character as Nelly, with her rich folk-culture and bit of self-education, could have presented the love-story of Cathy and Heathcliff so convincingly, and without imposing her own moral judgement on the reader. It is her language, with its unselfconscious allusions to folklore and to domestic detail that sustains the arch between the degenerate classicism of Lockwood's language and the equally degenerate romantic hyperbole which is all language can offer Heathcliff to express a passion for revenge worthy of the Jacobean theatre, and a love beyond death. At the same time, it is she who sustains the most crucial, and fruitful, tension in the novel: that between the civilized, Christian world and the rough pagan world of superstition.

Although the supernatural pervades the whole texture of *Wuthering Heights*, we are never allowed, finally, to believe or to disbelieve it. We keep Nelly company in this right to the end, to her remark after she comforts the shepherd-boy who believes he has seen the ghosts of Cathy and Heathcliff:

> He probably raised the phantoms from thinking, as he traversed the moors alone, on the nonsense he had heard his parents and companions repeat—yet still, I don't like being out in the dark now; and I don't like being left by myself in this grim house (XXXIV, 265).

But to say that Nelly, the old nurse with her fund of "nursery lore", is most responsible for the supernatural tremor that keeps us rivetted to her story, is not to claim that she is in any sense its villain. On the contrary, Nelly is the most fully-drawn, complete human being in the novel—or possibly in any novel, for that matter. She is enigmatic because she is so perfectly ordinary, a pragmatic peasant in a world of neurotic dreamers.[6] And because she is such a perfect creation, we have to go outside the novel to find some rule-of-thumb means of assessing her, and of appreciating Emily Brontë's achievement.

18

It is relatively easy to account for Emily Brontë's mastery of the supernatural: her reading in the Bible; her acquaintance with what Mrs Gaskell described as

> mad Methodist magazines full of miracles and apparitions, and pre-ternatural warnings, ominous dreams, and frenzied fanaticism; and the equally mad letters of Mrs Elizabeth Rowe from the Dead to the Living;[7]

then *Blackwood's*, with its tales of the supernatural, and finally her readings in the German romantics. Yet all of these together, one would be inclined to argue, would really only tend to endorse a more potent, because more intimate influence, there beside Emily Brontë every day, for almost the whole of her short life: that of the Brontë's servant, Tabby.

When Tabby came to Haworth she was already an "elderly woman", according to Mrs Gaskell, and old enough to remember "the 'bottom' or valley, in those primitive days when the fairies frequented the margin of the 'beck' on moonlight nights", and to have "known folk who had seen them". Mrs Gaskell also tells us – probably with one eye on *Wuthering Heights* – that Tabby had "many a tale to tell" to the Brontë children of

> . . . family tragedies, and dark and superstitious dooms; and in telling these things, without the least consciousness that there might ever be anything requiring to be softened down, would give at full length the bare and simple details.[8]

—just as Nelly does. Whether or not Tabby was the original for Nelly Dean is unimportant; what *is* important is that she was steeped in supernatural lore, believed much of it, and could reconcile these beliefs with the Christianity which became a parsonage servant. The ability to live with such an apparently vital contradiction in one's basic beliefs is not a mental feat; it is, rather, characteristic of human nature, and only the more obvious in the unsophisticated. Christianity did not eradicate superstition, as Mrs Gaskell makes plain in her comment on the state of belief in Haworth in the first quarter of the nineteenth century: "the people of this district are 'strong religionists;' only, fifty years ago, their religion did not work down into their lives".[9] The same would be true of the Scottish Highlands today, and, perhaps, of all isolated rural districts, for it would seem that the industrial

19

revolution had more to do with breaking down belief in unholy ghosts and fairies than Christianity did. By Emily Brontë's time —perhaps, even, after James Hogg—ghosts had begun to be metaphors or symbols of a disease of the soul. They were less substantial than they had been, but they were still there. And it is just at that point of ambivalence that Emily Brontë found them so useful to her purpose, beginning with Lockwood's "awakening" from a dream of Christianity at its grimmest to find the ghost of Cathy outside his window, and his unsuccessful attempt to dismiss the experience as a nightmare. In this scene (III, 32–3) it is made evident that Heathcliff does believe in Cathy's ghost, wholeheartedly. His anguish attracts the reader's sympathies, more especially after Lockwood's terrified cruelty, and from that it is but a step to the willing suspension of disbelief—then, enter Nelly Dean, whose role it is, for the purposes of the story, to sustain that state of mind in the reader, and, when necessary, to encourage it.

For Nelly herself, always so ready to dismiss other people's irrational fears as "a bit of superstition", has a mind full of automatic references to the supernatural. When Heathcliff leaves his supper untouched on Christmas Eve, for example, she says it "remained on the table all night for the fairies" (VII, 53). She later says of Heathcliff "it appeared as if the lad *were* possessed of something diabolical at that period" (VIII, 61) although there are perfectly good reasons for his asocial behaviour. It is Nelly who casually relates an experience of second sight:

> I gazed long at the weather-worn block . . . it appeared that I beheld my early playmate seated on the withered turf . . . I started—my bodily eye was cheated into a momentary belief that the child lifted its face and stared straight into mine! It vanished in a twinkling; but, immediately, I felt an irresistible urge to be at the Heights. Superstition urged me to comply with this impulse (XI, 94).

She then goes to the Heights, speaks to Hareton of his "devil daddy", catches sight of Heathcliff, and turns and runs down the road "as hard as ever I could race . . . feeling as scared as if I had raised a goblin" (XI, 95–6). This instance of the supernatural seems to be largely gratuitous, since Hindley does not die for at least another two and a half months, and Cathy's death takes place in the interim. All through the novel, in more subtle ways than this, Nelly is adding her little touches of the supernatural—as when, for example, she says to Cathy "We're dismal enough without conjuring up ghosts and visions to perplex us" (Cathy has made no mention of ghosts) . . . then adds an aside to Lockwood, "I was superstitious about dreams then, and am still" (IX, 72).

Nelly's Christianity partakes of the same ambivalence. It is the pragmatic Christianity of the Yorkshire peasantry, very much a religion of this world—a code of conduct for other people, and a present help to oneself—absorbed only imperfectly by a mind already saturated with folklore, and only then, at the points where it comes closest in its dogma to the ethic of the supernatural, with its rough justice. Try as she might, Nelly can't quite quell the still small voice that protests against the Christian doctrine of forgiveness. Watching Cathy's corpse, she reflects:

> I see a repose that neither earth nor hell can break; and I feel an assurance of an endless and shadowless hereafter. . . .
>
> To be sure, one might have doubted, after the wayward and impatient existence she had led, whether she merited a haven of peace at last (XVI, 137).

The comfort Christianity offers the living lies for the most part in its assurance of the finality of death: not that the soul doesn't go on into eternity, but that it goes on in a purified—or perhaps just neutralized—state.

All Nelly's account of Heathcliff's dying days, and of his death, suggests that he has gone to hell, and that hell is the concept which appeals most directly to the local imagination—"the country folk, if you asked them, would swear on their Bible that he *walks*" (XXXIV, 265). Heathcliff's smile in death terrifies Nelly, whereas Cathy's had comforted her. It is strange, but not surprising, that it never occurs to her to wonder how Cathy and Heathcliff could walk as ghosts together, with her soul in heaven and his in hell. The enigma of *Wuthering Heights* lies in such contradictions; in their being contradictions that the human mind does not resist, but, as often as not, actually welcomes. Nelly's pragmatism sustains this enigma at the deepest and most convincing level. For at the root of her irrational attitudes and be-

21

haviour is the fact that she is faithful to everything she has learned —whether from "sharp discipline", or the church, or the folklore she presumably absorbed at her mother's knee—and can only discard bits of her "wisdom" when they are *proven* false.

In many respects, Nelly is an archetypal mother figure. Much of her nature fits in with Jung's definition: "her life is lived in and through others, in more or less complete identification with the objects of her care. . . . Her Eros develops exclusively as a maternal relationship while remaining unconscious as a personal one. . . . The mind . . . usually remains in its original condition, altogether primitive, unrelated . . . but also as true, and sometimes as profound, as Nature herself".[10] If we see Nelly in this way, the contradictions in her attitudes and behaviour do not undermine her character, but actually enrich it, almost beyond the dreams of a critic's avarice.

There are some indications that we should see her as a mother figure, apart from the more obvious one that she is the only maternal person in the orphaned world of the novel—Emily Brontë having taken pains to ensure that Zillah is no substitute for Nelly. Chiefly these consist in the quality of her responsibility: her constant but well-intentioned interference, for example, is invariably passed over with no more than a rebuke by the other characters. This might be explained away with the excuse that she is, after all, a servant, but the fact remains that she is given far more responsibility, and hence far more power, than the ordinary servant would have: "the child Hareton fell wholly into my hands" (VIII, 60). And even when her "children" have grown up and become more or less free agents, she continues to assume a mother's cares:

> I seated myself in a chair, and rocked, to and fro, passing harsh judgement on my many derelictions of duty; from which, it struck me then, all the misfortunes of all my employers sprang. It was not the case in reality, I am aware, but it was, in my imagination, that dismal night (XXVII, 220).

She suffers, too, from a mother's emotional conflicts. When she agrees to deliver a letter for Heathcliff:

> . . . in the long run he forced me to an agreement. I engaged to carry a letter from him to my mistress; and should she consent, I

promised to let him have intelligence of Linton's next absence from home, when he might come . . .

. . . I fear it was wrong, though expedient . . . I remembered Mr Edgar's stern rebuke of my carrying tales; and I tried to smooth away all disquietude on the subject, by affirming . . . that this betrayal of trust . . . should be the last (XIV, 129).

Not only has she agreed to take the letter, she has promised to betray Edgar by letting Heathcliff into his house in his absence. But before this, she has stated flatly that her heart "invariably cleaved to the master's . . . side" (X, 93).

Like the archetypal mother, it is when her "children" grow up that Nelly cannot cope, and makes many mistakes, because she does not know herself, or them, as individuals. As long as they are children she does her duty faithfully, even when she is a child herself: "when the children fell ill of measles . . . I had to tend them, and take on me the cares of a woman at once" (IV, 40). Like the archetypal mother, she keeps going though the return she gets is embarrassingly small. We wonder, for instance, why Mr Earnshaw, having picked the "dirty, ragged" Heathcliff off the streets of Liverpool, should treat him as one of the family, and continue to use Nelly like a servant, even though she and Hindley had the same nurse, Nelly's mother. After Heathcliff's arrival, Nelly is "sent out of the house" for her "cowardice and inhumanity" in leaving him on the stair landing all night. When Mr Earnshaw sets out for Liverpool he asks Cathy and Hindley what they would like him to bring back, but tells Nelly he will bring her "a pocketful of apples and pears" (IV, 38–39), and later, when he gives Hindley a colt, he gives one to Heathcliff. There is no hint of resentment in Nelly's account of all this: she seems to have matured early in many respects, in the way of her class, and to have assumed the mother-role as soon as she could. She speaks of her childhood with Cathy:

In play, she liked, exceedingly, to act the little mistress; using her hands freely, and commanding her companions: she did so to me, but I would not bear slapping and ordering; and so I let her know (V, 43).

After Mr Earnshaw's death and Hindley's marriage, when Heathcliff and Cathy are allowed to run wild, she comments:

23

. . . many a time I've cried to myself to watch them growing more reckless daily, and I not daring to speak a syllable for fear of losing the small power I still retained over the unfriended creatures (VI, 46).

She becomes a mother-figure even to Lockwood, in her role as patient nurse, and it is in her conversation with Lockwood that one of her more obvious self-contradictions comes. She encourages him to think of marriage to Cathy, whom he has seen only twice and spoken to very little, shortly after she has been telling him of her reaction to Cathy's "love" for Linton: "Pretty loving, indeed, and both times together you have seen Linton hardly four hours in your life!" (XXI, 184).

If we look at such expedience with the cold eye of logic only, it would no doubt be possible to see Nelly as the villain in *Wuthering Heights*. But I believe we only employ such "logic" as a mask, to cover our child-like disappointment because we have read the novel as if it were a folk tale, but found no witch. When we do this, we are looking at the story *through Nelly's eyes*: it is she who sees it as a folk-tale, for the only way she can understand Cathy and Heathcliff's passion is in terms of myth. Far from learning about the nature of passion as she goes over it again for Lockwood, she is fixing it for herself into the unreal world of folk myth. It is not real to her, unless as a freak storm which disturbs the emotional atmosphere and suggests to its victims thoughts of supernatural agencies. What Emily Brontë achieves through Nelly is not to tell a Byronic tale in prose twenty-four years after Byron's death. Her achievement is far more difficult and complex than that; but unless we take Nelly to be an integral part of the whole novel, we shall miss it.

Nelly is the creation of artistic maturity. Instead of marvelling at what Emily Brontë created from her inexperience, we ought to marvel at what she created from her experience. For, individualized as she is, Nelly is both in the story and symbolically everybody's mother. And, as such, she is the perfect narrator for the story of *Wuthering Heights*, because, like everybody's mother, she is the mistress of the double-bind. Having created Nelly, Emily Brontë can thrust her reader into a double-bind situation virtually any time it suits her purpose.

The double-bind she most frequently and successfully achieves is to have us believe in the easy co-existence of the material, present, Christian world and the world of the supernatural. It is the supposition, without assurance, that there is a "world beyond" in which our individuality continues into eternity, that gives the love of Cathy and Heathcliff its tragic and heroic dimension. In the characterization of Heathcliff, Emily Brontë puts the whole credibility of the novel at risk—a step too far in one direction, and he could become a mere Caliban, the Caliban who complains

> You taught me language; and my profit on't
> Is, I know how to curse: the red plague rid you
> For learning me your language!

One step too many in the other direction, and the whole story would have fallen flatly into Macaulay's definition of the Byronic "system of ethics"; "compounded of misanthropy and voluptuousness, a system in which the two great commandments were, to hate your neighbour, and to love your neighbour's wife".[11] It is Nelly's effort to understand him, imperfect though it may be, that prevents our seeing Heathcliff as a mere monomaniac, or an immature poseur.

Because we see her actively building up the demonic picture of Heathcliff, we tend to set her more superfluous hints and dire, often melodramatic forebodings—" 'But where did he come from, the little dark thing, harboured by a good man to his bane?' muttered superstition" (XXXIV, 260) – to one side, and look at him for ourselves. When we do, we accept his curses as a Lear-like challenge against a supernatural enemy, rather than the demonic maledictions Nelly implies them to be, and we half-admire him for his courage in tempting the dark gods. He is, after all, a man: his frustrated passion is entirely human, even if its object is not. We can easily believe that it is possible to have a living passion for a dead person (especially when death comes on the very edge of consummation): eternal love is a very human aspiration. Yet the belief in such a love does not fit in with the Christian doctrine of an essentially sexless heaven. Lovers for eternity, therefore, are lovers committed to the untender mercies of the dark gods. Heathcliff acknowledges this when he gives Nelly the instructions for his funeral:

No minister need come; nor need anything be said over me. I tell you, I have nearly attained *my* heaven; and that of others is altogether unvalued and uncoveted by me! (XXXIV, 263).

Nelly relegates Heathcliff to the hazy world of superstition because she cannot understand him. Her superstitious world is, in the long run, as far removed from Heathcliff and Cathy's supernatural perceptions as is Joseph's with his belief that the young Cathy might be a witch and capable of killing off the red cow. Yet it is Nelly who teaches us that superstition is the poetry of life, and prepares our sceptical minds to accept the reality of a love beyond death.

In the second half of the novel the supernatural and the material worlds diverge; references to the supernatural are, significantly, diminished to about one third as many as there are in the first part, and these are largely confined to Nelly's conversations with, or remarks about, Heathcliff. The imagery is drawn from a more serene nature, and the tone of the whole is humanistic. Indeed, a certain ordinariness creeps in, and the world of the novel seems to shrink, not despite Emily Brontë's art, but because of it. Cathy's ghost is never so poignantly real to us after we witness her death, than when we read her life with Lockwood's experience in her room in mind. Nelly quite effectively lays that ghost with her comments on Cathy's serenity in death, and by comparing her to her daughter in such a way that we feel that we have been given a new, improved version of the original. Then, although Heathcliff is present in the second half, we begin to feel that as an interesting character, he died with Cathy. In fact, for the second half of the novel we might almost say that he is the ghost of Cathy. He is as ineffectual as a ghost:

I get levers and mattocks to demolish the two houses, and train myself to be capable of working like Hercules, and when everything is ready, and in my power, I find the will to lift a slate off either roof has vanished! . . . I have lost the faculty of enjoying their destruction (XXXIII, 254–5).

And anyway, by the time we have read Isabella's story, we can predict the course his revenge will take on Cathy and Hareton, none of whose lives are felt to have any cosmic significance beyond the commonplace, if charming, process of mating for the

26

continuation of the species. In another novel, one which could exploit the twentieth-century freedom in charting intimate relationships—*The Rainbow*, for instance—that might be enough, but not in *Wuthering Heights*, and especially not after what has gone before. The childishness of young Cathy, and Nelly's dilemma of being in the position of mother and servant at the same time, are no substitute for the mature passion of Heathcliff and the dying Cathy. It is, truly, Nelly's world: Cathy and Hareton are her children. The reader is left to mourn, and might lament with Emily Brontë (or Rosina Alcona):

> Once drinking deep of that divinest anguish
> How could I seek the empty world again?[12]

—or, on a less grand scale, we might feel as the Brontë children must have done, turning their eyes outward to the parsonage again after one of Tabby's rich tales of doom. But perhaps it is our immaturity that makes us feel the break so sharply; perhaps Emily Brontë intended that there should be no comfortable solution to the human dilemma, of which kind of significance to choose to aim for in life. Certainly, she provided us with two endings to the two worlds of the book—one to the story of Heathcliff and Cathy:

"They's Heathcliff and a woman, yonder, under t'Nab (XXXIV, 265)—and one which seems to fuse it with the story of young Cathy and Hareton:

> I lingered round them, under that benign sky; watched the moths fluttering among the heath and hare-bells; listened to the soft wind breathing through the grass; and wondered how anyone could ever imagine unquiet slumbers for the sleepers in that quiet earth (XXXIV, 266).

For even if the ghosts of Cathy and Heathcliff walk, it would seem they walk together, and in peace, with a quietness that haunts the reader.

. . . and if it haunts the reader, it haunts the critic even more. Yet, as the studies in this volume will show, we are at last moving towards a more mature way of reading *Wuthering Heights*, and of appreciating Emily Brontë's poetry. Two of the most superficial ideas of her art are finally scotched here. The first is that the mass of her poetry forms a wasteland of juvenilia, not worth consideration by the serious critic, and not offering any useful insight into the greater achievement of *Wuthering Heights*. The second is that *Wuthering Heights* itself is some kind of "freak" or "sport", interesting, but again, hardly rewarding for the critic to study at length, since it has its being somewhere outside "the great tradition"—as if "what happens when a new work of art is created" were *not* "something that happens simultaneously to all the works of art which preceded it". A new idea is replacing both: the idea that Emily Brontë was a conscious artist, far ahead of her time. The studies presented here will, it is hoped, establish that idea once for all, and point the way to a new era in the understanding of her art.

NOTES

1. Charlotte Brontë's "Biographical Notice of Ellis and Acton Bell", preface to the 1850 ed. of *Wuthering Heights*, reprinted in the Norton Critical Edition, ed. W. M. Sale Jr (New York, 1963). All references to *Wuthering Heights* in this book are to Sale's edition.
2. From "No coward soul is mine", in *The Complete Poems of Emily Jane Brontë* ed. C. W. Hatfield (New York, 1941), no. 191.
3. Mrs Humphry Ward, preface to the Haworth Edition of *Jane Eyre*, quoted by Miriam Allot in *The Brontës: The Critical Heritage* (1974) p. 1.
4. *The Brontës: A Collection of Critical Essays* (Twentieth Century Views, New Jersey, 1970).
5. The *Examiner*'s reviewer, for example, complained that "the language . . . is not always appropriate" (January, 1848, pp. 21–2; quoted in Allot *op. cit.*, p. 221), and G. W. Peck, reviewing it for the *American Review* (viii, June 1848, pp. 572–85, quoted in Allot, p. 235) went much further and accused Emily Brontë of "an ill-mannered contempt for the decencies of language".
6. Perhaps this is nowhere more amusingly evident than in chapter IX, when Hindley, drunk, threatens Nelly with the carving knife. Her response is reminiscent of Brer Rabbit's in similar situations: "But I don't like the carving knife, Mr Hindley . . . it has been cutting red herrings. I'd rather be shot, if you please" (67).
7. Life of Charlotte Brontë (1857; Thornton Edition, 1905) p. 108.
8. *Ibid.*, p. 65.
9. *Ibid.*

10. C. G. Jung: *Four Archetypes* trans. R. F. C. Hull (1972, extracted from *The Archetypes and the Collective Unconscious*, vol. 9 of his Collected Works) p. 22.
11. Review of Moore's *Life of Lord Byron*, *Edinburgh Review* LIII (June 1831), p. 572.
12. Hatfield, *op. cit.*, no. 182.

PART ONE
The Poetry*

*All references in this section are to the poem numbers in *The Complete Poems of Emily Jane Brontë*, edited by C. W. Hatfield (New York, 1941).

1

"It Would Not Do": Emily Brontë as Poet

by ROBIN GROVE

Had she deliberately set out to intrigue and mystify the public, Emily Brontë could hardly have done better. Her pseudonym, like Charlotte's, was a success: who were the Bells? and were they really one poet or three? for there was enough in their work to justify curiosity. And the even keener interest when they went on to produce their novels had scarcely reached its peak before Charlotte was telling of her sisters' lives and deaths and appending a further selection of poems to the new edition of *Wuthering Heights*. "It would not have been difficult to compile a volume", she declared,[1] but offered only a "nosegay" of verses instead. Throughout the remainder of the century the glimpses of the poet that could be had were tantalizingly few, and in such odd places as *The Woman at Home* (August, 1897), though students in the field knew that there was a large terrain of poetry still unexplored. The fascination of the material was not just that at least two collections of "The Complete Poems of Emily Brontë" (1910 and 1923) were misleadingly *in*complete, but that some powerful half-buried force seemed visible in the mass of writings. The clue to that force—and indeed, some commentators thought, the solution to *Wuthering Heights* and a good deal else besides—was the discovery of Gondal. It had been known of for years; even Mrs Gaskell came upon a reference to "Emily's and my best plays"[2] in the curious packet she carried away from Mr Nicholls after a visit to Haworth; but it was not until 1923, with Madeleine Hope Dodds's article "Gondaliand",[3] that particular poems by Emily Brontë were related in a determined fashion to her childhood game or "play". Since then, however, Gondal has exerted its spell. There is something mesmerizing about the very look of the Brontë juvenilia, those tiny books and scraps of manuscript, close-packed with minute descriptions of long-dead heroes, cities, landscapes: stifling, almost indecipherable fantasies cramming the page in laborious imitation of print. Besides, what increased the magnetism of Gondal was that only fragments of it remained: the lyric high-points, for the prose tale was lost, and enthusiasts were left with the task of reconstruction—"about as difficult", wrote Derek Stanford, "as would be that of reconstructing Shakespeare's plays (supposing them to have perished) from the snatches of songs they included".[4] Yet even so the attempt to make a coherent whole of the poems has continued, and both the difficulties and the interpretative persistence with which they are met are typical. Brontë it seems is one of those writers who demands that we make sense of her total *oeuvre*. Partly because so much is left out, of her novel, her poems, and her life, we feel a need to comprehend all of the little that is there—as though that, somehow, would solve the mystery of how she came to write one work of genius. And after all, the way forward may be through the tangle of myths and unanswered questions. What legends do stand between us and her poetry, then?

I

People write of "the Brontë story", and no wonder: its details are almost too gripping for un-organized real life, but have the effect of art instead—as though someone were composing the bare facts into suspenseful fiction. Frequently, as we now know, someone was, since to Charlotte Brontë, for one, even Haworth's heightened atmosphere was not bracing and dramatic enough; so, taking what was already remarkable, she ordered and dramatized it further, intensifying situations (sincerely, no doubt) in the cadence with which she recorded them, and converting her material into highly-charged Victorian legend. It is in that style that her 1850 introductions conclude:

> This notice has been written, because I felt it a sacred duty to wipe the dust off their gravestones, and leave their dear names free of soil.[5]

Throughout the Preface and Biographical Notice the same mode persists. Essentially, it is a style to render noble femininity, talents constrained but uncrushed; it is sensitive to aspiration above all —the aspirations of the house-bound, who refuse to suffer defeat but burn with undiminished purpose, looking outwards to Nature for inspiration, or inwards to the round of duties, like a nun. And as Charlotte writes of her life, her sisters, in this enclosed air, rarely crossing "the threshold of home", we feel her fierce enlargement of domestic commonplace. The homely touches of the Biographical Notice, together with its elegiac power, result in a simplicity where every detail contributes, poignant and larger than life.

> Resident in a remote district where education had made little progress, and where, consequently, there was no inducement to seek social intercourse beyond our own domestic circle, we were wholly dependent on ourselves and each other, on books and study, for the enjoyments and occupations of life.[6]

Isolated that existence certainly was; yet Charlotte's narrative makes the Parsonage sound like the narrow environment of her own governess-fiction where time and place, agents of isolation, are painfully registered by over-wrought nerves, and any incident may be magnified to crisis under the pressure of years-long hope and frustration. No one would underestimate the deprivations of such a life, and in so far as Charlotte suffered them it is the most natural thing in the world for her account to take this tone; once adopted, however, it casts her sisters as heroines of a recognizable kind, intellectual and lonely, their "secret power and fire" at odds with meagre circumstance. This is not quite the Haworth we glimpse in Emily Brontë's diary-fragments and birthday-notes ("We are all stout and hearty", 1841, "I am quite contented for myself . . . merely desiring that everybody could be as comfortable", 1845). And while banked-up intensity may mark out a Jane Eyre or Lucy Snowe, the same style transferred from fiction into biography gives the reserves of family life a dramatic configuration, till the very furniture, scrutinized, tells tales.

> One day, in the autumn of 1845, I accidentally lighted on a MS. volume of verse in my sister Emily's handwriting.

The discovery, expertly led up to, has an effect of theatrical surprise. Its underplayed preparation, the mounting excitement as the mystery unfolds and concentrates all eyes on the thrilling object—this handling of incident is masterly. Whether it is, strictly speaking, accurate is another matter. Rather, we might prefer to say that Charlotte is creating the *quality* of events, and to her they were heroic. The story she sets out, therefore, is one of courage undimmed by defeat and not vanquished even by death. In some ways, the Life of Emily Brontë is her most compelling work of art, though it does not offer itself as art at all, but as the simple truth. At any rate its influence has been immense; through public writings, letters, anecdotes, Charlotte succeeded in displaying her sister's career as passionately original, sombrely self-determined throughout. Emily Brontë now becomes the unapproachable genius, centrepiece of the legend.

This image of her as a brooding solitary is impressive, and we will find it in the context of the poems too; indeed, it so dominates that we are likely to miss the subsidiary but formative role played by Charlotte as dramatist and fellow-actor. Yet examined again, the letters and Biographical Notice half-show, even as they half-conceal, that second figure on the stage. It is Charlotte who lights upon her sister's poetry and endeavours to fan the "sparks of honourable ambition" to flame; Charlotte to whom the other characters stand in (sometimes unwilling) relation. To her, Anne Brontë's poems are brought as to an arbiter of taste: "I could not but be a partial judge, yet I thought that these verses too had a sweet sincere pathos of their own". And when both sisters die it is she who witnesses to the inexorable spirit of the one and the calm Christian triumph of the other.

> My sister Emily first declined. The details of her illness are deep-branded in my memory, but to dwell on them, either in thought or narrative, is not in my power. Never in all her life had she lingered over any task that lay before her, and she did not linger now. She sank rapidly. She made haste to leave us. Yet, while physically she perished, mentally, she grew stronger than we had yet known her. Day by day, when I saw with what a front she met suffering, I looked on her with an anguish of wonder and love.[7]

"I looked on her": between first- and third-person pronouns the writing pulses with an insistent beat. Of course, as survivor it is Charlotte's *place* to speak for her sisters and testify to their lives. What I am pointing to is the extent to which her consciousness, throbbing and eloquent, explaining, highlighting, playing over the painful facts, is the central actor of the Biographical Notice—a document which fulfils, even as it proclaims, her wish for Emily Brontë: "An interpreter ought always to have stood between her and the world." Since 1850, it would seem, an interpreter always has.

Yet even as we learn to identify this intervening presence, a more interesting problem appears. For the difficulty of sorting out the Brontë legend is not just a matter of detecting Charlotte at work reorganizing facts. That is comparatively easy: as when she describes the fate of their *Poems*—"Ill-success failed to crush us. . . . We each set to work on a prose tale"—whereas the correspondence shows that they had already offered fiction to their publishers before the poems appeared, and well before any reviews could have come in at all.[8] Nor is it much trouble to see that Charlotte, in stage-managing her sisters' posthumous reputation, is also presenting *herself* in a dramatic light—openly in places, covertly elsewhere, and not always aware that that is what she is doing. No, the complication lies deeper, so that, despite Charlotte, the question still remains, what responsibility did Emily Brontë take for her own career as author? One detail for a start throws an unexpected crosslight on events, for whereas Charlotte's story tells of discovering "a MS. volume of verse", the fact is that Emily at the time was transcribing her poetry not into one manuscript book, but two. Moreover, her contribution to the *Poems, by Currer, Ellis and Acton Bell* comes from both sources, and just as it shows the finest talent of the sisters, so too it shows keener judgement than Charlotte or Anne could manage. Someone—Emily herself?—had a sense of what would be most publishable, and extracted those six additional pieces from the Gondal notebook to provide the best poems the Bells were able to offer. But this hardly squares with the talk of an Emily contemptuous of reputation and holding her territory private against all intruders. Gondal especially (one might think) would be the region guarded most fiercely. So the image of the rapt, unaccommodating recluse will not answer the facts. On the contrary: when the challenge was put to her and the prospect of publishing opened up, she met its demands better than either of her sisters. They produced *The Professor* and *Agnes Grey*; she produced *Wuthering Heights*. And the author of that book is not unself-knowing in the way that Charlotte judged ("Having formed these beings, she did not know what she had done");[9] instead, I will argue that she maintained a most complicated relation to her own achievements.

Partly because of her own efforts, though, and partly because of Charlotte's, it is not easy to define the responsibility Emily Brontë took for her own productions. If we ask in what way they represent *her*—in what way, that is, they are deliberately formed works of art—we find ourselves facing perplexities on two fronts. On the one hand there is the character we glimpse through the Biographical Notice and the Preface: "stronger than a man, simpler than a child."

> In Emily's nature the extremes of vigour and simplicity seemed to meet. Under an unsophisticated culture, inartificial tastes, and an unpretending outside, lay a secret power and fire that might have informed the brain and kindled the veins of a hero; but she had no worldly wisdom. . . .[10]

That is, against the literary world and its pretensions (so the phrasing implies), a country girl like Emily Brontë embodies values which the *littérateurs* who attacked her simply cannot understand: they have no chance with a personality so beyond the reach of ordinary minds—unable to obey, even to comprehend, their strictures:

> if it was complained that the mere hearing of certain vivid and fearful scenes banished sleep by night, and disturbed mental peace by day, Ellis Bell would wonder what was meant, and suspect the complainant of affectation.[11]

That seems to answer the notorious first reviewers of *Wuthering Heights*, with their accusations of unscrupulousness or deliberate perversity, and their way of talking as though a bad book were likely to start an epidemic. But combined with this account of character, is an exculpation of Emily Brontë on larger, theoretic grounds as well. For she is to be seen not only as an heroic innocent, but also as an artist. "The writer who possesses the creative gift", urged Charlotte, "owns something of which he is not always master—something that at times strangely wills and works for itself":

> Be the work grim or glorious, dread or divine, you have little choice left but quiescent adoption . . . your share in it has been to work passively under dictates you neither delivered nor could question—that would not be uttered at your prayer, nor suppressed nor changed at your caprice. If the result be attractive, the World will praise you, who little deserve praise; if it be repulsive, the same World will blame you, who almost as little deserve blame.[12]

This strenuous tone is a measure of the seriousness with which popular moral ideas are being defied. And indeed, despite a rather panting rhetoric, Charlotte's Preface to *Wuthering Heights* is more to the point than much professional criticism of the time. Yet what dangerous temptations it provided. To the image of the unyielding heroine, it adds a whole inspirational doctrine of the artist: as possessed by some daimon, and thus carried beyond conventional praise or blame. All that is lacking is the notion of Emily the mystic. Complete with that, as the legend was in a very few years,[13] the author could be freed from accountability altogether, and every critic absolved from the responsibilities of his task. On those terms the distinctive greatness of *Wuthering Heights* is inevitably concealed. Not only the novel, however, has suffered: much the same expectations have helped obscure Emily Brontë as poet.

II

I would not myself make high claims for her poetry, but it is clearly the work of a more interesting, if less thrilling, personality than Charlotte's presentation allows. That is why the first task is to escape the aura of the myth. Once outside it, everything looks different: the unapproachable monolith has gone; Emily Brontë appears to have been capable of critical reception and in-interchange, not just "inspiration", so that we see in her verse the very complexities the Brontë legend denies: influences adopted and forsaken, conventionalities, sophisticated tastes. This is not pure gain, of course: many of those influences were bad; yet, inferior stuff and all, a more valuable living poetry remains. Instead of a creativity aloft in its eyrie, obedient to nothing but its raptures, we encounter a mind whose best strength is in resistance, self-checking, self-combat—a sensibility that yearns for ideal freedom, yet finds *in* that intensity of yearning a strength to bear the weight and limitation of "reality". This is the poet in whom my interest centres, although from the tradition we would hardly guess that she exists.

Her achievement is represented by poems such as "The night is darkening round me", "Stars", "Cold in the earth", and perhaps a dozen more. (It is not an extensive claim.) Yet in putting the emphasis on these pieces one runs the risk of normalizing what is no ordinary body of work but a very strange *oeuvre* indeed. For one thing, it is astonishingly mixed in quality. For another, it shows no convincing chronological development, so that to work through C. W. Hatfield's edition, reading the poems in order, is a disconcerting experience. To be sure, a number of the finest and best-known come where we might expect, near to the end of Brontë's life; but the first lyric in the book is quite as good as most of her writing ten or twelve years later, while her last extant piece (September 1846–May 1848) handles its revenge-theme—all "taunts" and "noble gore"—as if she had never read, let alone written, *Wuthering Heights*. What we seem to have is an author who gained access to her talents rarely: from time to time, and apparently at random, wrote poems of real worth; suddenly, in the winter of 1845–46, created a masterpiece; then lapsed into melodramatics again. If that is so, then the figure of Emily Brontë becomes more, not less, perplexing the nearer we approach. Over all we might agree that the other-worldly side of her nature has been exaggerated and that, put to the test, she was capable of judging shrewdly (so that the first selection of her poems, made when she was alive, is considerably superior to the second, made by Charlotte in 1850). But taste did not stop her including a number of feeble verses, and it allowed her to settle even strong original poems into a heavily-moralized frame—their titles, sounding like those of Victorian narrative-painting, are pencilled into the manuscript not in Charlotte's but in Emily Brontë's hand.[14] She is a bewildering mixture, then, of the conventional and the free, the profound and the jejeune, and her poems taken on the whole are a more Victorian product than it is quite comfortable for admirers of the novel to admit.

Not to take the poems as a whole therefore seems to me a first requirement. Whatever prodigies of stitching and unstitching have been performed by Miss Ratchford in order to assemble her "novel in verse", *Gondal's Queen*, the plain fact is that the pieces are too uneven in quality to sustain even a suppositious plot. With some that find a place in Miss Ratchford's romance, the kindest thing is to look the other way. Yet in doing so we are likely to miss the one value these poems have—namely, their defining a point of contact between the writer and the myth. For I want now to suggest that Charlotte did not create this image of the resolute solitary without considerable help from Emily Brontë herself. It was she after all who adopted in poem after poem a high heroic pose and tried to live its implications out—as the Biographical Notice tells, however much it magnifies the facts. Indeed, so often do the poems present a sort of martyrdom that images of captivity are practically their identifying mark. Imprisonment, stoicism, the unyielding spirit: the metaphors are typical of Brontë, and so is her recurrence to them: that in itself was a need. So to start with the dominant image of her myth:

> Strong I stand, though I have borne
> Anger, hate, and bitter scorn

Such attitudes of defiance are not unique in the nineteenth century, but they appear to have been a deep necessity to Brontë. Without them, we should never have had her best poetry, and to that extent they are essential, underlying even her lyric outcries ("Through life and death a chainless soul") with a courage not just stated, but felt, in the swift buoyant accent:

> Riches I hold in light esteem
> And Love I laugh to scorn
> And lust of Fame was but a dream
> That vanished with the morn
> (Hatfield 146)

On the other hand, though, there are dangers in seeing oneself as a spiritual victor. The defiance Brontë recommends is liable to degenerate into emotional displays.

> I flung myself upon the stone,
> I howled and tore my tangled hair,

41

And then, when the first gush had flown,
Lay in unspeakable despair.

Sometimes a curse, sometimes a prayer
Would quiver on my parchéd tongue;
But both without a murmur there
Died in the breast from whence they sprung.

(H. 15)

Coleridge has something to answer for here, and so does the
Byron of *The Giaour*, all temperament and attitude-striking. Such
bad verse need not detain us, except to notice how derivative it is,
and how helplessly puppet-like the speaker appears in the grip of
her "passions"—flung down, torn, and abandoned once the first
gush of violence has gone. Assertions are taking place alright, but
they are not exactly self-assertions, despite the pronoun "I".
Rather, these attitudes which vaunt their defiance look impotent
if seen from the other side: the two states being interchange-
able, when nothing more than a notional figure—a manipulated
persona—comes between.

The first questions therefore we might ask about Brontë's verse
concern the odd status of the persona. Gondal of course she
populated with an automatic cast, and the reader might wonder
why, for her writing *appears* self-declarative, yet frequently it is
not the "self" which is being declared (not even the self of a
Gondal figure) so much as extreme states of feeling, which issue
through it and use the "I" of the poems as a mouthpiece. In this
sense the verse is impersonal—indeed, more accurately, super-
personal; and drawn to extremes as she was, she quite naturally
admits as her speakers shadowy heroes, titanic lovers, winds,
spirits, abstract qualities, and the like. Under their aegis, the pride
and undying courage most prevalent in Gondal, its passions and
Marmionesque chivalry (as Muriel Spark has called it),[15] tend to
flourish independently of character and take on a life of their own.
In fact, what seems to have drawn her to ballad-themes in the
first place is the impersonalized pattern they enable her to display. Back she came in poem after poem to the one set of situations: the prison, love betrayed, the victor and the vanquished
in the wars. Over these themes the poems mime an anguish which
only in a handful of cases is brought to impinge on and pene-

trate the self, for mostly the martial sufferings and glories are quite formulaic.

> There swept adown that dreary glen
> A wilder sound than mountain wind:
> The thrilling shouts of fighting men
> With something sadder far behind.
>
> The thrilling shouts they died away
> Before the night came greyly down;
> But closed not with the closing day
> The choking sob, the tortured moan.
>
> Down in a hollow sunk in shade
> Where dark heath waved in secret gloom,
> A weary bleeding form was laid
> Waiting the death that was to come.
>
> (H. 89)

The soldier going into battle is, evidently, a satisfying image for Brontë, just because death is foretold in his very bearing, in the splendour and bravery assigned to his part. And his recurrent figure in her verse sums up the fatalistic pattern whereby high states of being are bound to their opposites and, by a turn of Fortune's wheel, laid low. But what a very Victorian ballad this is. Despite the "inspiring" theme, its energy is at low ebb; the gloomy colours of foreboding are heavily applied; the wildness is there to give place to the weariness, as "The thrilling shouts they died away" and the night comes greyly down; indeed, there hardly seems life enough to die, so that the poem ends still "waiting". From Brontë of all people such passivity is not what we expect, but her acquiescence permits the pageant-like remoteness and the complacent rhythms. What is more, as under some nineteenth-century ethic, it is men's work to fight and die for empire's cause, and the poet's task to hymn them in her lay— a domestic concert-form from which all disturbing particularity is excluded. Instead of particulars, therefore, impressionism offers "The choking sob, the tortured moan" as *features* of the battle-field, which, since they belong to nobody, merge with the background wailing of a vague "something sadder" in the wind. It is impossible to believe in the pain and destruction of this battle-poetry, for there is nobody—nothing—to die. So, far from preparing her for the creation of *Wuthering Heights*, Brontë's production of Gondal, I want now to suggest, was often a means of shielding and sealing off the self.

It would be wrong to suppose that nothing comparable happens in the novel. The strange impression many of its episodes make, of an energy at once violent, and innocent or free from taint, is perhaps the result of checks and insulations in the psyche. One sign of it is the way savage incidents are caught in the calm, even slightly pedantic rhythms of the prose.[16] But whereas the effort of *Wuthering Heights* is not merely to express but to isolate and define intensities, Gondal's attempt is rather to evade them. Often it seems no "self" worth speaking of is, really, engaged. So it is not just the narrow hymn-forms of Brontë's verse which at moments remind us of Blake: both poets prefer to confront the world through a series of masks, rather than dramatize a presence for themselves in their poems; both are extremists too, and are drawn towards allegory and the mythologizing of patterns of life. But whereas Blake in the *Songs* habitually sets one part of his vision in dialogue or contest with another, opposing the Nurse of *Innocence* to the Nurse of *Experience*, or answering the Pebble with the Clod—and thus going some way to meet the dilemmas his absolutist temperament provokes—Brontë manages a genuine dialectic much less often. Indeed, *her* extremism is such that the attempt to turn it against itself is liable to strengthen the hold of heroics on her mind—as in the poem I started to quote before.

> Strong I stand, though I have borne
> Anger, hate, and bitter scorn;
> Strong I stand, and laugh to see
> How mankind have fought with me.
>
> Shade of mast'ry, I contemn
> All the puny ways of men;
> Free my heart, my spirit free;
> Beckon, and I'll follow thee.
>
> False and foolish mortal, know,
> If you scorn the world's disdain,
> Your mean soul is far below
> Other worms, however vain.

Thing of Dust—with boundless pride,
Dare you take me for a guide?
With the humble I will be;
Haughty men are naught to me.

(H. 35)

The dialogue-form, opposing each point of view to the other,
suggests that Byronic defiance is being criticized here, not indulged. But the bullying reply that comes from the "Shade of
mast'ry" is no more attractive than the contemptuous pride of
stanzas 1 and 2. On the contrary, instead of answering the attitudes posed in part one, the second speaker annihilates the first,
substituting a superiority more inhuman still, before which "men"
shrink to "worms" and Dust. And in all this, where is Brontë?
Her dialectic, unlike Blake's, ends by cancelling the terms of the
contest, not making them richer or more intense.

Evidently, then, she had trouble providing a speaker or voice
which would admit her real strength into the poems, and was
inclined to substitute false images of heroism, as her biographers
sometimes have done. For the moment it is enough to say that,
paradoxically, the strongest of her poems seem those in which the
martial stance of "scorn" gives place to a certain kind of yielding.
It is a naturalizing touch, allowing time and pain to assume their
poignancy, so that the "I" of the poems is no longer a vent for
superhuman forces, but suffers, resists, endeavours to make in and
of itself something new. On however constricted a scale, the
Brontë-presence actively seeks to define its predicament, and
thereby gains dignity and weight.

> The night is darkening round me,
> The wild winds coldly blow;
> But a tyrant spell has bound me
> And I cannot, cannot go.
>
> The giant trees are bending
> Their bare boughs weighed with snow,
> And the storm is fast descending
> And yet I cannot go.
>
> Clouds beyond clouds above me,
> Wastes beyond wastes below;

But nothing drear can move me;
I will not, cannot go.

(H. 36)

Quiet as this poem sounds, it is none the less richer and fuller in self-assertion than any so far. Those we have looked at have been abstractly intellectualized, with the speaker no more than a set of postures. Dungeons and chains are quite suitable for striking these postures in, since the only activity needed is to reiterate one's defiance or whatever it may be. But here, highly formal and patterned though the landscape is, it does have a sensuous hold on the imagination. Size, and the failing light in which the scene shelves away to "Wastes upon wastes below"; the pressure of the storm coming down through a height of clouds, the snow weighing on the branches: all are felt as palpable equivalents to that "tyrant spell" by which the speaker is bound. So, mysterious and deliberately irrational the state may be, yet it is dramatized completely. And with unusual complexity. For the incapacity to move is also a refusal to *be* moved: that is the one power left to the speaker; and it is by seizing that power and simultaneously yielding to the spell of motionlessness that impotence is transformed into a new strength of will: like the giant trees which threaten to give way, but whose "bending" (poised in the rhythm) is a form of holding their own. Here, if anywhere in Brontë's verse, the spirit does stand firm. Yet even so the lyric's finest quality, perhaps, is its sensing of the queer disablement undergone—a disorienting inner shift, experienced as arrested time (where actions are suspended in participial forms, and the present tense unresolved), and in the note of burden and bewilderment in the speaker's voice. The resoluteness here exacts its price, and the poem earns a right to that altered declaration with which —at its loneliest point, significantly—it ends:

I will not, cannot go.

III

That line deserves its memorableness. Dissolve the legends surrounding Brontë, both those she spun herself and subsequent overlays, and the haunting image we are left with is still, as the last poem brings it into focus, a figure resisting but transfixed. Admittedly, we now know from surviving autobiographical fragments that she was not altogether the dramatic recluse her sister Charlotte described,[17] but she was a strange and secretive personality beyond doubt, and despite her famous and appalling acts of courage there is a fending-off, an unwillingness to risk the world, in the day-to-day actions of her life. At Haworth she occupied herself, and there as far as possible she stayed. Psychologically too, her fantasy of Gondal begun in childhood clung to her the rest of her life, and its recurrent themes and images dominate her verse, while her one great achievement, so local in setting that its action fits into sixteen square miles, is enthralled by Heathcliff's "ghost of my immortal love"—the "spectre of a hope" pursued through eighteen years, and dead but unchanging in the grave. Whatever else the reader comes to her poems for, these matters of time and landscape inevitably occur: we start to consider their pressure on her imagination, and the freedoms she was able to achieve.

One attempted freedom, that of heroic defiance, we have seen already and it will appear again. For many years, though, the Brontë who inspired her public with a sense of liberation was either the moorland poet, or the mystic: the poet, that is, who celebrated the Yorkshire landscape, or (on the other hand) ecstatically left it behind; and dedicated readers have found it possible to admire both these achievements at once. To take them seriatim, however: while her reputation as a "nature poet" has stood high, a firm basis for it is hard to discover. There are surprisingly few poems of landscape among Hatfield's 193; just as few of those descriptions of Catherine and Heathcliff roaming the moors can, actually, be found in the novel. Most of the time, after a stanza or two, the poems relinquish *rapport* with an outside world, and this may be why so many of them are fragments—

> Only some spires of bright green grass
> Transparently in sunshine quivering
>
> (H. 20)

—but more even than that, very often for Brontë's imagination landscape is at its most vivid when mapping out inner shifts, in energy and time.

Mild the mist upon the hill,
Telling not of storms to-morrow;
No; the day has wept its fill,
Spent its store of silent sorrow.

Oh, I'm gone back to the days of youth,
I am a child once more;
And 'neath my father's sheltering roof,
And near the old hall door,

I watch this cloudy evening fall,
After a day of rain:
Blue mists, sweet mists of summer pall
The horizon's mountain-chain.

The damp stands in the long, green grass
As thick as morning's tears;
And dreamy scents of fragrance pass
That breathe of other years.

(H. 113)

For all the quite developed sensuous life of phrases here and
there, the poem as a whole has little interest in an autonomous
outside world. Rather, it is deriving satisfactions from Nature,
but at her expense, in a typically Victorian way. The "dreamy
scents of fragrance" carry no hint of origin: nostalgia, not natural
perfume, is what they breathe. And the vague thickened langour
of the scene ("Blue mists, sweet mists . . .") does not even rest in
its reported present time, but draws the imagination on to yearn
towards other tenses—a future which has not arrived, or a past
which may come again, as the landscape spends itself in sympathy
and the rhythms, receiving the overflow, fill up:

Oh, I'm gone back to the days of youth,
I am a child once more.

Only with that opulent, re-possessing shift is the speaker felt at
all fully.

Preoccupation with the past of course colours much nineteenth-
century writing—not just in poetry, either, if we bring the grave,
deterministic rhythms of *Middlemarch* to mind. What distinguishes Brontë is the completeness with which, for her, intensity

48

resides in a past accomplished, *and* recurrent, both at once. Often
that is true even of unsuccessful poems: the emotion towards
which they are striving belongs neither to present nor to past, but
to a curiously circular, fatalistic time-scheme, as the syntax betrays:

> King Julius left the south country
> His banners all bravely flying;
> His followers went out with Jubilee
> But they shall return with sighing. . . .
>
> (H. 98)

The participial form is made to work—as it were—time and a
half; it is not just that the past, being over, is fixed, but that
what will be is already contained in *what was*, leaving no active
present tense. Thus, such poetry having abolished present time
has no room for an "I" or persona to stand—except of course
outside events, looking forward or back on them as being already
fated. And this passivity (as is typical of Gondal) can serve to
protect imagination from change and the unmanageableness of
daily, random life. In a preliminary way, one can guess why
Brontë's imagination revolved round stock situations such as
these, and the repetitive chiming ballad-forms in which she mostly
wrote have the effect of holding the mind in a reassuring rhythmical order. It was not so with prose. Once free of the rhyme-
scheme and the containing, limiting "music" of her verse, she
was laid open to new intensities of feeling which her intuited
theme forced up, at the same time as she gained—from unex-
hausted areas of her personality, and above all from homeliness
of speech and all that it implied of her environment—strengths
with which to express and control what her imagination produced.
Being a remarkable woman, she had the daring to face the enter-
prise; and now, in *Wuthering Heights*, her feeling for the past
assumes greater intensity still.

Of all famous novels, in fact, this is surely the one which has
least to do with present time. Its extraordinary vividness of
presentation is, actually, heightened by the effect of narratives
stretching inwards and back in time, each one enclosed by the
next, and not even the outermost story coming closer to its day
than by a distance of forty years. "1801", decisively past, is the
opening word of the novel. And yet its past does not *feel* com-

pleted: rather, there comes a sense, at points of maximum immobility too, that what has been done is still *being* done, postponing conclusion until finality has ceased to exist and death itself is transferred, imaginatively, backwards out of the future in which it waits.

> 'Disturbed her? No! she has disturbed me, night and day, through eighteen years—incessantly—remorselessly—till yesternight; and yesternight, I was tranquil. I dreamt I was sleeping the last sleep, by that sleeper, with my heart stopped, and my cheek frozen against hers.'[18]

It is a culminating vision of arrest within non-arrest; but even it is not the end, which comes with final ambiguous effect in a paragraph of fluttering moths, and soft wind breathing through the grass, to rouse "the sleepers in that quiet earth" *and* to lay them to rest. With these things in mind we may see Brontë, in her great novel, as empowered by two attractions: on the one hand, the ordering and intensifying of life as a fated pattern of events—all accomplished, like the naming of Catherine Earnshaw for her destiny, Heathcliff—Linton, before the drama has begun. On the other hand, though, there is her fascination with recurrences in nature and in human lives. It drew her strongly, this feeling for the way one event—one person, even—can recur in another, as Catherine's eyes reappear in her family: a haunting promise of likeness which can never be fulfilled. And the qualifying clause is needed. For if times and situations seem transfixed, turning back on themselves—

> It was the same room into which he had been ushered, as a guest, eighteen years before: the same moon shone through the window; and the same autumn landscape lay outside[19]

—there is an equal and opposite stress in the book: that identity is *not* repeatable, even Catherine's identity with Heathcliff. Her claim that it is, "he's more myself than I am", is not just upheld, it is (simultaneously) combated by the book. If we listen to the great speeches, we may be persuaded to believe in this passion on Catherine and Heathcliff's terms: such is the power of the writing. Attend to the structure of incident, though, and to the way the passion is "placed", and clearly Brontë is offering a

critique of this love, at the same time as her extremist temperament urges her to endorse it. It is the doubleness of attitude in
these central things that secures greatness for *Wuthering Heights*.

But to return to the poems. I do not know that she achieved
a comparable equipoise there. Rather, she seems inclined either
to passivity—diagnosed by Charlotte in her own way ("you have
little choice left but quiescent adoption"), but registered by us
in particular sensations—as when, in the poem quoted earlier,
the damp "stands" in the long green grass; or else, with what
has been called a mystical purpose, she reaches out for thorough-
going liberation. "High waving heather" (H. 5) is one poem where
what we are promised is escape; what we actually get, as the eager
dactylic rhythm betrays, is a changing from state to state in endless
cyclic return. So the ecstatic blending of spirit into nature is an-
nounced, but remains a mere wish unachieved. The same might be
said of a good many poems acclaimed as examples of Brontë's
ascent, from nature-poetry into mysticism.

> Aye, there it is! It wakes to-night
> Sweet thoughts that will not die
> And feeling's fires flash all as bright
> As in the years gone by!
>
> And I can tell by thine altered cheek
> And by thy kindled gaze
> And by the words thou scarce dost speak,
> How wildly fancy plays.
>
> Yes, I could swear that glorious wind
> Has swept the world aside,
> Has dashed its memory from thy mind
> Like foam-bells from the tide—
>
> And thou art now a spirit pouring
> Thy presence into all—
> The essence of the Tempest's roaring
> And of the Tempest's fall—
>
> A universal influence
> From Thine own influence free;
> A principle of life, intense,
> Lost to mortality.

51

Thus truly when that breast is cold
Thy prisoned soul shall rise,
The dungeon mingle with the mould—
The captive with the skies.

(H. 148)

As distinct from those poems which picture only cyclic alterna-
tions of power, this lyric does suggest both the fixed condition of
the "prisoned soul", and some sort of escape. It is when we try
to define it further that difficulties begin. For who or what *could*
be said to escape, once the body is left behind and self-hood dis-
solved to "A universal influence"? And if spirit is pouring out
itself, what then is left to retain "Sweet thoughts that will not
die"? But so fecklessly eager is the verse to dash the world aside,
it hardly notices how, in losing *that* resource for imagery, it might
lose everything. After all, if the memory of earth disappears like
foam-bells, we cannot be blamed for wondering what permanence
other thoughts and fancies have. The very attempt to render their
kindled ardent states where feeling's fires flash bright, is likely to
remind the reader that flames, the higher they blaze, the more
rapidly they burn out. And it is in line with these self-confound-
ing metaphors and the unresisted extremism which leads each
stanza increasingly to discard the familiar world that, as the lyric
approaches its climax (stanzas 4 and 5), not even its pronouns
can support their burden:

A universal influence
From Thine own influence free

—that capital is particularly puzzling. But even without it, the
system of relationships, between the "thou" to whom the poem
is addressed, its anonymous speaker, their (her?) spirit, and the
wind, is not transcended or transformed in an intelligible way,
it is merely obscured.

But it would be wrong to blame a poem too harshly when its
ambitions and weaknesses alike spring from deep temperamental
sources. The concealment of the speaker, and the passivity of
the poem's recipient, help to ensure that there is neither centre
nor human limit to these feelings of uplift. But more to the point
is the lack of pungency in the rhythms: their unexploratory, un-
liberating non-resistance. It is true that they show some variety,

52

and that gives impetus to the verse. But since there is nothing for the impetus to work against and break through, its effect is mere enthusiasm, not the transforming metaphysical drive for which, by Denis Donoghue for one, the poem has been praised (*Harvard English Studies* 1, 1970). Ostensibly, then, it is presenting strange liberations indeed, yet tested at any point its "strangeness" feels commonplace—and never more so than when it challenges comparison, as in stanza 5, with that genuinely New World Victorian, Emily Dickinson. The comparison, I think, is revealing. For even in

> A principle of life, intense,
> Lost to mortality

the holding-back of movement to staccato abstractions has little of the American poet's stringent intensity. On the contrary, Brontë is inclined to equate intense emotion with fulsomeness and passionately open utterance, whereas for Dickinson it is in-gathered, in-driven force. Again, in general Brontë's verse prefers an amplifying, plangent music, surging over line-ends, and even then through feminine rhymes and metres seeking to prolong its expressive capacities still further; whereas Dickinson's sensibility —a much odder, if not deliberately bizarre affair—persists in curtailed rhythms: not plangent at all, but keeping as their characteristic punctuation the dash or break in rhythm, so that we feel her imagination gather itself daringly, to leap across the gap. Hence, in part, the extraordinary wit of her poems: that is one of their constant features; hence also their intensification from point to point, as though by a series of *coups*. This wit and this disorienting strangeness have no parallel in the bulk of Brontë poems. "Mystical" experience, indeed, is something she barely touches at all, but Dickinson's case is different. To call *her* a mystic would be unhelpful, but we can see in her work the imagination under siege multiply its powers, and the effect is visionary in its strangeness. We pass from one order of experience to another.

> It was not Death, for I stood up,
> And all the Dead, lie down—
> It was not Night, for all the Bells
> Put out their Tongues, for Noon.

It was not Frost, for on my Flesh
I felt Siroccos—crawl—
Nor Fire—for just my Marble feet
Could keep a Chancel, cool—

And yet, it tasted, like them all,
The Figures I have seen
Set orderly, for Burial,
Reminded me, of Mine—

As if my life were shaven,
And fitted to a frame,
And could not breathe without a key,
And 'twas like Midnight, some—

When everything that ticked—has stopped—
And space stares all around—
Or Grisly frosts—first Autumn morns,
Repeal the Beating Ground—

But most, like Chaos—Stopless—cool—
Without a Chance, or Spar—
Or even a Report of Land—
To justify—Despair.

The halting strike-by-strike of the rhythms, and the hard-pressed negatives (It was not Frost, it was not Night), force on the reader a bringing to definition of fears. The consciousness here is peculiarly perplexed and extreme—one might say neurotic—in its subjection and dread; but it is also daring to an extent that Brontë never is. And so, the tighter the compulsion to define and know and set these Figures "orderly", the more the poem is determined to expose imagination *to* that unknown which it dreads. The speaker here is not swept away like the persona of Brontë's poem, whose thoughts are wakened and feelings altered but who says nothing for herself; instead, Dickinson's persona enters inanimacy so far that siroccos crawl on the flesh and "everything that ticked" stops into staring space—yet out of that, from the further side of nature as it were, pulses a new vitality to "Repeal the Beating Ground". There is an inhuman intensity to that; and the poem ends in psychic dissolution of a sort; but it does uphold a weird adventurousness of spirit, sailing into uncharted Chaos,

"Stopless—cool". And as against this creative power, and the personal victory for Dickinson it represents, Brontë's lyric sounds like earnest wishful declamation.

IV

We might suppose, then, that her positive achievement as a poet lies in learning to reject such wishful clamourings, and find a quieter, more genuinely personal voice. To some extent that *was* the way she took, but what could be gained in those directions she had gained early on. The following poem is placed by Hatfield before May 1837.

> All day I've toiled, but not with pain,
> In learning's golden mine;
> And now at eventide again
> The moonbeams softly shine.
>
> There is no snow upon the ground,
> No frost on wind or wave;
> The south wind blew with gentlest sound
> And broke their icy grave.
>
> 'Tis sweet to wander here at night
> To watch the winter die,
> With heart as summer sunshine light
> And warm as summer sky.
>
> O may I never lose the peace
> That lulls me gently now,
> Though time should change my youthful face,
> And years should shade my brow!
>
> True to myself, and true to all,
> May I be healthful still,
> And turn away from passion's call,
> And curb my own wild will.
>
> (H. 10)

Showier lyrics, "High waving heather" and "Aye, there it is", portrayed a cyclic procession of states and seasons, unresistingly metamorphic and escaping like water into clouds into rain; but

55

this poem carefully prefers a human scale. It is through modest precisions of "learning" that the first stanza comes to its tranquillity, where "toil" is distinguished from "pain" and both set in a rhythm of the day's labour giving place to evening quiet. In the hushed double-beat of the phrasing, wind and wave, snow and frost are released from *their* labours too, in a natural and welcomed dying-out of winter, the gentleness of which persists even through the poem's sentimental album-verse strain. So at the heart of the lyric is this present moment's peace—

> There is no snow upon the ground,
> No frost on wind or wave

—but what is characteristic of Brontë (and here, as for other insights, I am grateful to my colleague Beverly Hahn) is the inability to rest in that lulling condition. No sooner has the third stanza admitted its sweetness, than the forth casts forward into a possible future: "O may I never lose the peace. . . ." In weaker poems that melting away of present time is a disadvantage, a way of confirming passivity; here, on the other hand, the future is foreshadowed only to turn the speaker back, prepared, to herself; and the result is a fifth stanza which, ending the poem, seems retrospectively to tighten and reshape the whole.

"All day I've toiled" is an attractive poem I think, though slight and old-fashioned surely even in 1837. (It feels Late Augustan in a number of respects, from the gentle stress on discipline, right down to particular tropes—"learning's golden mine"; one recalls that Cowper was much read at Haworth parsonage, and that only three years earlier Charlotte had been recommending Goldsmith, Thomson, Campbell to Ellen Nussey.)[20] Had Brontë done no more than sustain a poise of this kind, therefore, her best poetry would have remained unwritten. The one germinating moment of this piece comes in its final line—

> turn away from passion's call,
> And curb my own wild will

—where the tightening of movement is felt, not just as a check on the self, but as a tension, a tremor of resistance, *from* the will even as it is imaginatively reined in. This double response, both against and on behalf of passion, is the creative condition of her

writing at its best: so the novel shows. Thus her achievement
(I want finally to suggest) was not to overcome her impulses, but
to find a mode—a presented voice—through which the real power
of her yearnings could speak. "Yearnings" they continued to be:
she saved her humour, her realism, and most of her shrewdness
for *Wuthering Heights*, and into her poetry went those feelings
that have to do less with living in the world than with intensifying and cherishing themselves. Memory, and the "bliss" or
"anguish" that it brings, are of major importance, as subjects and
enabling forces in her verse. So too is the exultancy denominated
by the adjective "wild", and the corresponding opposites of desolation: "dreary", "lonely", "despairing" states of mind. The
core of her achievement is in the realization of these essentially
private, self-intensifying states.

> Fall, leaves, fall; die, flowers, away;
> Lengthen night and shorten day;
> Every leaf speaks bliss to me
> Fluttering from the autumn tree.
> I shall smile when wreaths of snow
> Blossom where the rose should grow;
> I shall sing when night's decay
> Ushers in a drearier day.
>
> (H. 79)

For Brontë, the slow varied rhythms of this lyric are unusual, but
the engagement with autumnal states of dying and decay is not.
Her poems are full of these desolations, but mostly without the
sensuous gravity they have here; here, with fulness of texture,
comes fulness of feeling too—not mere ritual welcomings of
"death", but a verse-movement that spreads and rises to one
moment of intensity, "I shall sing . . .", delivering us to that verb
with an ardour at once defiant and yearning. What is called for
is night-time and winter, but not because they are final like our
humanity's death. However lengthened out the night, it is—by
its very prolongation—not an end at all, but a means to "usher
in a drearier day". And as with the day's cycle, so with the
seasons': in the fluttering leaf and blossoming wreath of snow,
life is not ending, or even decaying (it feels), but rather replacing itself.

There is something finely Romantic about this sense of self-renewing powers, and the poem's composed blend of elegy and triumph claims a place for human life in nature's grand responsive scheme. Yet how untouchable the speaker sounds. Calm, musical, her feelings extend and deepen, but they show no sign of any mortal limit at which death might be felt, either by nature or by her. The cadences are too self-intensifying for that, too rich and lingering—"die, flowers, away"—to render an authentic pain and ending. And in view of the prevalence of death in Brontë's poems, this is an important reservation. Compared with the intense disturbing power of Emily Dickinson's work, how like death *is* death as depicted by Brontë? Its most memorable images are not those of the dead as unliving, but as "cold" in the earth, still feeling the weight and chill of the deep snow piled above. Death in fact seems a kind of banishment, in which men are far "removed"— as though there are *two* survivors after it is over, one either side of the wall of the tomb. Which of course increases the passion of loss: for mourning does not meet a vacancy "Without a Chance, or Spar", but reaches instead towards the state of exile into which "the Dweller in the land of Death" has gone. Less startling therefore than Dickinson's poems in their alienation from life, Brontë's lyrics attempt (initially, at least) a reconciliation with death as something external, experienced *out there*: this is the imagery of that lovely *berceuse*, "The linnet in the rocky dells", where heather-bells "hide" my lady fair, and behind the grave's wall her form is still "retained". Supremely, in that poem, mortality brings not an end but a replacing, of life by life.

> The linnet in the rocky dells,
> The moor-lark in the air,
> The bee among the heather-bells
> That hide my lady fair:
>
> The wild deer browse above her breast;
> The wild birds raise their brood;
> And they, her smiles of love caressed,
> Have left her solitude!
>
> (H. 173)

What distinguishes the poem is not its sense for death, but for continuance in life. Now, it is by coming alive to the sounds and

58

movements of an on-going world and yielding to its claims, that the freedom of spirit which Brontë sought in so many infertile ways is, finally, achieved.

> Blow, west wind, by the lonely mound,
> And murmur, summer streams,
> There is no need of other sound
> To soothe my Lady's dreams.

That ending is far from the universalism of the "mystical" poems, but it is no facile resignation all the same; instead, the subterranean victory by which tranquillity has been won leaves its trace on the phrasing of the central stanzas: the checked tide of grief, the retaining wall of the grave, the source of sorrow which has in imagination been wept dry. The loss, identified in nature first, has shifted inwards, where it conduces to, just as it re-enacts, a discipline of self.

And with better poems still, the capacity of the self to absorb change and triumph in it is realized all the more.

> Cold in the earth, and fifteen wild Decembers
> From those brown hills have melted into spring—
> Faithful indeed is the spirit that remembers
> After such years of change and suffering!
>
> (H. 182)

The brown hills, says Leavis,[21] do not themselves "melt", but neither does the speaker relinquish her task of bearing in the memory what one might call a living absence—the gap in nature where her beloved used to be. It is time itself (as in *Wuthering Heights*), the length and grief of fifteen wild Decembers, which is the scale by which we are to measure the intensity of this love; and through memory, the agent of time, that love continues to intensify itself: not through mourning the loss, but through recognizing it finally, without despair.

> Then did I learn how existence could be cherished,
> Strengthened and fed without the aid of joy;
>
> Then did I check the tears of useless passion,
> Weaned my young soul from yearning after thine;
> Sternly denied its burning wish to hasten
> Down to that tomb already more than mine!

"Then did I learn" to be "cherished", to be "fed": these verbs which carry the rapturous longing of the speaker are the same which define her self-resisting, self-intensifying will, and prepare the way for the identifying of love *with* Memory in the final stanza:

> Once drinking deep of that divinest anguish,
> How could I seek the empty world again?

To drink deep of one's yearnings, and to know the dangers of doing so—that, not any lesser self-discipline, is the strength this poem has.

And the last poem I will quote, "Stars", dramatizes this double necessity, making it quite directly the subject. I give the poem's original punctuation (14 April 1845) to replace the slight normalizing of Hatfield's transcript.

> Ah! why, because the dazzling sun
> Restored my earth to joy
> Have you departed, every one,
> And left a desert sky?

> All through the night, your glorious eyes
> Were gazing down in mine
> And with a full hearts thankful sighs
> I blessed that watch divine!

> I was at peace—and drank your beams
> As they were life to me
> And revelled in my changeful dreams
> Like petrel on the sea.

> Thought followed thought—star followed star
> Through boundless regions on
> While one sweet influence, near and far,
> Thrilled through and proved us one.

> Why did the morning rise to break
> So great, so pure a spell,
> And scorch with fire the tranquil cheek
> Where your cool radiance fell?

Blood red he rose, and arrow-straight
His fierce beams struck my brow
The soul of Nature sprang elate,
But mine sank sad and low!

My lids closed down—yet through their veil
I saw him blazing still;
And bathe in gold the misty dale
And Flash upon the hill.

I turned me to the pillow then
To call back Night, and see
Your worlds of solemn light, again
Throb with my heart and me!

It would not do—the pillow glowed
And glowed both roof and floor
And birds sang loudly in the wood,
And fresh winds shook the door.

The curtains waved, the wakened flies
Were murmuring round my room
Imprisoned there, till I should rise
And give them leave to roam—

O, Stars and Dreams and Gentle Night.
O Night and Stars return!
And hide me from the hostile light
That does not warm, but burn—

That drains, the blood of suffering men—
Drinks tears, instead of dew—
Let me sleep through his blinding reign
And only wake with you!

There are good reasons for thinking this Emily Brontë's best poem. For the most part it is less passionately phrased than "Cold in the earth", but perhaps because its emotional pitch is lower, one is aware of a specifically erotic note that no other poem has sounded. Erotic, but movingly vulnerable: for there are *two* sexual claimants to the woman, and she is subjected to both. It is in fact the very thankfulness with which she accepts the mastery of the stars ("All through the night, your glorious eyes / Were gazing down in mine") that makes her plight the more poignant: for the language in which she commits herself to night is sensitive to truths she will not, cannot, consciously allow; the day restores her earth to "joy", the stars are drunk-in as *though* they were life, and their cool remoteness is a "spell"—but any recognition of these facts is hidden from us beneath the speaker's demeanour, grateful to be passive. This unwillingness of the persona to wake to herself or the day is, perhaps, expected; what is unexpected I think is the vigour with which the masculine demands of the sun are made:

> Blood red he rose, and arrow-straight
> His fierce beams struck my brow

—the combative, outward-striding rhythm transfers initiative onto that warrior-sun, blazing, dazzling and bathing in gold, so that the speaker's attempt to wrest it back again, in stanzas 7 and 8, is the more difficult, when what has been challenged is not her psychological unpreparedness only, but (so to speak) the consciousness of her body:

> My lids closed down—yet through their veil
> I saw him blazing still

As that curiously passive syntax suggests, the divisions in the self are driving deeper, allowing the body of its own accord to half-resist the world, while the senses, through the body, are resisting the woman's will as well. And the more she yearns for that breach to be healed—

> and see
> Your worlds of solemn light, again
> Throb with my heart and me

—the brighter and louder nature's protest grows: the pillow, to which she turns for darkness, glows; the very flies are murmuring with purpose; and as though in anger *and* invitation, fresh winds "shake" the door, to bring the beating and throbbing of her wishes in stanza 8 into the open at last. "It would not do": that phrase which I have taken as title for my essay has its full doubleness of meaning here, uttered both against the speaker, and in her character, on her behalf.

"Stars" is not one of the poems copied into the Gondal note-book in February, 1844, when Emily Brontë was transcribing the verses she wished to keep. It comes from her other, untitled notebook of that year; and in some respects, as we have seen, it does indeed stand as a critique of one strain in her tempera-ment, self-protecting, wishing to return to that sheltering trance of nature rhapsodies and "mysticism" and the Gondal world which would not bear exposure to daylight. A self-checking, then; but at the same time the poem is alive to the raptures of the night-time world, and strong though her moment of rejection is—"It would not do"—it is back to those Stars and Dreams and Gentle Night that the formal emphasis of the monologue returns. That in itself seems to typify the character-istic direction of Brontë's interests. Or (to put it another way) even this poem, which I think her finest, is preoccupied with Yearning and the extent to which that emotion is not at home in the ordinary world: hence the vocabulary—*glorious, divine, thrilled, pure, elate, solemn, throb*—otherworldly in a Victorian style, and striving to transcend the homeliness of the curtained bedroom-setting. The strength of the poem is of course that its morning-world is so vigorously and variously felt: half-mytholo-gized as it may be in the warrior-sun, it still has a homeliness quite unlike Gondal where feudalism and castle-loyalties reign. But when all is said, a great deal of the energy of the presented Brontë-self goes into the ardent aspiring note of the final stanza:

> Let me sleep through his blinding reign
> And only wake with you!

"I know no woman that ever lived ever wrote such poetry be-fore", declared Charlotte in a letter to W. S. Williams.[22] Char-lotte's literary judgement, which allowed her to produce that diluted edition of *Wuthering Heights*, is not altogether to be trusted. Nowadays, we are more likely to feel that, however un-womanly by nineteenth-century standards Brontë's subjects are, the poetry itself, by and large, is more Victorian than Charlotte was able to see. But it would be wrong to leave the last emphasis there. For in the same letter, listening to Charlotte recount her discovery of the poems, we are reminded of how odd a relation Emily Brontë maintained to her own achievements.

The deep excitement I felt forced from me the confession of the discovery I had made. I was sternly rated at first for having taken an unwarrantable liberty. This I expected, for Ellis Bell is of no flexible or ordinary materials. But by dint of entreaty and reason I at last wrung out a reluctant consent to have the 'rhymes', as they were contemptuously termed, published. The author never alludes to them; or, when she does it is with scorn.

For years, the assumption has been that Charlotte was right, Emily Brontë wrong, in their estimates of the latter's poetry. But what I have been arguing in this essay is that a great deal of that poetry was, for its author, a means of protecting, occupying, sealing-off the self from the demands of the adult world. And whether it was wise to intrude on this activity is, I think, an open question. But at any rate, thus shielded by her work, Emily Brontë had no trouble in striking the heroic attitudes which she herself hankered to see. The challenge was to admit the world of adult passions, rather than to renounce or proudly defy it; and even in *Wuthering Heights*, I am not sure that that, exactly, was what its author did. Certainly, in her poems it happens so rarely that it is hard to find real intimations of present time, choice, sexuality, death. But the image of an heroic death she failed to achieve in her poems, she did achieve in her life. And here, finally, is the irreplaceable value of Charlotte's Biographical Notice: for it presents her sister Emily's life *as* an image—part of what I began by calling the highly-charged Victorian legend. To Charlotte, involved in her own responses, the heroic stance she discerned in her sister's career was promoted at the expense of domestic, day-to-day life:

> I am bound to avow that she had scarcely more practical know-
> ledge of the peasantry amongst whom she lived, than a nun has of
> the country people who sometimes pass her convent gates.

Yet it was *in* the domestic context that, day by day, real heroism was achieved.

> She sank rapidly. She made haste to leave us.

In those anguished, moving cadences we are brought to realize that homeliness does have an heroic significance after all: the significance proved and conferred by death. Even the most humble life—and all the more, Emily Brontë's—dying amid the close proximities of the nineteenth-century household might have left behind it an image of stoic endurance, and the sacred duty to wipe dust from the gravestone and keep the dear name free of soil.

NOTES

1. *Memoir of Emily Jane Brontë*, included in the second edition of *Wuthering Heights*, 1850.
2. "The History of the Year 1829", quoted by Mrs Gaskell in her *Life of Charlotte Brontë*, chapter V. Actually, the phrase should read "Emily's and my bed plays": these, explained Charlotte, "mean secret plays they are very nice ones all our plays are very strange ones there nature I need not write on paper, for I think I shull always remember them. . . ."
3. *The Modern Language Review*, vol. XVIII, pp. 9–21. This essay was followed by "A Second Visit to Gondaliand", vol. XXI, pp. 373–9, in which Angrian poems by Charlotte and Branwell Brontë are attributed to Emily Brontë—an error which Miss Dodds corrected in the following issue of *M.L.R.*, 1927, pp. 197–8.
4. *Emily Brontë: her life and work*, Muriel Spark and Derek Stanford, 1953, p. 121.
5. *Biographical Notice of Ellis and Acton Bell*; my references are to the Penguin English Library text of *Wuthering Heights*, ed. David Daiches, 1965, p. 36.
6. *Ibid.*, p. 30.
7. *Ibid.*, pp. 34–5.
8. See the letter from Charlotte Brontë to Aylott & Jones, 6 April 1846, Shakespeare Head Brontë, *Lives, Friendships and Correspondence*, II, p. 87.
9. Editor's Preface to the New Edition of *Wuthering Heights*, 1850: P.E.L., p. 39.
10. *Biographical Notice, ed. cit.*, p. 35.
11. *Preface*, p. 39.
12. *Ibid.*, pp. 40–1.
13. Swinburne's *Note on Charlotte Brontë*, 1877, sets the tone: "There was a dark unconscious instinct as of primitive nature-worship in the passionate great genius of Emily Brontë" (p. 73), a "passionate reverence for the All-mother" (p. 75), "a prayer to the indestructible God within herself; a psalm of trust so strangely (as it seems) compounded of personal and pantheistic faith, at once fiery and solemn, full alike of resignation and of rapture . . . wholly stripped and cleared

and lightened from all burdens and all bandages and all incrustations of creed" (pp. 79–80), etc.

14. See Appendix: "Poems published under Emily Brontë's Supervision".

15. In her Introduction to *A Selection of Poems by Emily Brontë*, 1952.

16. Some careful analysis of the novel's prose-qualities is given by F. H. Langman, *Essays in Criticism*, XV, no. 3, and Vincent Buckley, *Southern Review*, I, no. 2.

17. Whereas Charlotte, back from Brussels, sank by degrees into brooding and despair ("I can hardly tell you how time gets on here at Haworth", she wrote to Ellen Nussey, "There is no event whatever to mark its progress—one day resembles another—and all have heavy lifeless physiognomies. . . . I feel as if we were all buried here": 24 March 1845), Emily Brontë's birthday-note of July 30th sounds as different as can be. Occupied, jaunty, her style is almost boisterous: "The Gondals still flourish bright as ever—I am at present writing a work on the First Wars—Anne has been writing some articles on this and a book by Henry Sophona—We intend sticking firm by the rascals as long as they delight us—Which I am glad to say they do at present. . . . I am quite contented for myself—not as idle as formerly, altogether as hearty and having learnt to make the most of the present and hope for the future with less fidgetness that I cannot do all I wish—seldom or ever troubled with nothing to do—and merely desiring that everybody could be as comfortable as myself and as undesponding and then we should have a very tolerable world of it."

18. *Wuthering Heights, ed. cit.*, chapter 29. p. 320.

19. *Ibid.*, p. 317.

20. See the letter of 4 July 1834, in which Charlotte draws up an approved reading-list of literature, biography, natural history.

21. In the essay "Reality and Sincerity", *Scrutiny*, XIX, now republished in *The Living Principle*.

22. The letter, dated September 1848, is printed in the Shakespeare Head Brontë, *Lives, Friendships, and Correspondence*, II, p. 256.

APPENDIX:
POEMS PUBLISHED UNDER EMILY BRONTË'S SUPERVISION

Emily Brontë contributed twenty-one pieces to the *Poems, by Currer, Ellis and Acton Bell* (Aylott & Jones, 1846), six of them from her Gondal notebook, and fifteen from the manuscript headed "E.J.B. Transcribed February 1844". Both sources show that she herself adapted and titled poems for publication, having chosen them from what was, broadly speaking, her best work of the previous five years. The following list gives the printed title first, then the opening line and number of each poem in Hatfield's edition. An asterisk indicates poems from the Gondal notebook.

1. FAITH AND DESPONDENCY: *"The winter wind is loud and wild" H. 177
2. STARS: "Ah! why, because the dazzling sun" H. 184
3. THE PHILOSOPHER (In Emily Brontë's handwriting, "The Philosopher's Conclusion" has been added at the head of the poem in Notebook A): "Enough of Thought, Philosopher" H. 181
4. REMEMBRANCE: *"Cold in the earth, and the deep snow piled above thee" H. 182
5. A DEATH-SCENE: *"O Day! He cannot die" H. 180
6. SONG: *"The linnet in the rocky dells" H. 173
7. ANTICIPATION: "How beautiful the Earth is still" H. 188
8. THE PRISONER—A FRAGMENT: *"In the dungeon crypts idly did I stray" H. 190
9. HOPE: "Hope was but a timid friend" H. 165
10. A DAY DREAM: "On a sunny brae alone I lay" H. 170
11. TO IMAGINATION: "When weary with the long day's care" H. 174
12. HOW CLEAR SHE SHINES!: "How clear she shines! How quietly" H. 157
13. SYMPATHY: "There should be no despair for you" H. 122
14. PLEAD FOR ME: "O thy bright eyes must answer now" H. 176
15. SELF-INTERROGATION: "The evening passes fast away" H. 155
16. DEATH: "Death, that struck when I was most confiding" H. 183
17. STANZAS TO——: "Well, some may hate and some may scorn" H. 123
18. HONOUR'S MARTYR: *"The moon is full this winter night" H. 179
19. STANZAS: "I'll not weep that thou art going to leave me" H. 136
20. MY COMFORTER: "Well hast thou spoken—and yet not taught" H. 168
21. THE OLD STOIC: "Riches I hold in light esteem" H. 146

2

A Baby God: The Creative Dynamism of Emily Brontë's Poetry

by ROSALIND MILES

It is never easy to say anything worthwhile about a great writer;
and among poets Emily Brontë was perhaps the most heedless of
her future critics and biographers, pitilessly suppressing the raw
materials needed for the task of describing and assessing her.
The hopeful commentator finds himself handicapped by the existence of two central puzzles or mysteries in her life, which have
a direct bearing upon her work. The necessity of coming to terms
with these forms the first imperative in any approach to Emily
Brontë's poetry.

First, despite the wealth of primary and secondary material,
Emily Brontë remains extraordinarily remote from us. Not for
nothing does the comparison with Shakespeare so readily and
repeatedly present itself, from the earliest recorded comment
upon "the Bells". Like Shakespeare's her work stands alone
and challenges us, forces us, to do without the authorial gloss or
"personal touch" which academic and general readers alike so love
to have upon or read into a work. Mrs Humphry Ward summed
this up in her perceptive preface to the Haworth edition of
Wuthering Heights:

> The artist remains hidden and self-contained; the work . . . has
> always that distinction which belongs to a high talent working
> solely for its own joy and satisfaction, with no thought of a spec-
> tator, or any aim but that of an ideal and imaginative whole. . . .

She has that highest power . . . the power which gives life, intensest life, to the creatures of the imagination, and, in doing so, endows them with an independence behind which the maker is forgotten. . . .[1]

Emily Brontë was, of course, a determinedly private individual, both as an artist and as a person; so much so that she succeeded in intimidating even her sisters from any intrusion upon her inner self. She was, simply, without that urge to communicate, to explain, defend, elaborate and describe the ups and downs of her mental, emotional, and creative life which has brought Charlotte so endearingly close to us; and thus, as with Shakespeare, we know so little about the writer's process of creation that we are but tenuously justified in drawing personal inferences from the result. We may *feel* that a certain poem "must" be autobiographical, but we can never know, as we can, for instance, with Keats.

Keats indeed expressed, on Emily Brontë's behalf, as it were, the artistic attitudes which we know from her behaviour to have been hers. She too could well have declared, as he did in a letter to Reynolds of 9 April 1818, "I never wrote one single Line of Poetry with the least Shadow of public thought"; or again, "my imagination is a monastery, and I am its monk" (letter to Shelley, August 1820). Who more than Emily Brontë felt able to "refuse the poisonous suffrage of a public" in the knowledge that "the soul is a world of itself, and has enough to do in its own home" (Keats's letter to Reynolds, 25 August 1819)? By the adoption of such attitudes, implicit though unarticulated, Emily Brontë repels rather than invites critical attention, discouraging any casual or trivial approaches to her work.

The second source of Emily Brontë's enigmatic quality lies in the importance of the Gondal saga in her life and poetry. Emily Brontë herself distinguished between "Gondal Poems" and others, to which she gave no group title (Hatfield's A and B manuscripts). But all her work does not fall conveniently within these two volumes and categories. There are many poems which we could not definitely say belong either in the "personal" or in the Gondal group; this tantalising fragment, for instance (Hatfield 161):

> Had there been falsehood in my breast
> No thorns had marred my road,

69

> This spirit had not lost its rest,
> These tears had never flowed.

Clearly there is a very real sense in which the distinction ceases to be relevant. To borrow her own unforgettable dream image from chapter 9 of *Wuthering Heights*, from its length and centrality in her life, the Gondal saga must have gone through Emily Brontë like wine through water, and altered the colour of her mind.

This fusion is very evident from any scrutiny of the poems with definite Gondal attributions. Gondal experiences, despite their lurid, often quite ghastly trappings, are often in essence plainly borrowed from and blended with those of Emily Brontë herself. The Gondal saga, what we know of it, was melodramatic, but then so was some of Emily Brontë's own life. Are we to take it, for instance, that given the narrowness of her daily round, and the rule of her well-intentioned but hardly imaginative aunt and the domestics, she would not know at first hand the sense of being constrained, the denial of her "wild will", even "the agony of still repining" (15), however she disguises these emotional events, masks them as Gondal characters, Gondal voices, Gondal plights and disasters? Why should we doubt that the young woman who spent so many nights gazing at the moon and stars should, when she slept, have dreamed as often and as vividly as her creatures do?

> "Dreams have encircled me," I said,
> "From careless childhood's sunny time;
> Visions by ardent fancy fed
> Since life was in its morning prime."
>
> (H. 27)

Similarly it seems clear that the memories, fantasies, and experiences of the past remained alive to her, and rose up to revitalize a newly contrived Gondal situation with a reservoir of emotional truth from a previous occasion; see H. 102, for instance, where she makes a character say, "Old feelings gather fast upon me / Like vultures round their prey". Inevitably, too, the weight of her emotional experiences, both real and vicarious, increased as the years went by, so that she was, by and in herself, carrying a growing burden of the knowledge of "torment and madness, tears and sin"; she was able to relieve this pressure by voicing through her characters attitudes which progress from a rather down-hearted pragmatism (H. 118 and 119), through an occasionally hysterical cynicism—"the poison-tainted air / From this world's plague-fen" (H. 143)—to a generalized disillusion and despair (H. 157, 174). Again, though, to borrow from one of her characters, we know that Emily Brontë herself could "journey onward, not elate, / But *never* broken-hearted" (H. 122; Emily Brontë's italics).

This blending of personal and Gondal material is well illustrated in H. 97, "By R. Gleneden". This poem, written on 17 April 1839, a week after Anne left home to go as a governess, repeatedly laments the absence of "one" for whose loss "cheerless, chill is our hearthstone". How could Emily not grieve for the loss of Anne, whom both Charlotte and Ellen Nussey tell us was as a twin to her? And yet, with her obsessive reticence, how could she treat the subject except under the Gondal cover, from behind the mask, on this occasion, of Gleneden? Even in the poem's theme of noble self-sacrifice for the general good there is an echo of the motive underlying Anne's departure—for none of the Brontës ever went into the joyless servitude of tutoring except to make their contribution towards relieving the common economic burden.

Again, in H. 99 and 100, in the theme of degeneration and the hardening of a young heart, we see behind the fictional portrait the shadow of Branwell's condition. Nine years were to pass before his eventual death, but it was by now abundantly plain that he would not fulfil the great destiny that he had once seemed to flourish, and that he could not even make his living as a portrait painter. In the lament for the "ardent boy" (is there a punning reference here to Branwell's distinctive flaming red hair?) we see a version or incarnation of one whom, temporarily at least, Emily dismissed as "a hopeless being", having seen him from adolescence depending upon increasingly strong doses of merry company, drink, and opium, to relieve him from cynicism and despair. Yet this personal element is informed, transformed, strengthened and distanced by its interweaving with the threads of the Gondal narrative into a cloak which allowed her in another poem, "Well, some may hate, and some may scorn" (H. 123), to anticipate not only Branwell's distressing and ignominious death, but also the wrestling of her own proud nature against feelings of contempt for those who could not match up to her exacting standards of behaviour.

What would we not give to have more knowledge of the lost Gondal stories? Of all the 'might-have-beens' of English Literature—the poems of Keats's full maturity, the novels of Jane Austen's middle age, the ending of *Edwin Drood*— the survival of the Gondal material is among those which Emily Brontë's admirers are bound to wish could have occurred. It is highly possible that some of the poems now rather loftily dismissed as weak and pretentious would gain in strength if we knew, as Emily Brontë did, the supportive context in which they were conceived and written. The posturing strain, the vein of melodramatic extremism, the thrill of what can strike the reader as a false excitement, may have proved legitimate in their original surroundings.

It is almost as if Homer had left us only snatches of the *Iliad*; as if we had, for instance, Andromache's lament for Hector without understanding the implications of his fall for her, for Astyanax, for his aged parents and all his people. Again, imagine what we should make of *Njal's Saga* if we possessed only Hrut's first enigmatic response to Hallgerd, his distrust of her beauty and her "thief's eyes", without knowing what sinister use she was to make of these attributes. The devout may still continue to make it their morn prayer that, like *Love's Labour's Wonne*, the *Life of Emperor Julius* or even Anne's *Solala Vernon's Life* will somehow, somewhere, surface. But since it is not possible to recapture Gondal in the present state of our knowledge, any more than it is to make Emily Brontë herself "abide our question", we must, simply, come to terms with what we have.

This, in fact, like so much else in life, is easier said than done. Emily Brontë's strangeness, her remoteness, have meant that even her keenest commentators may mislead, pointing the way confidently up blind alleys or side tracks. The magnitude of her achievement, taken with her reticence and the private, teasing, enclosed nature of the Gondal world, make her techniques and processes difficult to analyse and pin down. Some critics fall back on the assumption that this body of work just happened, by itself, and treat it as some tremendous awe-inspiring natural phenomenon, like Niagara Falls or the Grand Canyon. Even her admirers may play down the idea of her work as something *made*, the product of a controlling intelligence of acute creative ability.

For, from the beginning, the stress has been on Emily Brontë's "unconscious felicities", "instinctive art", side by side with her lyrical power. These remarks were made by an early reviewer, who, while praising *Wuthering Heights* honestly and perceptively, pronounced it "the unformed writing of a giant's hand; the 'large utterance' of a baby god".[2] Another reviewer (Allott, p. 323) says, "she has not to do with intellect, but emotion . . . the passion she has chosen is love", later identifying in her work "that *original* cadence, that power of melody" as the sign of "the born poet".

Praise of the art, which yet gives insufficient credit to the artist, is no praise at all. In this way Emily Brontë has been done something of a disservice, even by those who have felt most strongly for her. Charlotte Brontë, in her love for one who must have been a most awkward person to love, mourned her sister in strange ways, recreating an idealized Emily in Shirley, and trying to obtain from the world a posthumous pardon for the "rude and savage" *Wuthering Heights*. Charlotte Brontë in fact contributed to notions of Emily Brontë as an untutored genius piping her native woodnotes wild, with her stress upon the physical limitations of Emily Brontë's life (her rarely going out, or talking to people, and so on), and also with placing so much emphasis upon the mysterious and uncontrollable power of genius as "something that strangely wills and works for itself" (Allott, p. 287). Notice too Charlotte Brontë's concentration upon the "wild", and, paradoxically, the "homely" in Emily Brontë—but the whole line of thought posits a truly classical belief in the need and efficacy of training for genius—something that to our way of thinking has been amply disproved, for example by Emily Brontë herself.

It seems curiously difficult, with Emily Brontë, to accept what is there; to begin with and from the authority of the text itself. Red herrings abound, and we are too readily drawn into such irrelevancies as poor loving Charlotte Brontë's talk of Emily Brontë as she would have been "in health and prosperity", had she been in contact with "other intellects", or even the unwittingly

73

comical "Ellis will not be seen in his full strength till he is seen as an essayist" (Allott, p. 245). Needless to say, Emily Brontë's French *devoirs* have since been given to the world[3] without dislodging *Wuthering Heights* and the poems from their supremacy in our estimation.

Another potentially misleading area of discussion, and one which needs to be approached with caution and precision, is the question of the dramatic in Emily Brontë's poetry. It is true that she shows herself capable of using the dramatic technique of direct address in an enormous variety of different situations and *personae*. Among these we may isolate the simple approach of H. 14, "I saw thee, child, one summer's day", or that of H. 80, "Geraldine, the moon is shining"; the Blakean H. 3, "Tell me, tell me, smiling child"; or the differing moods of exclamation and apostrophe, as in A.G.A's paean, "There shines the moon" (H. 9), and "How still, how happy!" (H. 93). Few poets are so free with the vocative; she is mistress too of the tone of effortless command—"Come, sit down on this sunny stone" (H. 93) and "Light up thy halls!" (H. 85)—although in the nature of things Gondal other characters may question or reject the demands made upon them, and her direct address technique often modifies to a question and answer structure; or even, more typically perhaps, a wild questioning which, as in H. 82, "Where were ye all? and where wert thou?", perfectly conjures up for us the silent faithless ones around the speaker. Not uncommonly, too, she uses a question to end a poem: "Geraldine, wilt thou delay?" (H. 80). Variations of this are the voices of cursing, exhortation and lamentation, which may modify into self-address or self-question: "Forget them—O forget them all" and "Why return / O'er such a past to brood and mourn?" (H. 15). Without in any way undervaluing her more reflective mood, it remains a remarkable feature of her work just how many of her poems plunge in in this direct and startling way, with a direct address—and how central is this technique for stimulating and involving the readers, not relaxing the poetic hold upon them even at the end.

A unique and arresting feature of Emily Brontë's poetic world is the number of speaking parts it contains, the wide-ranging *dramatis personae* with exotic names, desires and capacities. Browning indeed seems her poetic inheritor here, with his well-

peopled monologues and scenes. We may readily conceive of his
handling the recurrent figures of the outcast boy, the tyrant queen,
and the betrayed lover; or indeed the common soldier of H. 28,
the dying maiden of H. 42, the minstrel apostrophizing his harp
in H. 59, or the soothing maternal voice of the lullaby in H. 62.
Nor, with Browning's interest in morbid psychology, would we
feel that the spirit who haunts the doomed "child of dust" in
H. 14, or the other weird manifestations of Emily Brontë's
haunted and guilt-ridden characters, who carry their past about
them continually, would be outside his range.

Yet the comparison with Browning can take us farther into the
heart of Emily Brontë's mystery. While she may, with him, cover
a range of character-types and situations, we could never say that
she achieves the delineation of personality, the sound of the individual voice with all the notes of anger, weariness, or resignation so intensely peculiar to each well-observed human being, as
Browning was to do. "How long will you remain?" (H. 114)
illustrates this. It is couched in the form of a dramatic monologue;
but the reader's ear is perplexed by the alternation of question
and answer, since both voices sound the same. Ultimately here,
as in much of her work, the effect is not *dramatic* as we understand the term (though doubtless so in the original vivid conception).

This is not to underestimate the gripping quality of the poetry,
which links with the riveting power of *Wuthering Heights*; it is
very rare to have a volume of poems which it is, in the standard
phrase, "impossible to put down". Incontestably she possessed
the ability to speak with a strange magic, dark fascination and
mesmerizing intensity; see, for instance, "I am the only being
whose doom" (H. 11), with the unexpected and shocking turn in
the last couplet:

> 'Twas grief enough to think mankind
> All hollow, servile, insincere;
> But worse to trust to my own mind
> And find the same corruption there.

Yet with all this, her gift is not that of the creator of characters
as people, who move and talk in imitation of human action. Hers
is not that "one touch of nature" that "makes the whole world

kin". Like Shakespeare she did not need to be king, queen, despot or victim in order to delineate the condition; but unlike him she never penetrated it. She deployed her characters with a powerful flourish, but the conviction with which they move and speak is Emily Brontë's, rather than their own; she dons the robes, the crowns, the fetters, the boots and spurs at will, and her creations are truly hers, they speak in her voice, in her accents of defiance, rage, and love. Truly she played the "baby god" with the inhabitants of her created world; and a tyrannical one, too.

This is her peculiar gift, and the source of her fascination. We long to be admitted to share her megalomaniac fantasy. But the essentially Shakespearean facility of so entering a character as to *become* it, the greatness so to diminish oneself as to dwindle into nothing but the other, the ability to allow the character to speak not in his creator's voice but in his own—this is not Emily Brontë's, and the comparison with Shakespeare, helpful as a way in, at this point becomes misleading. Whatever the requirements of the ability to make us feel that we are hearing the words and thoughts of one person, and that one only, Emily Brontë did not have them. Hers is a ventriloquial gift, not a dramatic one, and this is a paradox indeed, in view of the dramatic nature of much of what she writes, the dramatic basis of the original Gondal "play" itself, and the intensity and energy of her mind which naturally caused her to project outward, in the more public form of drama, what she thought and felt. One final example in summing up. Her poem, "If grief for grief can touch thee" (H. 138), is a perfect illustration of her Gondal manner. A brilliant, haunting lament of betrayal, whose pain, but that the "worn heart" of the poet "throbs" rather more "wildly", recalls that of Shakespeare in the *Sonnets*—yet it is plainly not personal in the way that Shakespeare's poems are, nor could we say with any conviction which of Emily Brontë's *dramatis personae* it properly belongs to. It is, inescapably, a cry from the soul—but whose?

If, as Keats said, we hate poetry that has a palpable design on us, then that is why we love Emily Brontë. But, even in our admiration of her effects, we should not therefore confuse her masterful confidence with effortless ease and unconscious facility. Hers is the art that conceals art; the result, at its best, is truly that of "carefullest carelessness". Far from being the product of an untutored genius, her work everywhere conveys an overwhelming impression of conscious artistry. Charlotte knew this; in a letter of 16 November 1848 to W. S. Williams she declared her belief that "Ellis" possessed "the very finish and *labor limae*" which she herself lacked.

We must, though, distinguish between the dynamic of creativity, the self-generated and astonishing momentum of the poems, and the helpless headlong flow which Charlotte elsewhere describes. While we should probably all agree that poets are born, not made, poetry itself certainly isn't. It has to be generated, delivered, shaped and assisted into life. Poetry should, and rightly, come as naturally as leaves to a tree; but it will not write itself. "The road lies through application study and thought" (Keats's letter to Taylor, 24 April 1818)—any examination however cursory, of Emily Brontë's poetry, will show how carefully she attended to the techniques of creation, how painstakingly she sought the appropriate expression for her provocative vision. The success, the excitement of the result, should not blind us to the difficulties she needed to overcome in achieving it, in finding the variations of form, rhyme and rhythm to meet the challenge of the content. We can only marvel at how hard she must have worked, at the energy of her endeavour.

This energy, expressed as honesty and directness, is the source of her impact and attraction. Her hold upon her readers (and most of her admirers would agree that this hold is little short of mesmeric in its intensity) is rooted in two elements. Both are equally compelling, both are manifestations of her extraordinary drive; the one is of content, the other, style.

What is exciting about Emily Brontë's style is its astonishing confidence. Her sureness of touch would be impressive in a much older practitioner of the demanding art of versification; but in an inexperienced girl, who had hardly begun upon her mature life before she was torn out of it, it is little short of miraculous. There are, of course, the moments when her flowers are just fragrant, her grass green, and her skies blue; there are some attention-seeking archaisms like "yesternight" and "verdant"; there is perhaps an over-reliance upon certain favourite words, "drear", "dazzle", wild", "ghastly" and "gloom" (though it could be argued that this kind of insistence is a contributory cause of her hypnotic effect). On the whole, however, we may rather wonder that her poetry is so free of youthful weaknesses and self-indulgences than waste time picking up the errors she does commit. So to do is to close our eyes to the great and good things which lie scattered about throughout her work.

One of these is certainly the gift for the memorable phrase. Who would not be haunted by "the sea of death's eternity", the "child of dust", the "portals of futurity", the "moonlight wild", "sweet as amber", or "that wide heaven where every star / Stared like a dying memory"? This facility in evocation is part of a wider gift, that of creating a variety of impressive visual images; we remember the Emily Brontë landscape in a series of photographic representments—the arch of heaven, the moor at night with one solitary inhabitant, the full moon and the lone star. Later, these natural images are interwoven with those of startling fantasy, expressing surreal moments of perception like that of the little twittering glittering spirits, sparks of fire, evoking subliminal memories of Stoic theories of reincarnation in H. 170; in this context we think too of the vision of "The Philosopher" in H. 181:

> "A Golden stream, and one like blood,
> And one like Sapphire, seemed to be,
> But where they joined their triple flood
> It tumbled in an inky sea."

Many of Emily Brontë's images are built upon the ancient principle of contrasts; not, in her case, the gradations of tone or subtle shades of meaning, but that of stark opposition. Extremes lent themselves readily to the presentation of her own intense and strongly-varied apprehension; extremes were her natural mode. Hence, for instance, the importance of one of her favourite images, that of the grave, which in itself catches up much of what she wishes to say about living *and* dying. It implies the same apposition between the stillness of death and the busyness of life which is the stuff of much of her imagery; we see constantly in her poems a recurrence of all the physical images associated with being free, and with its opposite; birds, animals, adventurers male and female, are set against tyrants, their victims, and their paraphernalia of dungeons, fetters and coercion, their reluctant prey.

This simplification may appear to convey a reduction of her associative power; the grave, in her work, stands too for the paradox of life in death among the mourners beside it, for the strength of the spirit after death, for the walking ghost, the memory that is the ghost, so strong that it lives on, and for the dead, who, Banquo-like, refuse to keep their graves or take their eternal rest —as against the living death of being confined, constrained, tormented.

Extremes characterize too her remarkable use of colour; remarkable for its evocation of all the brilliant effects of nature and art without much overt employment of the epithets of colour in themselves. That is to say, while she does use for example "blue", usually in conjunction with "clear", or green, red, brown and so on, her colour effects are most frequently accomplished by the introduction of phenomena of nature which suggest ideas of colour without actually declaring them; dawn, sunset, frost, mist, the robin, blood, snow.

Among this group, and probably the most memorable of them, are all the terms of light and dark. Although predominantly a night person, Emily Brontë did not neglect the effects of day, but throughout her poetry is revealed as a "watcher of the skies" in all their phases and moods. "Darkness and glory" are everywhere opposed and contrasted through the use of such terms as "sparkling", "cloudless", "dazzling", "bright", "cloudy grey", "dim", "gloomy"; colour is defined in Emily Brontë's work as much by its absence as by its presence. Indeed, any colour pattern of her world as a whole must present itself to our imagination as a blackness shot through here and there with brilliant or vivid contrasts; "midnight and moonlight and bright shining stars". As we see from this, no one word is particularly fresh or powerful in itself; but, as with Keats's "Ode to Autumn", the effect is cumulative. "There shines the moon" (H. 9) is an early example of this method. Even in this poem of her eighteenth year we note, too, another characteristic feature of her use of colour, and one which was to increase in importance; that is, the way in which adjectives are supplemented by verbs of colour in such a way as to add weight and vigour, and to make her poems, in her own verbs, "gleam", "glow" and "flame":

... And bursting through the leafy shade
A gush of golden sunshine played,
Bathing the walls in amber light
And sparkling in the water clear
That stretched below—reflected bright
The whole wide world of cloudless air ...

With maturity, too, Emily Brontë perfected even more striking and sophisticated colour effects. Even as early as "Will the day be bright or cloudy?" H. 2), her "golden flowers" are partly literal (the next line has them "sparkling in sunshine and dew") but mainly they suggest an other-worldly vision of the promised glorious future. Later we have the fascinating and complex pattern of contrasts between the "golden suns", the blackness of night and death, the prophetic "rose-red smile" of dawn, and the shining brightness of morning achieved in stanza seven of "The busy day has hurried by" (H. 104). Equally exciting is the colour pattern in "On the Fall of Zalona" (H. 156); the Gondal adventures, naturally perhaps, stimulated the formation of gaudy scenes, painted in arresting primary colours—blue, bright, light, white, gold and emerald assault our visual sense in the first two stanzas alone.

Another striking element of Emily Brontë's verse, and one which is perhaps the most expressive of the energy of her mind and style, is her use of verbs of movement. From her earliest ventures into poetry-making she displayed a grasp that older hands might envy on one of its fundamental laws; that the force of a piece of writing lies in its verbs, not in its decorative adjectives and adverbs. So we have, in "High waving heather", for example, a torrent of verbs, bending, blending, descending, bursting, breaking, rending, extending, shining, lowering, swelling, dying, roaring, flying and flashing—in this piece (H. 5) Emily Brontë celebrates, with all the vigour of her eighteen years, a delirious frenzy of movement. She is not always to be so active again, but like Cathy's heaven in *Wuthering Heights*, hers is a busy universe; even over Elbe's quiet grave the ferns toss in the breeze. Later, in "Lines by Claudia" (H. 102), the verbs "burning", "bending", and "brooding" in three successive lines of the first four-line stanza add power and intensity to what could otherwise be a conventional pastoral scene, while in stanza two the "mellow hum of

bees / And singing birds and sighing trees" again recall the young
Catherine's "perfect idea of heaven's happiness" in chapter 24
of *Wuthering Heights*. It is through her verbs, too, that Emily
Brontë achieves her much-admired effects of balladic simplicity
and fervour; "for which we fought and bled and died" (H. 102).
This use of verbs to lend authenticity and muscularity to verse
lines was a skill which Emily Brontë was still perfecting at the end
of her life; its culmination lies in the almost intimidatingly magnificent "No coward soul is mine" (H. 191), where of the nineteen words in the fifth stanza, nine are verbs:

> With wide-embracing love
> Thy spirit animates eternal years
> Pervades and broods above,
> Changes, sustains, dissolves, creates and rears.

Movement and colour, then, are vital elements of this work;
and, of the other senses which Emily Brontë sought to stir through
her poetry, well to the fore was that of hearing. A main source
of the satisfaction and delight which we derive from Emily
Brontë's poems lies in her creation of rich and varied sound patterns. Her lines are full of memorable resonances—that of
"thunder . . . a mournful story" (H. 2), of wind (*passim*), of "inspiring music's thrilling sound" (H. 4), of stormy blasts, of the
robin's "wildly tender" song (H. 7). Then, too, her lines in themselves make agreeable sounds, fall into patterns which strike very
acceptably upon the ear. Her use of rhyme, for instance, simple,
bold and strong, never disappoints with feebleness or evasion; she
will not cheat for the sake of a rhyme, working in a redundant
"deceiving elf" or "little fay" as Keats and Hardy do. Occasionally
she attempts feminine rhymes: forever/never, falling/palling,
weeping/sweeping, are some examples; sometimes too acceptable
near-rhymes (heaven/even, laid/head, return/mourn) give way to
near-misses like showered/adored, or hard/sward. But in general
the overwhelming reliance upon monosyllables ensures success;
her rhymes chime with an astonishing accuracy upon the mind's
ear. Her manipulative skill is well illustrated in "Lines by Claudia"
(H. 102), with its intricate rhyme scheme; she readily alternates
four-line stanzas rhyming *abab*, with six-line stanzas rhyming
aabcbc:

I heard the mellow hum of bees
And singing birds and sighing trees,
And far away in woody dell
The Music of the Sabbath bell.

I did not dream; remembrance still
Clasped round my heart its fetters chill;
But I am sure the soul is free
To leave its clay a little while,
Or how in exile misery
Could I have seen my country smile?

Rhyme goes hand in hand with its sister, rhythm; and the conscious artist in Emily Brontë never shrank from the often enormous technical problems implied in rhythmic variation, practising and experimenting in an impressive range of metres. Her favourite was always the brisk tetrameter, for which she showed a constant fondness over the more conventional pentameter. Yet this basically simple line—"I gazed upon the cloudless moon" (H. 110) – was constantly modified by the introduction of a trochaic inversion in the first foot, as in H. 9, "There shines the moon", where, of sixty-eight lines, twenty-three begin with the inverted foot. Notice the effect of this in line two of the third stanza of H. 113, "Mild the mist upon the hill" (which further displays her refusal to accept as a tyranny her chosen rhythm, her ability to pack a line almost to overflowing with sound and meaning):

I watch this cloudy evening fall,
After a day of rain:
Blue mists, sweet mists of summer pall
The horizon's mountain-chain.

See too "Loud without the wind was roaring" (H. 91) where the introduction is constructed upon the basis of the tetrameter, which then modulates into a running parlour-ballad rhythm which is quite different.

This ability to change gear within a poem (as also in "Alone I sat", H. 27), is only part of a general interest in different forms of stress and emphasis. Emily Brontë liked too the trimeter, an aggressive little line very demanding of the reader, and potentially hypnotic in intensity, especially when, as here, it gives way to a fuller line and then reverts again:

> And truly at my side
> I saw a shadowy thing
> Most dim, and yet its presence there
> Curdled my blood with ghastly fear
> And ghastlier wondering.

(H. 12)

She always reserved to herself the freedom of adding to or subtracting from one of the regular rhythms, so that the reader is stimulated by a beat which recalls, but yet does not sound like, one that he knows well in other contexts. Interesting here is the balladic "A.G.A. to A.E." (H. 16), which is roughly based on an anapaestic measure like *Lochinvar*, and "Awake! awake!" (H. 40), which has an iambic pentameter with an intermittent feminine ending. This has the effect of making it sound like a hymn, a battle-hymn; one can readily imagine it as a sung rhythm, and also as a marching one. Some of the unfinished pieces or fragments are particularly fascinating in a consideration of Emily Brontë's use of rhythm; one manuscript sheet holds "Iernë's eyes were glazed and dim" (H. 46), where many trochaic lines unite to produce an urgent and balladic effect, and also this skilfully-wrought snippet:

> All hushed and still within the house;
> Without—all wind and driving rain;
> But something whispers to my mind,
> Through rain and through the wailing wind,
> Never again.
> Never again? Why not again?
> Memory has power as real as thine.

(H. 45)

In her handling of rhythm as much as in her presentation of her characters Emily Brontë knew how to be flowing or terse, knew how to storm or soothe. In H. 74, for instance, the long lines have a smooth and elegiac glide to them:

Old Hall of Elbë, ruined, lonely now;
House to which the voice of life shall never more return;
Chambers roofless, desolate, where weeds and ivy grow;

Windows through whose broken arches the night-winds sadly mourn;
Home of the departed, the long-departed dead.

Yet in stark contrast is the sinister manipulation of the trimeter
in H. 111, "Shed no tears o'er that tomb", where every syllable
carries a doom-like beat of grief and reproach; the same technique
is used again in H. 163, "In the earth", which contains many such
heavily impressive lines charged to capacity with thought, feeling,
and stress. Even in her last years, when the bright future which
had beckoned to the members of her family in their teens had
given way to a world of doubt and despair; when Charlotte, Branwell and Anne had all been disappointed in their ambitions, and
the two girls were suffering, with an immediacy which revitalizes
a tired phrase, the pangs of unrequited love—even amid all this,
the pulse of the true artist continued to beat strongly in Emily
Brontë. Within one year, 1844, she ranged from the simplicity of
her old favourite, the ballad refrain of the tetrameter which she
had by now mastered as well as any other writer in English was
ever to do, through a more complex set of six-line stanzas in "To
Imagination" (H. 174) whose metrical pattern recalls the second
part of a Shakespeare sonnet, rhyming *abab* with a final clinching
couplet, *cc*, through to the extraordinarily daring and complex
"D.G.C. to J.A." (H. 175):

Come, the wind may never again
Blow as now it blows for us;
And the stars may never again shine as now they shine;
Long before October returns,
Seas of blood will have parted us;
And you must crush the love in your heart, and I the love in mine!

All this unites to form, for the reader, her quite unmistakeable
tone. Her variety and skill exist to serve a rare talent, and one
with some quite unique features of perception. Her awareness
of the dark side of nature, for instance, of the underworld of
human affairs, and her reliance upon the Gothic element as
its objective correlative, lend backbone to her work—it is this
which can transfigure what might otherwise be the utterances of
a versifying pet lamb. The opening couplet of H. 94, "The blue
bell is the sweetest flower / That waves in summer air", could
almost come from any nineteenth-century miss's notebook of

poetic effusions. But even in stanza two we recognize a different and weightier talent—"There is a spell in purple heath / Too wildly, sadly dear"—the intense and unexpected adverbs here so entirely characteristic of her mode of apprehension. The poem as a whole indeed, so apparently artless in its inception, moves us on through a complex progression of aural, tactile, and emotional sensations—the remembered scent of the violet, the mourning tears and lamentation of the narrator, the silvery, sapphire and emerald of the flower, its colours artificially heightened by the passion of the moment of perception of it; until the poem builds to a climax which is inescapably Emily Brontë, in tone, form and content:

> If chilly then the light should fall
> Adown the dreary sky
> And gild the dank and darkened wall
> With transient brilliancy,
>
> How do I yearn, how do I pine
> For the time of flowers to come,
> And turn me from that fading shine
> To mourn the fields of home.

What was the aim, the drive behind Emily Brontë's poetry, the struggle of her artistry to be at all costs accurate? She put the honesty of her energy to work at one of the most unusual and difficult task of poetry, the account of her mystical experiences. If her style is, as we have seen, sinewy, personal and impressive, how much more so is the content of this theme—uniquely personal, uniquely impressive. An important preconditioning influence, here, and one we may do well to begin with, is that of nature.

Emily Brontë is, *par excellence*, our poet of nature's less benign aspects. Few writers have so consistently celebrated, or at least incorporated, the action of relentless rain, dreary winds, storms, mist, and the sunless hours of a "heaven lorn". Did any better know than Emily Brontë how to "form [her] mood to nature's mood", and vice versa? In places, of course, there is considerable degree of reliance upon the standard "props" of nature, snow, frost, summer, sun, and so on, occasionally conveyed in archaic and self-conscious poetic terminology: "Cynthia's silver morning", for example. But this type of pseudo-pastoral effect was to give way to the truly-felt and simply moving "How clear she shines! How quietly / I lie beneath her silver light" (H. 157). This in fact summarises for us the constant style of Emily Brontë's nature references. The environment is all important. The details are observed in their place, but they are rarely particularized, or presented with the startling immediacy of the freshness of first observation.

There are exceptions to this, occasions when her epithets are wonderfully apt, unpredictable, and vivid. Her "iron clouds", for instance, the "waves in their boiling bed", or "the blue ice curdling on the stream"; all these waken our own duller senses to the singularity and strange beauty of what is described. On the whole, however, nature is present rather as the essential background and preconditioning factor without which the thoughts of the poem could not have birth, rather than as a subject in itself; and consequently its contours, its peculiarities and landmarks, are not isolated and specified. In Emily Brontë's landscape we grow accustomed to seeing a wood, a lark, an aged tree; while in "I've been wandering in the greenwoods" (H. 128), with its casual catalogue of flora and fauna, there is more than a hint of the sublime Wordsworthian vagueness of "a violet by a mossy stone"—the very phrase of which occurs in Emily Brontë's "blue bell" poem (H. 94): "And that wood flower that hides so shy / Beneath its mossy stone."

Wordsworth seems at first to have more than a passing connection with Emily Brontë, as the other great nature-lover and mystic of English poetry; and Emily Brontë displayed a continuous response to the ebb and flow of the seasons, to the action and interaction of the elements of wind, sun, night and stars, and to the very sounds of nature's working, which we associate with this type of mystic, the Wordsworthian. Yet at other times she shows an infinitely calm and objective recording of nature rather than a response to it: "The deer are gathered to their rest / The wild sheep seek the fold" (H. 19)—in a mood which recalls Sappho's immortal evening piece, "O Hesper, you bring homeward . . . the sheep to the fold, the goat to the stall, the child to the mother".

This was because, like so much else, her mystical appreciation

86

grew and developed during the course of her life. We have to trace its maturing from stage to stage as she realized and concentrated her powers. From the very first her poems are full of references to visions, tremendously clear mental images both real and imaginary; in H. 3, "Tell me, tell me", for instance, the "smiling" child "sees" in a brilliant evocation both the "green and flowery spray" with the bird poised for flight, and also the sea of glorious infinity. There is, too, the frequent representation of Gondal characters being "rapt", and "unheeding", in intensely engrossing spiritual states. What we may feel is the first declaration of this capacity finds voice in H. 12, "The night of storms had passed", although Emily Brontë still felt it necessary to present it very conventionally as "I dreamt". This however may be less of a fictional evasion for her, than a conventional excuse for us, if we are unable or unwilling to accept the implications of such visionary possession. Described here are features which we come to recognize as inextricably associated with the mystical experience; physical paralysis, the sense of space and time being different in the "dream" from that of the "real" world, the ideas of eternity and of bridging the unbridgeable void. All these strands are bound up in a sensation of horror, as if in this early version Emily Brontë had to offer it in a conventionalized Gothic treatment; also although it contains no conclusive evidence internally, it is fairly plainly a Gondal poem, and therefore a dramatic mask for Emily Brontë's personal preoccupations, from its position amid a cluster of leaves which also include "Woe for the day! Regina's pride" (H. 13).

The fragmentary H. 23, "And first an hour of mournful musing", gives us our first unmasked treatment of the onset of the mystical experience. Central here is the reference to the focusing upon one significant star. Is it the concentration upon the one bright object that induces the onset of the trance-like state (as, at a much lower level, in hypnosis)? Or is the star to be taken simply in the symbolic sense of the final line, the "star of love"? If so, whose? and for whom? It seems most likely that it is the love of and for the mysterious spirit "He", who comes, as explicitly as he ever does in this body of poetry, in H. 190, "Julian M. and A. G. Rochelle"; but there were to be various developments before this stage was accomplished.

It is of course entirely characteristic of Emily Brontë that, with this key area of her experience, we are reduced to combing the poems for clues, and piecing together the evidence. In H. 24, "Wind, sink to rest in the heather", we have the assertion of what is plain throughout, that the moon, and sometimes "dreary weather" are imperative for the right mood for the onset of the visitant. This is picked up again in "I'll come when thou art saddest" (H. 37), which Fannie Ratchford, in her Gondal notes to Hatfield's edition of the poems (p. 19), describes as showing A.G.A's "triumph . . . clouded by loneliness and remorse". But even allowing for the fact that "A.G.A." is Emily too, this curious first-person account of the visitant as ghost is surely an effort to come to terms with these strange occurrences, and with the fact that they are not always pleasant or rewarding; H. 55, again, "It's over now", carries a reference to "the fearful vision".

With maturity Emily Brontë's capacity to fleet away an hour at a time, "with raptured eye / Absorbed in bliss so deep and dear" (H. 92) appears to have extended and become more frequent. H. 102, "Lines by Claudia", in its description of her vision specifically disclaims now any idea of day-dreams—"I did not dream", is the declaration of the first line. Emily Brontë further insists as a fact that "the soul is free / To leave its clay a little while"; this type of suspense of animation is later to be described in more detail. But we need to distinguish between this type of vision of a scene, and her real visitant, her soul's partner, "that never comes with day". Also, in these visionary trips to another known place, rather than into the higher consciousness as indicated in the mystical poems, there does not seem to be the wrench of "bitter waking", the terrible return to the chains of the flesh.

Amid all the other wealth of her material, the endless explorations of Gondal situations, Emily Brontë repeatedly returned to the attempt to catch and set down in poetry the nature and effect of this happening. At times she is emphatic in her assertion of its pre-eminence, as in the telling fragment of (H. 105):

> What though the stars and fair moonlight
> Are quenched in morning dull and grey?
> They are but tokens of the night,
> And *this*, my soul, is day.

At others she is more hesitant, giving expression to mixed feelings:

> It is too late to call thee now:
> I will not nurse that dream again;
> For every joy that lit my brow
> Would bring its after-storm of pain.
>
> Besides, the mist is half-withdrawn;
> The barren mountain-side lies bare;
> And sunshine and awaking morn
> Paint no more golden visions there.
>
> (H. 135)

Then again, in H. 140, "The Night-Wind", she attempts a
version of her visitant in a dialogue with the night wind; there
is an interesting hint of pantheism in what he breathes in her ear,
that the "myriad voices" of the leaves rustling "instinct with
spirit seem". From this it seems that Emily Brontë's visitant
was as real as a human being to her, more real perhaps; he is
endowed with the capacity for affection—"Have I not loved thee
long?"—he bestows kisses, even playing the part of a seducer with
"I'll win thee 'gainst thy will". There is a suggestion, too, that his
appeal is to Emily Brontë's sensuous emotions, and that she resists his "power to reach [her] mind".

Between May and July of 1841 Emily Brontë seems to have
made a sustained effort to pin down her mystical experiences. In
H. 147 "Shall earth no more inspire thee?", an outside being
addresses the poet as a "lonely dreamer". This visitant appears
to reprove the dreamer for permitting useless intellectual questing
in an unknown void—"regions dark to thee"—and as the poem
progresses we gain renewed intimations of the poet as Pan,
seducing the poet-dreamer, "I know my mountain breezes / En-
chant and soothe thee still", reminding the poet of past depend-
ency, "I've seen thy spirit bending / In fond idolatry", and
demanding a return to the old allegiance, "I know my mighty
sway"; finally blandishing, "Return, and dwell with me". It is as
if at this stage Emily Brontë is progressing beyond an earlier un-
critical rapturous surrender to sensuous natural delights, in the
direction of an experience in which her considerable intellect
sought to play its part, and that a dominant one.

In the even more interesting H. 148, "Aye, there it is!", Emily
Brontë adopts the distancing *persona* of an outside observer. The
poet describes the appearance of the effect of the visitant upon
the subject; it comes in a "glorious wind", sweeps "the world
aside" and kindles "feeling's fires" as vividly as in former times.
The narrator continues relentlessly, as if hypnotizing the subject:

> And thou art now a spirit pouring
> Thy presence into all—
> The essence of the Tempest's roaring
> And of the Tempest's fall—

We should notice too the reference to the suspense of animation
in the last line—"lost to mortality"—not least for its expression
of another fascinating paradox, that of the poet of the "wild will"
voicing, however transiently, a desire for a surrender of personal
identity.

Is it with the "mystical" group of poems that we should place
the tantalizing "My comforter" (H. 168)? The grim couplet "What
my soul bore my soul alone / within its self may tell", if nothing
else, indicates the iceberg nature of Emily Brontë's poetry—most
of the meaning lies beneath the surface of the text. We can at least
exclude such poems as H. 170, "A Day Dream", from consideration. Winifred Gérin, in *Emily Brontë* (Oxford, 1971), p. 152,
describes this as an account of a mystical experience. But this
overlooks Emily Brontë's own way of referring to her different
states. Here she tells us firmly that she sinks into "a reverie", in
which she still consciously reflects upon what she sees. Her consciousness of the outside world is reflected in the awkward dis-
claimer, "Now whether it were really so / I never could be sure",
as she introduces a Coleridgean scene of "a thousand thousand
glancing fires" which "*seemed* kindling in the air" (my italics). The
"little glittering spirits" of this poem are too artfully wrought, too
moral, too well-drilled, like a professional choir, to convey the sublime strangeness of a mystical experience—a fact acknowledged by
Emily Brontë in the last stanza—this is a "noonday dream", a
"fond creation", the product of "fancy", not fervour.

"O thy bright eyes", H. 176, brings us a little nearer to understanding something of this experience which much of the time
appears to defy comprehension. Here there is at least some degree

of personification of her "God", when she appeals to the "bright eyes" and "sweet tongue" of her visitant to check the frown of Reason. Here, too, Emily Brontë is perhaps at her most explicit as to the nature of her visitant. It is, she seems to imply, an irrational thing (this links with earlier hints of sensuousness and emotional significance). It is a "radiant angel", "ever-present", though "phantom"; it is "slave", "comrade", and "king". This last is the operative noun; he is her "God of visions"; *this* is his gift to her. It is not without its cost—she refers to her "darling pain", and the oxymoron effectively glances at the painful tensions within her. He also offers escape by "deadening [her] to real cares". Yet stirrings of orthodoxy cast doubt upon the validity of her experiences, where instinct alone, faith and hope, support and sustain her choice. Another paradox presents itself here; Emily Brontë's is a self-seeking sufficiency—"My own *soul* can grant my prayer"—which, when pursued, leads to a total annihilation of self and selfish preoccupation with "wealth", "power", "glory", and "pleasure", all the things of this world.

Inevitably the more intense her visions grew, the duller in comparison lay the world outside, robbed of its colour by the vividness of the dream world. H. 184, "Ah! why, because the dazzling sun", shows us Emily Brontë going more and more into her inner existence, the night life of spirit and thought. The "glorious eyes" that watch in this poem are pretty clearly those of the stars. But their power is not only to soothe her into peace—once her spirit is lulled into serenity they provide too the stimulus for the free association of thought and feeling which lifts her into the desired but unknown state of unknowing:

> Thought followed thought—star followed star
> Through boundless regions on,
> While one sweet influence, near and far,
> Thrilled through and proved us one.

This state, virtually indescribable because virtually unimaginable by others, achieved its finest poetic rendering in the famous central section of H. 190, "Julian M. to A. G. Rochelle". This poem catches up and illuminates afresh all the vital elements of Emily Brontë's mystical experiences as we have noticed them in earlier references; possibly it was not until this stage that she had sufficiently refined and clarified her own perception of what was taking place within her. We see again, evening, wind and stars; we have the visitant identified as "He", and for the first time set forth as a "messenger of Hope". He brings "visions", in the plural, which "rise and change", indicating plainly that for Emily Brontë mystical possession was not a static state, but one which progressed in itself and also hinted at further progression towards an even more desirable goal—"kill me with desire". There is a brief reference to her having passed through an earlier emotional stage, of strong but confused emotion, which was unlike what she now feels; this supports other suggestions of some sort of emotional apprenticeship served before the full harmonious spiritual union was realized.

The mystical experience itself is described as occurring in two stages. First comes the cessation of physical life, and especially the irritability of expectancy. Paradox again is the natural, indeed perhaps the only, mode of expression here—"mute music . . . unuttered harmony". Then, in one brilliant movement, the inner self ("essence") leaps to commune with a being which can only be described in terms of negatives—the Invisible, the Unseen. Yet despite the use of these (to us) rather chilling abstracts, this being or condition is warm and welcoming to the poet; note Emily Brontë's use of the two supreme metaphors of safety and reassurance in line eighty-three, "home" and "harbour". In agonizing contrast to this certainty, this poem gives the fullest account of what Emily Brontë elsewhere refers to simply as her "bitter waking". It is clear that the freedom which she elsewhere highlights as an essential of her life is more totally hers in this state of mystical possession than in any other mode of her life. Nothing can make her lose her faith in this; again we see the flicker of doubting orthodoxy, when she concedes that her vision may be "robed in fires of Hell, or bright with heavenly shine"; but she remains insistent upon its (ultimately) divine origin.

In the face of an achievement like that of Emily Brontë, the imagination staggers, the self-esteem creeps away rebuked. The startling originality of her experiences combines with her mastery of poetic techniques to dwarf the accomplishment of many poets who are yet often higher in the general esteem. It is a final paradox that one of the most honest of our writers, who emphasized so strongly, using such passionate and authoritative rhythms because she wanted above all to make herself plain, has been taken so oddly at times; especially when the treatment of her as an instinctive, unconscious creature results in a major critic writing off *Wuthering Heights* as a "sport", as Leavis did. Yet this is the writer who consistently, and with amazing resources of technical skill, dealt on our behalf with all the great intolerables of life— pain, loss, and cruelty—who put her originality to work in the service of clarifying for us all the great unoriginal occurrences of human nature and daily existence.

Emily Brontë, as a poet and as a person, was quite devoid of that winning flirtatiousness, that capacity to charm and flatter, that gratitude for guidance and attention which is still felt in some circles, even today, to be a prerequisite of a literary female. While her true greatness has long been acknowledged, perhaps we can now pay her the further tribute of an ungrudging, *unsurprised* admiration of her achievement. We should be able to accept with grace the idea that a young female could, without faltering, create works whose only fellows in literature are the Greek tragedies, the Norse sagas, *King Lear*. We must see the beauty of her artistry and skill, or see her all wrong.

NOTES

1. Reprinted in *The Brontës: The Critical Heritage*, edited by Miriam Allott (1974) p. 456.
2. Sydney Dobell, writing on "Currer Bell" and *Wuthering Heights*, *Palladium* (September 1850) pp. 161–75. Reprinted by Allott, *op. cit.*, pp. 277–283.
3. Perhaps most accessibly in Winifred Gérin's biography (1971), or see *Five Essays Written in French by Emily Jane Brontë*, trans. L. W. Nagel, ed. F. E. Ratchford (Austin, 1948).

3

The Lyricism of Emily Brontë

by BARBARA HARDY

The act of writing verse is sufficiently distinct from that of writing prose to deter most novelists from being poets as well. Among early narrative artists Swift is an exception, and then there is no one until Scott and Emily Brontë. Emily Brontë resembles her two great successors, Hardy and Lawrence, in being capable of controlled and sustained lyricism in prose and poetry.

Whatever we forget of *Wuthering Heights* we remember its moments of strong feeling. There is Catherine's declaration of her identification with Heathcliff, "I *am* Heathcliff", and the distinction between her love for Edgar Linton, which she pictures as "foliage in the woods", and her love for Heathcliff, which she calls "the eternal rocks". She dreams of exile in heaven and of joyful waking on earth. There are as well the second Catherine's definitions of heaven and happiness, which softly echo her mother's harsher vitality, and contrast with Linton's imagery of tranquil happiness. Then there are Lockwood's nightmare panic and cruelty, Heathcliff's unmoving vigil outside Catherine's window, and the last stages of his life when he is possessed by joy and racked by terror. At the end are the hints of foreboding and haunting, succeeded but not cancelled by Lockwood's elegy for the sleepers in a quiet earth.

Emily Brontë instils strong feeling in most of her characters, even in the feebler frames of Linton and Lockwood. Passion is no guarantee of moral strength, and she seems to anticipate that breaking-up of the old stable ego and moral pattern which Lawrence thought typical of nineteenth-century fiction. Emily Brontë's presentation of character depends more strongly on the flux and reflux of passions than on the kind of moral classification

94

found in Jane Austen, Thackeray, Charlotte Brontë, Dickens and George Eliot. These other writers are all novelists of passion, as all good novelists must be, but they work to a rational moral scheme which controls and limits lyrical flights.

In *Wuthering Heights*, however, the lyrical moments stand in an unusual relationship to the novel's action. Feeling may precipitate action, but not invariably, and often it exists as an almost independent entity. Heathcliff is exiled from Wuthering Heights when he overhears an extract from Catherine's emotional confession, "It would degrade me to marry Heathcliff now", but the main import of her statement, its acknowledgement of his central position in her thoughts, is kept from him. Her feeling is not subject to change or development. It contains some features which are cut off from action, like Catherine's dream of being evicted from heaven, which she tells to illustrate her feelings. She tells this dream after she has tried to tell Nelly Dean another dream which has changed and pervaded her "like wine through water". Nelly refuses to listen, it is never told, and the attempt turns into a silence which moves us more ominously than the incidents which are expressed. The gaps in Heathcliff's history, like the mystery of his origin, permit and check speculation, opening cracks and crannies through which possibilities furtively intrude. Critics have attempted to read into the novel precisely that kind of rational background and explanation which the novelist chooses to leave out, and in so doing have provided explanations more obscure than the problems they try to solve—like the crass proposal that Heathcliff is Earnshaw's illegitimate son[1]—and show an insensitivity to the mutenesses and implications of Emily Brontë's lyrical novel. Unlike the fuller and more explanatory plots of Victorian novels, the action of *Wuthering Heights* depends on the unspoken.

Catherine's dream of being exiled from earth to heaven, and her daughter's heaven of wind, sun, trees and birds, augment our sense of human passion without contributing moral or social explantations. Emily Brontë does not show visible ghosts, but she creates visible states of desire, obsession and fear which haunt and terrify the watchers. Heathcliff's haunted dying is directly observed by Nelly Dean. The erratic and unexplained rhythm of his feelings emerges through her story of what she sees, but cannot understand. Emotional experience is registered without cause and effect. Emily Brontë's narrative device of reticence and implication permits the feelings to appear before the observer, without moral or psychological analysis. Events are left out, feelings made dominant. Like all observers of other people, Nelly and Lockwood wonder and speculate, but the variety and incompleteness of their interpretations help to register a course of feeling, intense and concentrated because freed from explanations, analyses and judgements.

In this way, the novel abjures the usual privileges of prose fiction, to analyse and judge its affective action. But it would be a mistake to speak of *Wuthering Heights* as if it contained no more than a trajectory of feeling. Emily Brontë's intensities particularize—at times unnervingly—certain concepts or commonplaces of romantic love: elective affinity, deathless passion, love's torment, overwhelming feeling, constancy, the inaccessible or impossible love. She hits on a narrative form which removes certain elements of fiction in order to shape and intensify others. She creates remoteness so as to produce an intimacy and intensity not usually found in prose fiction.

If her novel's achievement is to create a medium for such intensities, it is not surprising that her lyrical poetry reveals them more extremely. The refusal to tell, the refusal to develop, and the refusal to make linear patterns of cause and effect are all prominent in her verse. Just as the passions of *Wuthering Heights* prove and particularize abstractions, so too does her poetry. She is interested in showing the shape of the affective life, but not just for its own sake. Although she does not let judgement or analysis of feeling inhibit the intense and strong utterance, the affective life of her poetry depends on concepts as well as passions. The outbursts of feeling are not so simple or so indulgent as to fail to evoke ideas about feeling. The achievement of the poetry at its best, is to join impassioned experience with a grasp of the significance of that experience. Emily Brontë occasionally writes love poetry, more frequently poetry expressing experiences of nature, religion and death, but she joins all these subjects or experiences in an exploration of the nature of Imagination.

Some of the poems belonging to the Gondal saga contain fine lyrical passages in a context of weak, banal or melodramatic narrative. Most readers will have their own anthology of lyrical fragments filched from bad verse:

> Sleep brings no strength to me,
> No power renewed to brave,
> I only sail a wilder sea,
> A darker wave. (Hatfield 34)

> I'm happiest when most away
> I can bear my soul from its home of clay
> On a windy night when the moon is bright
> And the eye can wander through worlds of light— (H. 44)

> Yet, still steeped in memory's dyes,
> They come sailing on,
> Darkening all my summer skies,
> Shutting out my sun. (H. 59)

> The world seems made of light; (H. 137)

> But Death has stolen our company. (H. 172)

> Blow, west wind, by the lonely mound,
> And murmur, summer streams,
> There is no need of other sound
> To soothe my Lady's dreams. (H. 173)

> Come, the wind may never again
> Blow as now it blows for us;
> And the stars may never again shine as now they shine; (H. 175)

There are fragments we take from poems, and also some fragments that are all we have: "I'm happiest when most away" (H. 44) or "Fall, leaves, fall" (H. 79). Some fragments are much larger pieces whose language, imagery and rhythmical line are powerfully individual in expression, but companioned by trite action, language and music. Poem 163 has an impressive beginning:

> > In the earth, the earth, thou shalt be laid,
> > A grey stone standing over thee;
> > Black mould beneath thee spread
> > And black mould to cover thee.

> 'Well, there is rest there,
> So fast come thy prophecy;
> The time when my sunny hair
> Shall with grass roots twinèd be.'

And there is one other stanza where a movement of feeling seems to be generated:

> Farewell, then, all that love,
> All that deep sympathy:
> Sleep on; heaven laughs above,
> Earth never misses thee.

But the rest of the poem consists of three extremely crude and exaggerated exclamations, unfortunately typical of much of Emily Brontë's verse-writing. The last verse can stand as an example.

> Turf—sod and tombstone drear
> Part human company;
> One heart broke only there—
> *That* heart was worthy thee!

The best known of her poetic fragments, powerful in a weak context, and gaining immeasurably when extracted from that context, is the description of Hope from "Julian M. and A. G. Rochelle" (H. 190):

> He comes with western winds, with evening's wandering airs,
> With that clear dusk of heaven that brings the thickest stars;
> Winds take a pensive tone, and stars a tender fire,
> And visions rise and change which kill me with desire—
>
> 'Desire for nothing known in my maturer years
> When joy grew mad with awe at counting future tears;
> When, if my spirit's sky was full of flashes warm,
> I knew not whence they came, from sun or thunderstorm;
>
> 'But first a hush of peace, a soundless calm descends;
> The struggle of distress and fierce impatience ends;
> Mute music soothes my breast—unuttered harmony
> That I could never dream till earth was lost to me.

'Then dawns the Invisible, the Unseen its truth reveals;
My outward sense is gone, my inward essence feels—
Its wings are almost free, its home, its harbour found;
Measuring the gulf it stoops and dares the final bound!

'Oh, dreadful is the check—intense the agony
When the ear begins to hear and the eye begins to see;
When the pulse begins to throb, the brain to think again,
The soul to feel the flesh and the flesh to feel the chain!

'Yet I would lose no sting, would wish no torture less;
The more that anguish racks the earlier it will bless;
And robed in fires of Hell, or bright with heavenly shine,
If it but herald Death, the vision is divine.'

She ceased to speak, and I, unanswering, watched her there,
Not daring now to touch one lock of silken hair—
As I had knelt in scorn, on the dank floor I knelt still,
My fingers in the links of that iron hard and chill.

This intense evocation was printed separately in *Poems by Currer, Ellis, and Acton Bell*, in 1846, and is the classical example of Emily Brontë's visionary verse. The visionary feeling, though present in the complete narrative poem, which belongs to the Gondal saga, is greatly intensified and transformed when background, story and character are eliminated. It is sometimes described as mystical, and the startling physical account of the withdrawal of vision does resemble accounts of mystical experience. The surrounding verses are undistinguished in language and uninteresting in character and action, and were evidently eliminated because of these inferiorities. As in her novel, vagueness becomes powerful. But the missing stanzas indicate that she had no aim of deliberate vagueness at the start. They provide explanations which make it hard to take the seven stanzas as being about spiritual trance or ecstasy. When we put the lines back in the context of its story of imprisonment and rescue, the first thing that changes is metaphor. In context, "chain", "torture" and "rack" are not images of spirit tormented by flesh but mean precisely what they say, literally describing a physical imprisonment. The "flesh" which feels "the chain" does not refer to the indifference of flesh to spirit, but to the metal chains, bolts and fetters which bind the

99

lady in the dungeon. The stings, tortures and racks refer to physical punishment, and not to the torture of life-in-the-flesh. The check and agony describe the pain and discomfort of being fettered. The "Desire for nothing known in my maturer years", and "The more that anguish racks the earlier it will bless" refer not to a desire for identity with spirit but to a hoped-for release by Death. Any death and any life-after-death will do. She is indifferent to the theological implications of her vision, 'robed in fires of Hell, or bright with heavenly shine, / If it but herald Death, the vision is divine". The vision of hope, and the return of reality, are more resonantly suggestive of rapture, ecstasy and liberation when removed from their setting but such reverberations are accidents of selection. Even the divine or diabolical vision, which sounds so interestingly reckless out of context, is conditioned by the imprisonment. Once there is a glimpse of possible rescue by the hero, the vision is indeed rejected: "Earth's hope was not so dead, heaven's home was not so dear; / I read it in that flash of longing quelled by fear".

Were Emily Brontë's powers of shaping feeling less, such transformation would of course not be possible. The religious and sexual penumbra of imagery does exist, but in the narrative context there is a restriction not only of feelings but of action and development. The heroine prefers release by rescue to the vision of death. The context of history and character is banal and histrionic, like most of Emily Brontë's narrative verse, but its sifting down to elemental feeling lends it an unearned strength.

What critical taste and accident have done to this poem reflect Emily Brontë's tendency to exaggerated intensity. What is excess in a particular context becomes interestingly expansive when melodrama is cut out. And the act of selection reflects the work of the poetic process itself. When James Joyce reproduces the act of making a poem in *A Portrait of the Artist as a Young Man*, he shows how event decomposes into feeling, how action reduces to image, how narratives of laborious memory are compressed under stress of sensation and feeling. Stephen Dedalus's villanelle concentrates events to distil feeling, standing as a lyrical "transsubstantiation", as he calls it, between two passages of narrative sequence. What Joyce illustrates is the transformation of history into lyric by that process of elimination which reshapes and telescopes event, bringing out new implications by removing context, exposing suggestion, developing nuance and turning actuality into metaphor, sequence into image. Emily Brontë seems to have conceived and written much of her lyric poetry in an expansive narrative context. There is no doubt about the patchiness of her writing in the Gondal poems where character and action are usually so wooden or strained as to be self-eliminating. Many of the lyric poems have gained from being broken off from the full history or story in which they once took a part. The Gondal saga is full of bondage and imprisonment, subjects that roused her sharpest sensations, and it may be that the powerful short poem, often known as "Spellbound" (H. 36), originally existed in a fuller context which explained what was happening, to whom, and why:

> The night is darkening round me,
> The wild winds coldly blow;
> But a tyrant spell has bound me
> And I cannot, cannot go.
>
> The giant trees are bending
> Their bare boughs weighed with snow,
> And the storm is fast descending
> And yet I cannot go.
>
> Clouds beyond clouds above me,
> Wastes beyond wastes below;
> But nothing drear can move me;
> I will not, cannot go.

The poem as it stands is an extreme example of lyric isolation. The withdrawal of narrative is not to be wished away. Lyric poetry removes more than it keeps in order to reproduce or produce pure forms of feeling. This poem is self-generative, growing and coming to an end when growth is complete. To move beyond feeling into explanation would not be an advantage. The first stanza may suggest some direct connection between the night, the weather, and the tyrant spell, since the night's darkening and the winds' wildness and coldness are aggressive and threatening. "And I cannot, cannot go" aids this preliminary sense of connection which continues into the second stanza, where the epithet "giant", more anthropomorphic than anything in the previous lines, adds its weight. But just as the identification seems to become clearer, it is checked by "And yet I cannot go", which discourages the identification of the tyrant spell with hostile nature. In the third stanza the dissociation from nature is complete, "But nothing drear can move me". The tyrant spell is left disturbingly unidentified as the poem's movement ends in the climax and conclusion of the last line. It is more than a negation, "I will not, cannot go". The will now seems to submit to the tyranny. We have gone further than the "cannot, cannot" of the first refrain. Moreover, nature's limited hostility is made clear; it defines constraint by its force of dreariness, but does not explain it. Nature does not explain the bondage. The dreariness accumulates, but only to create a theatre for feeling. And the reader is oppressed by the enclosure and refusal to tell, checked by the frustrated movement towards knowledge. The poem slowly acts out the state of bondage it describes, so going beyond description.

Such apparent opening and final enclosure depend on absence of information. The suggestiveness of what is not defined by nature, but is intensified by the natural harshness, reverberates like Catherine's dream and Heathcliff's vision, answering to Coleridge's praise of poetry that moves best by being imperfectly understood. For the lyric poetry of vision, this seems true. But the short poem's suggestiveness manages to combine feeling with idea, presenting the action of bondage in a way which is reflective and self-conscious, "nothing drear can move me". The self-consciousness, like Catherine's discriminations of love, stops short of analytic control. It is self-reflective but scarcely self-possessed, and its brief moment only occupies a small part of the poem and is perfectly compatible with the enactment of bondage.

The natural world often exists for Emily Brontë in order to suggest what is unnatural, and in this poem unnatural feelings are all we are given. Emily Brontë's lyric poetry is usually less extreme in reserve, but it is often inclined to be enigmatic. Sometimes a fully detailed and narrated action can stress feeling by withholding conventional development, arranging feeling in an erratic or unexpected way. Narrative is often allegorical in Emily Brontë's poetry, but the allegory is evasive, meanings and correlations often being suggested provisionally and then modified or withdrawn. In the incantatory poem, "Far away is the land of rest" (H. 32), the land of rest is not identified until the concluding stanza, and in the third stanza there is a deceptive possibility that it is not death:

> Often he looks to the ruthless sky,
> Often he looks o'er his dreary road,
> Often he wishes down to lie
> And render up life's tiresome load.

This permits a strange argument or apostrophe, in which the mournful man is encouraged—if that is the word—to continue, on the grounds of what has already been achieved: "Leagues on leagues are left behind / Since your sunless course began". The second stage of the poem's own progress, in the fourth and fifth stanza, seems to continue this argument from sheer mileage, and the poem's conclusion can only assert that the goal is rest. This is a limited goal, but rest cannot be timed to choice or convenience. It is an exhausted poem, exhausted perhaps in diction as in mood, and the attempt to prolong its own energy charges the abstract journey of life with feeling. Death was always the goal, but it has to be worked and waited for.

In the powerfully bizarre allegory, "Death, that struck when I was most confiding" (H. 183), Emily Brontë astonishingly creates symbols of faith and hope only to let them be destroyed. The poem describes a lost "certain Faith" most vividly, lusciously and vigorously, through a combination of images which are at once abstract and sensuously particular:

> Leaves, upon Time's branch, were growing brightly,
> Full of sap and full of silver dew;
> Birds, beneath its shelter, gathered nightly;
> Daily, round its flowers, the wild bees flew.

The human actor in this poem has a faith in the seasonal rhythm of the symbolism, and suggests it in the vigour of sapful leaves, sheltered birds, and fertilizing wild bees:

> And behold, with tenfold increase blessing
> Spring adorned the beauty-burdened spray;
> Wind and rain and fervent heat caressing
> Lavished glory on its second May.

> High it rose; no wingèd grief could sweep it;
> Sin was scared to distance with its shine:
> Love and its own life had power to keep it
> From all wrong, from every blight but thine!

The vitality can only be destroyed by Death, and the seasonal symbol is checked in its implications in order to make absolutely clear the frustration of human feeling. "Time for me must never blossom more!" is not allowed to be the last word. That is given to an image which is logical enough, "Strike it down, that other boughs may flourish / Where that perished sapling used to be", and—somewhat oddly—appropriates the imagery of natural decay and regeneration: "Thus, at least, its mouldering corpse will nourish / That from which it sprung—Eternity". Much of the passion in the poem goes into the imagery and action of frustration, but this is framed between the last verse and the first. The poem initially insists, before the story was told, that what is wanted is for Death to strike again—apparently for a third time, as we know by the time we get to the end:

> Death, that struck when I was most confiding
> In my certain Faith of Joy to be,
> Strike again, Time's withered branch dividing
> From the fresh root of Eternity!

The poem manages to contain, without conflict or rancour, the narrative of pain and loss, and the declaration of faith.

"The Night-Wind" (H. 140) is a full narrative argument, with a tense and developing dialogue establishing the relationship between the speaker and the wind. At each stage in the action there is an illusory sense of progress. What the wind first does and says is gentle, like the scene established in the poem's first lines:

> In summer's mellow midnight,
> A cloudless moon shone through
> Our open parlour window
> And rosetrees wet with dew.
>
> I sat in silent musing,
> The soft wind waved my hair;
> It told me Heaven was glorious,
> And sleeping Earth was fair.

The speaker's first rejection of the wind is simply made on the grounds that its thoughts are not necessary: "I needed not its breathing / To bring such thoughts to me," but this argument is immediately followed by a different suggestion:

> But still it whispered lowly,
> 'How dark the woods will be!
>
> 'The thick leaves in my murmur
> Are rustling like a dream,
> And all their myriad voices
> Instinct with spirit seem.'

This seductive whisper seems distinct from the first, with the stress placed on darkness—echoed in Robert Frost's "Stopping by Woods on a Snowy Evening". The darkness is qualified by a larger dream-like lure, and the plea seems to me to be made for spirit rather than humanity. The human actor now rejects the voice on the new grounds that its music has not "power to reach" the mind and recommending that it

> 'Play with the scented flower
> The young tree's supple bough,
> And leave my human feelings
> In their own course to flow.'

We then reach the last stage in the seductive appeal to old acquaintance, "Have we not been from childhood friends?", strengthened and made sinister by the suggestion, however sweetly sighed, that it can overpower the will. There is a seductive deepening of friendship to love. It is love on both sides, but what the wind has loved is the human being, while her love is not just for the wind, but also for 'the night / Whose silence wakes my song'. The invocation of beloved darkness introduces something new into the argument:

> 'And when thy heart is laid at rest
> Beneath the church-yard stone
> I shall have time enough to mourn
> And thou to be alone.'

All the lures and arguments are joined in these last words: death includes the darkness of the woods, the voices instinct with spirit, and the silent night. The conclusion implicitly explains the several rejections, the human being's sense of Heaven and earth, her desire for her human feelings to flow in their own course, the implication that this course is distinct from the world of vegetable nature, and her old affection for darkness, night, silence and the wind itself.

Only when we reach the conclusion do the various rebuttals and appeals become clear. This final darkness, silence, solitude and lamentation is what the wind has always been uttering, as it speaks both for surviving nature and for natural mortality. It can outlast the individual, like Keats's nightingale, but what this sweetness sings is less a solace than a threat. The attempts to distinguish what is human from what is natural meet the inevitable frustration.

Such an attempt to paraphrase calls attention to the poem's reliance on an erratic course of feeling. It does not move towards a climax but gradually and obliquely notes a shift in feelings. The speaker never fully comprehends what the wind's last words can tell the reader, for the telling turns back, giving the process a new and ironic sadness in the recapitulation. Feeling is met with feeling. Meaning is created by a wayward assembly of experiences, not by an intellectual argument. The feelings stop and start, rather than accumulate in an orderly curve.

Although Emily Brontë's poems show a variety of theme and passion, their symbolism and their attitudes come to cohere. There is, for instance, a body of poetry which enacts a clash of will, and an experience of half-desired, half-feared bondage. There is also a community and variety of conclusions about nature, spirit and death. The night-wind itself belongs to a set of images of wind, darkness, moonlight and starlight, which often represent an imaginative force which both bind and are bound by the human speaker. At times it utters an affinity with her mind, "Have we not been from childhood friends? Have I not loved thee long?" and "I needed not its breathing / To bring such thoughts to me", and at times speaks for a nature or a spirit which transcends the individual. The force may be expressed naturally and supernaturally, as in "The Night-Wind" or "Spellbound", There are theological rather than naturalistic implications in "No coward soul is mine" (H. 191), where the sense of a "God within" seems to

create the imaginative realization of a God which exists outside,
and beyond:

> With wide-embracing love
> Thy spirit animates eternal years
> Pervades and broods above,
> Changes, sustains, dissolves, creates and rears.
>
> Though Earth and moon were gone
> And suns and universes ceased to be
> And thou wert left alone
> Every Existence would exist in thee.
>
> There is not room for Death
> Nor atom that his might could render void
> Since thou art Being and Breath
> And what thou art may never be destroyed.

Emily Brontë often questions Imagination by analyzing and
evaluating its capacities. She does not regard Imagination as a
monolithic power. In "Often rebuked, yet always back returning"[2]
there is a separation between the natural imagination and a more
fantastic creative effort. The poem's typically expansive inclusions
create a tension between two efforts of mind. The poem begins
with a large negative invocation of an energy and area of imagination which is to be rejected:

> Often rebuked, yet always back returning
>   To those first feelings that were born with me,
> And leaving busy chase of wealth and learning
>   For idle dreams of things which cannot be:
>
> To-day, I will seek not the shadowy region;
>   Its unsustaining vastness waxes drear;
> And visions rising, legion after legion,
>   Bring the unreal world too strangely near.
>
> I'll walk, but not in old heroic traces,
>   And not in paths of high morality,
> And not among the half-distinguished faces,
>   The clouded forms of long-past history.

The "I will seek not" and "I'll walk, but not" are embedded in the long and detailed account of imaginative rejection, and the rejection, while clearly dismissive—"unsustaining", "drear", "unreal", "too strangely near", "clouded forms"—is sufficiently evocative to make the lure felt.

The positive movement of natural Imagination occupies only seven lines, of these only six remain uninterrupted and unqualified by negatives and rejections. The poem first registers effort, then the last undisturbed six lines create relief after struggle, in the two lines of simple natural celebration: "Where the grey flocks in ferny glens are feeding; / Where the wild wind blows on the mountain side", and the concluding stanza of energetic defence:

> What have those lonely mountains worth revealing?
> More glory and more grief than I can tell:
> The earth that wakes *one* human heart to feeling
> Can centre both the worlds of Heaven and Hell.

Everything that the shadowy region might hold can be found here —glory, grief, Heaven and Hell. Once more, there is the insistence that the individual Imagination can focus, concentrate, and contain extremity and multiplicities. The amorality of the last line, reminiscent of *Wuthering Heights* in its claim for Imagination, also makes a claim for something small and personal, "*one* human heart", and something large and impersonal, "both the worlds of Heaven and Hell". Both are claims for creativity. The retreat to "my own nature" and to earth's nature is not made in the interests of a simplified pastoral repose or pleasure. There is a defiant refusal of restriction, a claim for liberty made in the interests of bravely claiming and facing extremes of experience. But the defiance works both ways, to affirm and to state the pull away from nature. The poems dealing more explicitly and precisely with Imagination show a similar division, and a similar inclusiveness. They offer not a system but a variety of passionate moods which image ideas, and particularize abstraction, though neither steadily nor consistently. At times Imagination compels, at times it frees. At times it is fantastic, at times claims authenticity for vision. At times it seems lost, then found. At times there seems no incompatibility between the extent and force of the individual Imagination and a sense of totally reliable meaning, in a God,

an Immortality, and an Eternity. At times, there is a gap between the sense of imaginative power and its guarantees in religious experience.

Her poetry of Imagination always dramatizes effort and sometimes frustration. In the poem "Ah! why, because the dazzling
sun" (H. 184) there is a severance between a rejoicing nature, lit
and warmed by daylight, and the poet's Imgination, needing the
nourishment of night and stars:

> All through the night, your glorious eyes
> Were gazing down in mine,
> And with a full heart's thankful sighs
> I blessed that watch divine!
>
> I was at peace, and drank your beams
> As they were life to me
> And revelled in my changeful dreams
> Like petrel on the sea.
>
> Thought followed thought—star followed star
> Through boundless regions on,
> While one sweet influence, near and far,
> Thrilled through and proved us one.
>
> Why did the morning rise to break
> So great, so pure a spell,
> And scorch with fire the tranquil cheek
> Where your cool radiance fell?

The night ended, the necessary day rises, and the imagery of the
sun is aggressive, threatening and hostile, though it is what Nature
needs:

> Blood-red he rose, and arrow-straight
> His fierce beams struck my brow:
> The soul of Nature sprang elate,
> But mine sank sad and low!
>
> My lids closed down—yet through their veil
> I saw him blazing still;
> And bathe in gold the misty dale,
> And flash upon the hill.

The poet tries to turn back to Night, and the imagery of un-extinguishable day cannot be wholly harsh or unpleasant, though there is a clever blurring of beneficence and discomfort:

> It would not do— the pillow glowed
> And glowed both roof and floor,
> And birds sang loudly in the wood,
> And fresh winds shook the door.
>
> The curtains waved, the wakened flies
> Were murmuring round my room,
> Imprisoned there, till I should rise
> And give them leave to roam.

This violently physical invocation of day establishes the identification of creativity with night, partly through the logical associations of dream, magic, vastness, concentration, and solitude, the concept of the Imagination's dependence on the sleep of consciousness and the banishment of routine, but partly through invocations of purity, coolness and sweetness. The starlight can be gazed at, "I . . . drank your beams", as the sunlight cannot. The relationship between this brilliant piece of antithetical sensation and "Often rebuked, yet always back returning", brings out the impossibility of imposing a consistent pattern on this poetry.

In another poem about Imagination, "My Comforter" (H. 168), the imagery tells a very different story. There is a clear distinction between a hidden light in the soul, and a hysterically rendered gloom in daylit existence:

> Deep down—concealed within my soul,
> That light lies hid from men,
> Yet glows unquenched—though shadows roll,
> Its gentle ray can not control—
> About the sullen den.
>
> Was I not vexed, in these gloomy ways
> To walk unlit so long?
> Around me, wretches uttering praise,
> Or howling o'er their hopeless days,
> And each with Frenzy's tongue—

But the imagery blurs the simplicity: the outer experience is rendered in terms of an admittedly glorious sunlight, but this is

accompanied and qualified by another glare, "the glare of Hell".
The central statement of suffering transforms and restates a much
weaker verse which describes rather than expresses feeling:

> So stood I, in Heaven's glorious sun
> And in the glare of Hell
> My spirit drank a mingled tone
> Of seraph's song and demon's moan—
> What my soul bore my soul alone
> Within its self may tell.

The refusal to tell is more powerful than the telling. Similarly,
although the soothing power of Imagination's comfort is evoked,
it is provisional and tentative, ushering in and dismissing images
that will not quite render the solace:

> Like a soft air above a sea
> Tossed by the tempest's stir—
> A thaw-wind melting quietly
> The snowdrift on some wintery lea;
> No—what sweet thing can match with thee,
> My thoughtful Comforter?

And the poem ends where it began, with the beginning only of
comfort:

> And yet a little longer speak,
> Calm this resentful mood,
> And while the savage heart grows meek,
> For other token do not seek,
> But let the tear upon my cheek
> Evince my gratitude.

Emily Brontë likes to record imaginative effort and essay, the
process of feeling a mingled pain and consolation. Her concept of
Imagination is not stated but experienced, not understood or per-
ceived statically, but through particulars. In "How Clear She
Shines!" (H. 157) there is an impassioned invocation of Fancy
made in the full knowledge that dream will not last:

> How clear she shines! How quietly
> I lie beneath her silver light
> While Heaven and Earth are whispering me,
> 'To-morrow wake, but dream to-night.'

111

Yes, Fancy, come, my Fairy love!
These throbbing temples, softly kiss;
And bend my lonely couch above
And bring me rest and bring me bliss.

The world is going—Dark world, adieu!
Grim world, go hide thee till the day;
The heart thou canst not all subdue
Must still resist if thou delay!

The poem reverses the process of "Often rebuked, yet always back
returning", beginning with the willing of Fancy and dream, and
then stating Imagination's *fiat* through a string of bitter personi-
fications. They make their presence felt so powerfully that the
poem turns from the hope of consolation to an irony unusual
though not unparalleled in Emily Brontë. Irony admits what
Imagination will have to deny:

And this shall be my dream to-night—
I'll think the heaven of glorious spheres
Is rolling on its course of light
In endless bliss through endless years;

I'll think there's not one world above,
Far as these straining eyes can see,
Where Wisdom ever laughed at Love,
Or Virtue crouched to Infamy.

The concluding four stanzas admit the presences of everything
that will have to be dismissed. The poem dramatizes will and
imaginative intent, but then travels fast and harshly from moonlight
to the unlit world. The dismissal of Joy, Peace and especially Hope,
"a phantom of the soul", makes the invocation a startling gather-
ing-up of hostility and cynicism. The world which needs to be
changed by dreaming is established in all its undiminished horrors.
The poem moves through extremes of feeling, as does "O Dream,
where art thou now" (H. 86) where the feeling is a complex one
in which the memory of vision seems intolerable. Emily Brontë
uses Imagination while she probes its certainties and uncertain-
ties:

112

> Alas, alas for me
> Thou wert so bright and fair,
> I could not think thy memory
> Would yield me nought but care!

There are more poems energetically praising Imagination than poems which lament its passage. The transience is almost always acknowledged, even in poems of praise like "To Imagination" (H. 174) which prizes the world within admitting the "hopeless" world without. This poem vacillates from doubt to assertion, claiming that the important principle is

> . . . a bright unsullied sky,
> Warm with ten thousand mingled rays
> Of suns that know no winter days

but adding Reason's intrusive complaints and Truth's destruction. So it seems right that the concluding stanza gathers together welcome and trust:

> I trust not to thy phantom bliss,
> Yet still in evening's quiet hour
> With never-failing thankfulness
> I welcome thee, benignant power,
> Sure solacer of human cares
> And brighter hope when hope despairs.

One of the best-known poems about Imagination is "O thy bright eyes must answer now" (H. 176), which offers the most complex analysis of Imagination's struggle with Reason, defending Imagination as a "radiant angel" but one which has to speak eloquently at the Judgement seat of Stern Reason. The analysis runs through the sense of bondage and the sense of power:

> So with a ready heart I swore
> To seek their altar-stone no more,
> And gave my spirit to adore
> Thee, ever present, phantom thing—
> My slave, my comrade, and my King!
>
> A slave because I rule thee still;
> Incline thee to my changeful will
> And make thy influence good or ill—
> A comrade, for by day and night
> Thou art my intimate delight—

My Darling Pain that wounds and sears
And wrings a blessing out from tears
By deadening me to real cares;
And yet, a king—though prudence well
Have taught thy subject to rebel.

The poem becomes more lucidly a poem about itself, the constant process of qualification offers a rational yet tense account of imaginative complexity and tension. It is sufficiently assertive to tolerate uncertainty, sufficiently uncertain to confront objections. The final summons admits question, expects an affirmative answer, and asserts the personal and individual guarantee. It tries to claim at the same time the authority of a universal, in the apostrophe to a God, and a God of "Visions":

And am I wrong to worship where
Faith cannot doubt nor Hope despair
Since my own soul can grant my prayer?
Speak, God of Visions, plead for me
And tell why I have chosen thee!

The constant entertainment of acceptance and rejection is subtly at work in the strange poem "Enough of Thought, Philosopher" (H. 181). At the heart of this poem is an elaborately detailed vision of a Spirit standing by the golden, blood-red and sapphire rivers, and finding his unity in an ocean first darkened and and troubled by the joined waters, and then radiantly whitened. The transformation seems inseparable from an intensity of vision formed to see its splendour:

'The Spirit bent his dazzling gaze
Down on that Ocean's gloomy night,
Then—kindling all with sudden blaze,
The glad deep sparkled wide and bright—
White as the sun; far, far more fair
Than the divided sources were!'

The vision is asserted as an explanation, apparently made by the speaker to the "Space-sweeping soul" who uncaringly looks for annihilation since he believes in no possible Heaven or Hell. The speaker's position is different, since he has imagined what the Philosopher has never conceived, and shares the wish for a sleep without identity only because it has been seen but not found. The

114

poem sets a defence of one state of unbelief against another, but its religious feelings self-consciously rest on the dazzling but unreliable findings of Imagination. It weighs poetry against philosophy, to assert the poet's vision, lovingly but doubtingly. "It is too late to call thee now" (H. 135) declares the pointlessness of dream, since "every joy that lit my brow / Would bring its afterstorm of pain". The most powerful image combines barrenness and radiance:

> Besides, the mist is half withdrawn;
> The barren mountain-side lies bare;
> And sunshine and awaking morn
> Paint no more golden visions there.

The poem moves from the strongly asserted refusal to dream to the weaker expression of gratitude for past dreaming:

> Yet, ever in my grateful breast,
> Thy darling shade shall cherished be;
> For God alone doth know how blest
> My early years have been in thee!

In "No coward soul is mine" (H. 191) Imagination goes beyond nature, and the natural images are mostly sterile, "withered weeds / Or idlest froth". There is a striking attempt to use natural images to define transcience, though it is not carried out with complete consistency, for the imagery of light, "I see Heaven's glories shine" and strength, "The steadfast rock of Immortality", are natural images, invoked, magnified, and generalized in traditional religious language. As we have seen, the poem invokes the familiar sense of a vast existence beyond the individual by invoking and then dismissing nature:

> There is not room for Death
> Nor atom that his might could render void
> Since thou art Being and Breath
> And what thou art may never be destroyed.

Emily Brontë can only imagine spirit through nature. "Atom" and "Breath" are physiological terms being made into absolutes. The mind is felt to be capable of apprehending what is outside the mind; its light is part of the light outside: "I see Heaven's glories shine / And Faith shines equal arming me from Fear".

The effort involved in this invocation is rare in her poetry.[3] Whether dealing with the passions of love, nature, death or religious faith, her poetry commonly involves a sense of the gap between the human Imagination and the consequences of its powers. The poetry only once states that perfect equivalence between a light in Heaven and the light of the mind, an image made conventional in many hymns, but given a personal voice here. In the earlier poems, "Spellbound" (H. 36), written in 1837, and "The Night-Wind" (H. 140) written in 1840, there are affinity and acquiescence, but also struggle, reluctance and pain. In this respect, Emily Brontë's self-consciousness about vision is close to that of Wordsworth's and Keats's, also inclined to see the vision as impaired, doubtful, unstable or lost.

Even Emily Brontë's rare love poetry makes the same accommodation, and creates the same tension. In "R. Alcona to J. Brenzaida" (H. 182), the first three stanzas make a strong claim to fidelity in the form of question, not assertion:

> Cold in the earth, and the deep snow piled above thee!
> Far, far removed, cold in the dreary grave!
> Have I forgot, my Only Love, to love thee,
> Severed at last by Time's all-wearing wave?
>
> Now when alone, do my thoughts no longer hover
> Over the mountains on Angora's shore;
> Resting their wings where heath and fern-leaves cover
> That noble heart for ever, ever more?

The question, however, does not receive a negative answer. As with "The Philosopher" the mode is that of painful candour, not irony. The questioning prepares for a complex definition of remembrance, not through a claim of unchanged emotion, but through the admission of necessary change. The third stanza, with its memorable image, "fifteen wild Decembers / From those brown hills have melted into spring", creates movement and plurality to reduce time and yet to measure it. The last two lines of this stanza first appear commonplace in what they say about "years of change", but are then seen to assert a kind of forgetting:

> Cold in the earth, and fifteen wild Decembers
> From those brown hills have melted into spring—

116

> Faithful indeed is the spirit that remembers
> After such years of change and suffering!

The poem is no trite assertion of remembrance, but explains the nature of a survival of love, scrupulously allowing for the passage of time. Love has to forgive the necessary process of forgetting. The explanation makes a melancholy and rational account of a feeling which, though subject to change, remains a feeling of personal love. The speaker, Rosina Alcona, is no Heathcliff; she joins passionate lament with an unobsessed remembrance, eroded and distracted. Bliss has gone, but life has continued:

> No other Sun has lightened up my heaven;
> No other Star has ever shone for me:
> All my life's bliss from thy dear life was given—
> All my life's bliss is in the grave with thee.

Dreams have gone too, and passion has had to live on, qualified by dreamlessness. We are told this somewhat baldly:

> But when the days of golden dreams had perished
> And even Despair was powerless to destroy,
> Then did I learn how existence could be cherished,
> Strengthened and fed without the aid of joy

It is not simply a life and love-in-memory which is expressed. The memory has dangerously regenerated feeling, as imaginative memory can, and the poem moves out of its rational explanation to the point where reason is in danger of losing control. The individual words are flat, but what is being said is spiritedly conveyed. The poem must end at this point, because energy of remembrance is the force which it resists:

> And even yet, I dare not let it languish,
> Dare not indulge in Memory's rapturous pain;
> Once drinking deep of that divinest anguish,
> How could I seek the empty world again?

Emily Brontë's best love poem is imaginative in the fullest and most exact sense of the word. It recognizes the limits and the indulgences of Imagination, and controls its own passion by that act of recognition. Its dynamism and order show her lyricism once more melting abstraction into particulars. The growth of feeling seems to rely on the powerful syntax which checks, permits, drives and shapes sharp feeling. Like much of her poetry, it has lapses. Its phrases are weak, often conventional. Her ecstatic description often partakes of the vague and uncontrolled hyperbole of hymns: "rapturous pain" and "divinest anguish" are uncomfortably over-intense. But the direct utterance, while flouting restraint, does act as a medium for passion. The poem is characteristic of her strengths and her weaknesses. Emily Brontë can muster more intensity than greater masters of language.

NOTES

1. See Q. D. Leavis, "A Fresh Approach to *Wuthering Heights*", in F. R. and Q. D. Leavis's *Lectures in America* (London, 1969), p. 89ff., and Herbert Dingle, *The Mind of Emily Brontë*, (London, 1974), p. 69ff.
2. This poem is not included in the numbered collection of Emily Brontë's poems because Hatfield conjectures it is by Charlotte Brontë (p. 255). There seems to be little basis for this speculation.
3. "No coward soul is mine" is one of Emily Brontë's last poems, written in 1846.

PART TWO
*Wuthering Heights**

* All references in this section are to the Norton Critical Edition of *Wuthering Heights,* edited by William M. Sale, Jr (New York, 1963).

1

The Originality of
Wuthering Heights

by KEITH SAGAR

In the context of the ninteenth-century English novel, the most striking feature of *Wuthering Heights* is its originality. Other novelists, including her sisters, dealt with relationships, manners and morals in a highly civilized society. Emily Brontë had no social life, few relationships outside the household, and neither knew nor cared about the world beyond Haworth. Her inner life was turbulent and passionate. She found on the moors around her living manifestations (so it seemed to her) of those same forces which warred within her. There is little place for nature in the English novel before Hardy; none for wild nature, even in the rural novels:

> In George Eliot's *Adam Bede*, where there is relatively a great deal of 'outdoors', nature is man's plowfield, the acre in which he finds social and ethical expression through work; this is only a different variety of the conception of nature as significant by virtue of what man's intelligential and social character makes of it for his ends.
>
> (Dorothy Van Ghent, *The English Novel: Form and Function*,
> 1953, 251)

Emily Brontë's own nature led her to wild nature as its mirror, subsuming Heaven and Hell. She exulted in the freedom, wildness and purity of the moor, its summer profusion and blossom and birdsong, its space for the spirit to soar in; yet she knew also, and shrank from, the wuthering wind on the heights, the desolation, the inhuman cruelty of its storms and winters leaving nests full

121

of little skeletons. Still she chose the heath as her heaven, knowing that she was choosing exposure and death. She exulted even
in that, the release of her spirit from the body's prison. So the
landscape of the novel is also her own psychic and spiritual
landscape which she explores with single-minded unfaltering
honesty.

The amazing originality of *Wuthering Heights* can be aptly
illustrated by taking further the comparison suggested by Dorothy
Van Ghent with *Adam Bede*, a novel of twelve years later. In
chapter V of *Adam Bede* George Eliot introduces the reader to the
Irwine home:

> Let me take you into that dining room, and show you the Rev.
> Adolphus Irwine, Rector of Broxton, Vicar of Hayslope, and Vicar
> of Blythe, a pluralist at whom the severest Church reformer would
> have found it difficult to look sour. We will enter very softly, and
> stand still in the open doorway, without awaking the glossy-brown
> setter who is stretched across the hearth, with her two puppies
> beside her; or the pug, who is dosing, with his black muzzle aloft,
> like a sleepy president.
>
> The room is a large and lofty one, with an ample mullioned
> oriel window at one end; the walls, you see, are new, and not yet
> painted; but the furniture, though originally of an expensive sort,
> is old and scanty, and there is no drapery about the window. The
> crimson cloth over the large dining-table is very threadbare, though
> it contrasts pleasantly enough with the dead hue of the plaster on
> the walls; but on this cloth there is a massive silver waiter with a
> decanter of water on it, of the same pattern as two larger ones that
> are propped up on the sideboard with a coat of arms conspicuous in
> their centre.

Before commenting on this, let us set it against our introduction
to the interior of Wuthering Heights:

> One step brought us into the family sitting-room, without any
> introductory lobby or passage: they call it here 'the house' pre-
> eminently. It includes kitchen and parlour, generally, but I believe
> at Wuthering Heights the kitchen is forced to retreat altogether into
> another quarter; at least I distinguished a chatter of tongues, and
> a clatter of culinary utensils deep within; and I observed no signs
> of roasting, boiling, or baking about the huge fire-place; nor any

glitter of copper saucepans and tin cullenders on the walls. One
end, indeed, reflected splendidly both light and heat from ranks
of immense pewter dishes, interspersed with silver jugs and tank-
ards, towering row after row, in a vast oak dresser, to the very
roof. The latter had never been underdrawn: its entire anatomy
lay bare to an inquiring eye, except where a frame of wood laden
with oatcakes, and clusters of legs of beef, mutton, and ham, concealed it. Above the chimney were sundry villainous old guns, and
a couple of horse-pistols, and, by way of ornament, three gaudily-
painted canisters disposed along its ledge. The floor was of smooth,
white stone; the chairs, high-backed, primitive structures, painted
green, one or two heavy black ones lurking in the shade. In an arch
under the dresser, reposed a huge, liver-coloured bitch pointer
surrounded by a swarm of squealing puppies, and other dogs
haunted other recesses. (I, 14–15).

Perhaps the first thing to strike us here is the very different
relationship each author seeks with her reader. George Eliot
speaks with a cosy familiarity and is able to take for granted the
reader's trust which her style has bought with certain assurances:
that you and I, dear reader, are the same sort of honest, decent,
homely people, sharing a set of common values; that through this
door are no monsters, nothing which cannot be wholly known
and placed in accordance with those values, only people very like
ourselves. This is, of course, partly trickery, for George Eliot
does intend that her novel shall widen the reader's sympathies.
But only partly. There is no real violation of permitted attitudes.
We know a good deal, from other sources, about George Eliot's
advanced ideas and moral non-conformity, but such was the burden
of being a Victorian and a woman writer that very little of this
gets into the novels, which extend the range of experience of her
less intelligent readers only so far as that of her rather more intelligent ones.

The price paid for the reader's acquiescence in the passage
under discussion is clearly too high. The complacency is achieved
by narrowing the lives of the characters to the point where they
become little more than articulate pieces of furniture. Class can
be deduced from the cut of nostril and upper lip, age from "con-
servatism in costume". With the eye of the connoisseur of antiques
we are invited to "look at that stately old lady, his mother, a

123

beautiful aged brunette, whose rich-toned complexion is well set off by the complex wrappings of pure white cambric and lace about her head and neck".

In her Preface to the 1850 edition of *Wuthering Heights*, Charlotte Brontë spoke of those many readers who had been puzzled or repelled by the book as

> Men and women who, perhaps, naturally very calm, and with feelings moderate in degree, and little marked in kind, have been trained from their cradle to observe the utmost evenness of manner and guardedness of language. . . . (9).

Emily Brontë writes without a care for such readers. Let them squirm and flounder with their representative, Lockwood. The presence of moor and rock is not lessened by the absence of human onlookers, nor can her fictional world be in the least diminished by the defection of faint-hearted readers. The prose dares the reader to leave the padded security of urban and urbane life to confront that which is other, savage and unknowable (perhaps also, if Lockwood is not indeed their double, within themselves).

Lockwood is made to speak a language very like George Eliot's. Heathcliff says "walk in", but "the gate over which he leant manifested no sympathizing movement to the words". When he asserts his fellow-feeling for Heathcliff—"a sympathetic chord within"—he exposes himself as incapable of any real feelings or any understanding of them in others. Of course the whole book is spoken by Lockwood. But Emily Brontë quickly establishes her own convention of flashback. As the narrative gets under way, the narrator, whether Lockwood, or, through him, Nelly Dean, fades away, so that one is never aware of being asked to believe that Lockwood is able to reproduce perfectly the idiom of all the other characters, including Joseph's thickest dialect. The convention also allows for the subject-matter to generate its own intensity of language, its poetic resonances, without forcing us to ascribe a poetic imagination to Lockwood, even though the very same sentence may have begun in his unmistakable voice. The paragraph in question begins as Lockwood; we remain aware of him about as far as the phrase "culinary utensils". But already there has been one hint of what is to come: that the kitchen should be "forced to retreat" hints at the forces at work in the house investing inanimate objects with a sinister presence and threat. The roof, never underdrawn, generates the terrible image of a dissected body, the skeleton exposed, clusters of legs hanging from it. This is the first of many images of cruelty which merge with the real incidents of sadism—the hanging of dogs and cats, the drawing of human flesh across broken glass.

> "Had I been born where laws are less strict, and tastes less dainty, I should treat myself to a slow vivisection of those two, as an evening's amusement" (XXVII, 215).

Though bright and hot, the room seems surrounded by dark recesses in which dogs and black chairs lurk, while the "repose" of the "huge, liver-coloured bitch pointer" under the dresser proves short-lived indeed.

Emily Brontë's utter contempt for the proprieties of her sex, art and time is instanced again and again:

> The dog was throttled off, his huge, purple tongue hanging half a foot out of his mouth, and his pendant lips streaming with bloody slaver (VI, 48).

Aunt Branwell once severely corrected a servant for using the word "spit". It is not only a matter of daring to use proscribed words and phrases: it is a matter of stark candour informing every aspect of her art, her imagination itself. It is not that other writers would not have dared to use the word "anatomy"—they would not have dared to conceive it.

George Eliot expects us to be interested in the furniture and decor of the Irwine dining-room because it reveals, in a most obvious way (the coat-of-arms and the threadbare tablecloth) a social history. The author herself then tells us how we respond:

> You suspect that the inhabitants of this room have inherited more blood than wealth. . . .

The Irwines themselves have little significance (as opposed to charm) as individuals. Like most of the characters of *Adam Bede*, they go to make up a community. As Dorothy Van Ghent says:

> It is the community that is the protagonist of this novel, the community as the repository of certain shared and knowledgeable

values that have been developed out of ages of work and care and common kindness.

The continuity and stability are of real value. But George Eliot overlays the scene with such a nostalgic, autumnal haze that she seems to be holding up not so much a mirror as a golden gauze. It is this same Mr Irwine who is to make explicit the book's intended resolution when he comments on the marriage of Adam and Dinah:

> "What better harvest from that painful seed-time could there be than this?"

What more bland dismissal of the suffering and death of Hetty could there be than that? These terms, for all their appeal to the pastoral values the book has so fully embodied, are quite incommensurate to her actual suffering. The world just isn't that comfortable. Nelly Dean is much less complacent than Mrs Poyser, her wisdom rooted in a far greater depth and variety of experience. Nevertheless, Emily Brontë is at pains to indicate the inadequacy, indeed the perniciousness of such homely wisdom, "common-sense" and "decency" when it offers to comprehend the full range of human experience. She is like someone confidently approaching the sea with a mop.

Nelly is afraid to hear what Cathy has dreamed because the possibility that dreams may be significant represents a threat to her common-sense conception of time as a simple chronological sequence of causes and effects. She tries to tell her story to Lockwood in this way and so subtly but drastically misrepresents. Emily Brontë is at pains to dislocate this sequence for the reader. She creates a double time-scheme, one in which the past dies, one in which it does not. Cathy suffers "derangement" when she is "wrenched at a stroke" from the world of being to that of acting. She dies in the attempt to get back. After her death, Heathcliff lives on agonizingly suspended between the two. Time stops at that moment for him; yet he must live through the charade while Hindley drinks himself to death, Linton grows up, marries and dies, the younger Cathy and Hareton mature and come together, and Lockwood pays his social calls. He is "stalled". His life is in that timeless world where Cathy waits for him.

George Eliot's conception of community ("There is no private life which has not been determined by a wider public life") implies a definition of morality in terms of the public life which is utterly opposed to Emily Brontë's almost Lawrentian insistence on the sacredness of selfhood. There is no public life in *Wuthering Heights*. There is no such thing as society, except as a rather unreal concourse of marionettes to whose existence only Lockwood testifies.

Lockwood enters *Wuthering Heights* in much the same spirit as George Eliot and her reader enter the Irwine dining-room, bringing the same easy assumptions that what he finds there will be easily comprehended in terms of what he takes to be common human experience and values. The result is hilarious and savage comedy at both Lockwood's expense and the reader's. The "canine mother", he soon learns, is "not kept for a pet". As soon as he is left alone for a moment, the whole room seems to spring to snarling life:

> Half-a-dozen four-footed fiends, of various sizes and ages, issued from hidden dens to the common centre. I felt my heels and coat-laps peculiar subjects of assault; and, parrying off the larger combatants as effectually as I could with the poker, I was constrained to demand, aloud, assistance from some of the household, in re-establishing peace (I, 16).

The Irwine dining-room had offered us an image of peace much too stable to be shaken even by an infanticide or last-minute reprieve from the gallows. Peace at *Wuthering Heights* is a condition most insecure and ephemeral. We feel that tumult and savagery are the norms which reassert themselves when not actively held in check. The dogs are "fiends" to Lockwood, they seem "possessed". He next uses the word "fiend" of the pathetic ghost which taps at his window. Anything which is not manageable, orderly, tame, is fiendish. For Lockwood, that which is beyond control should be leashed, muzzled and preferably hidden; that which is in the darkness beyond the window must at all costs remain there.

The destructive comedy continues in the second chapter, is indeed, the purpose of that chapter. For by the time we reach Lockwood's first confused inklings of the family history, his dreams and his report of them in the third chapter, Emily Brontë must be sure that Lockwood has become for us a buffoon and a bore. We do not know, we must learn the hard way, how to respond to these strange people and events. We know only how not to respond—as Lockwood does, with premature assumptions and irrelevant judgements. Moved by the same curiosity the reader also feels—who are these people? what are their relations to each other?—he conjectures that the "amiable lady" is Heathcliff's wife (the phrase produces "an almost diabolical sneer" on Heathcliff's face); then, still less happily, that the "beneficent fairy" is Hareton's ("She had thrown herself away on that boor, from sheer ignorance that better individuals existed"). Already the word "better", which might be found and understood, unqualified anywhere in *Adam Bede*, seems ludicrously irrelevant. At long last, Lockwood begins to feel "unmistakably out of place", and, assuming the role of King Lear, he demands to be let out into the storm. Acting the part too vigorously, he brings on a nosebleed, has a pint of icy water splashed down his neck by the kindly Zillah, and is constrained to stay the night.

How, after this, can the reader be so impertinent as to demand that these people account for themselves, or to risk a judgement or assumption of any kind. The reader gets no privileges, but must struggle with Lockwood to piece together the past, and use it to cast intermittent but growing light upon the present. Not until the last chapter are we allowed to feel that perhaps we know enough to hazard some tentative moral judgements, but by that time we are surely past wishing to do so.

The largely hostile reception *Wuthering Heights* received from contemporary reviewers was predictable, given the current notions of what a novel should be ("the aim of fiction is to afford some sensation of delight"), and of the function of the critic as guardian of public taste and decency. The reviews are full of such words as "disagreeable", "coarse", "painful", "shocking". The novel is criticized for its improbability, but is not required to be too realistic either, since "there never was a man whose daily life constituted fit materials for a book of fiction". It is as though Lockwood, on his first visit to the Heights, had discovered not Cathy's diary, but the manuscript of this novel, and had proceeded to review it. In spite of his finding himself perpetually out of his depth, he would never have questioned his own qualifications as judge. Nor, in spite of his disapproval on both artistic and moral grounds, would he have been able to deny its fascination.

The word which occurs more frequently than any other in the reviews is "original". But, finding themselves committed to the word, the reviewers don't know what to make of it—they don't know whether to use it as a term of approval or disapproval. They saw that the book's originality was a matter of its power and freshness and honesty, but equally, of its crudity and lack of art. The author's creations, the *Britannia* reviewer wrote,

> are so new, so wildly grotesque, so entirely without art, that they strike us as proceeding from a mind of limited experience, but of original energy, and of a singular and distinctive cast.

He goes on to suggest that this distinctiveness and energy derive from the author's seizing on "one single aspect of nature", which would be "permitted to painting", "but in fiction this kind of isolation is not allowed". What would have been recognized as art in painting (and perhaps even in poetry and drama) is seen only as the utter lack of it in fiction, though the reviewer has to admit that it is directly responsible for the "singular power" which at times "approaches to sublimity".

The *Atlas* reviewer also strides confidently into the same cul-de-sac:

> The reality of unreality has never been so aptly illustrated as in the scenes of almost savage life which Ellis Bell has brought so vividly before us.

Yet the book is "inartistic". In other words, the ability to reveal truth in fiction with unique power is not art.

G. W. Peck in *The American Review* goes still further. *Wuthering Heights* is "*very* original":

> It does in truth lay bare some of the secret springs of human action with wonderful clearness. . . . If the rank of a work of fiction is to depend solely on its naked imaginative power, then this is one of the greatest novels in the language.

But his conclusion is that *Wuthering Heights* is *not* one of the greatest novels in the language because Emily Brontë is not sufficiently concerned to please.

We need no further examples to demonstrate that in the mid-nineteenth century "art" and "imaginative power" are completely distinct concepts which may even be at odds. Art is a technique for processing the products of the imagination to make them pleasing to the sensibilities of the "readers of light literature", to which class the novel is assumed to belong.

It is not a matter of foolishness and incompetence among the reviewers. Even Charlotte felt that Emily's ideas were too "daring and original" for fiction, and that she would be well advised to become an essayist. (Letter to W. S. Williams, 15 Feb. 1848).

The first critic to affirm that the originality of *Wuthering Heights* was a triumph of art was Sydney Dobell in a remarkable review of the 1850 edition in *Palladium*. He saw that a prose work can be structured like a poem:

> The *thinking-out* of some of these pages . . . is the masterpiece of a poet

that, like a poem, it can embody its central meanings in imagery. He claimed that successful art is that which best serves the demands of the imagination, imagination working in obedience to no external principles, but to "the nature within her". Dobell resolves the problem which had baffled nearly all the earlier reviewers by coining the phrase "instinctive art", which he applies not only to Emily Brontë, but to all writers whose art serves to release their deepest "powers of insight", "intuition of character" and "infallible inspiration". He was echoed three months later by G. H. Lewes in the *Leader*:

> The artist does not possess, but is possessed. . . . There is at such time a *momentum* which propels the mind into regions inaccessible to calculation, unsuspected in our calmer moods.

Despite this early breakthrough, no nineteenth-century critic offered any detailed interpretation of the novel in these terms. In 1857 Émile Montégut took a step in the direction of an interpretation of the Heathcliff–Cathy relationship:

> He and she are, so to speak, but a single person; together they form a hybrid monster, twin-sexed and twin-souled; he is the male soul of the monster, she the female. In him, Catherine recognizes her own energies no longer confined by the reserves imposed on her

sex; in him, she sees in full bloom, like poetic, poisoned flowers, all her own secret perversities.

(*The Brontës: The Critical Heritage*, ed. Miriam Allott, 1974, 377–8)

Montégut's emphasis is, I think, wrong, but at least he is allowing Emily Brontë's art work to work upon him in an appropriate way.

The first critic to offer a coherent interpretation of the whole novel was David Cecil in *Early Victorian Novelists* in 1934.

The ability to read *Wuthering Heights* in an appropriate way is no guarantee that it will be so read, nor that it will be recognized as the great novel that it is. Nor does it dispose of the problems associated with that word "originality". There is, for example, that notorious note on Emily Brontë at the end of the first chapter of F. R. Leavis' *The Great Tradition* (1950). The great tradition of the English novel, we have just been told, is Jane Austen, George Eliot, Henry James, Conrad and D. H. Lawrence. Emily Brontë was, of course, a genius; and *Wuthering Heights* is an "astonishing work". But she so obviously cannot be accommodated in the great tradition that her novel has to be more or less dismissed as a "sport" or at best relegated to a minor tradition "to which belongs, most notably, *The House with the Green Shutters*". The judgement seems to have been taken over from, or to coincide remarkably with, that of George Saintsbury in 1899:

—a kind of 'sport', as botanists say, in the mid-nineteenth century, as Beckford's Vathek is in the late eighteenth, a wonderful and isolated tour-de-force very unlikely to be in any way germinal, to found a school, and still more unlikely to revolutionize or at least herald the revolutionizing of the novel generally.

(*Emily Brontë*, ed. Jean-Pierre Petit, 1973, 67)

The tradition Leavis discusses is certainly a great one, and he demonstrates very forcibly the advantages of belonging to it. But it seemes to me quite staggering that he should go on to imply, in the Brontë note, that only by belonging to it could a writer be great. If a great novel were to be discovered tomorrow, having lain in a drawer unpublished for a century, I do not see that its greatness would be in any way reduced by the fact that it could not have had the slightest effect on the subsequent history of the novel. What tradition has "come from" *Moby Dick?* But Melville finds his way into the rather less parochial list Leavis offers us in *D. H. Lawrence, Novelist* (1956) of the great novelists from Jane Austen to Lawrence:

> I think of Hawthorne, Dickens, George Eliot, Henry James, Melville, Mark Twain, Conrad. (17–18)

These, we are told, are the "successors of Shakespeare". In any case, it is not true that *Wuthering Heights* is a sport, only that it belongs to a much older and much less limiting tradition than that of the English realistic novel of the late eighteenth and nineteenth centuries. Behind her is certainly Shakespeare—what novel is closer to *Macbeth* or *King Lear?* Ahead of her is *The Heart of Darkness, The Rainbow, Women in Love, St. Mawr.* She opened the way for developments in the novel which Lawrence was able to exploit only when he had weaned himself of the influence of George Eliot.[1]

But I should rather have *Wuthering Heights* outside all traditions than admitted to the Great Tradition on Q. D. Leavis's terms. In "A Fresh Approach to *Wuthering Heights*" (*Lectures in America*, 1969) her approach is fresh indeed, since I recall no earlier critic, not even a Marxist, who has so mutilated the novel to make it fit a preconceived pattern—in this case that of the orthodox mid-nineteenth century novel with its concern for "correct behaviour". She leaves out the body of the novel. Having attributed to Emily Brontë various rather commonplace and prosaic ends, Mrs Leavis then berates her for using such disproportionately dramatic, poetic and even metaphysical means. There is a great deal in *Wuthering Heights* which is bound to strike the reader as larger than life, exaggerated, or melodramatic. I don't think we can shrug this off as "older material" which has somehow survived. It is at the centre of the novel and at the source of its power. In order to be able to praise the novel in terms one might use to discuss the work of George Eliot, Mrs Leavis has to argue that the "poetic" passages have been over-rated, that the symbolism is largely the invention of American critics, that the mysticism is accounted for by the "older material" theory, and that Heathcliff's role in the novel, even in the first part, is not the dominant

132

one it has normally been taken to be. I believe that she is wrong on all these counts. Her essay might have been called "*Wuthering Heights* as Non-Dramatic Non-Poem*", for Mrs Leavis ignores or attempts to devalue precisely those qualities in the novel which made it such an excellent choice for the *Scrutiny* series on "The Novel as Dramatic Poem", a series which also included F. R. Leavis's splendid essays on *The Rainbow*, *Women in Love* and *St. Mawr*.

Apart from the name Heathcliff and the incongruity in the mouth of the affected Lockwood of the phrase "Heathcliff and I", it is not until we reach, on the second page, the description of the exterior of Heathcliff's house that we begin to realize how different this novel is to be from any earlier novel:

> Wuthering Heights is the name of Mr. Heathcliff's dwelling. "Wuthering" being a significant provincial adjective, descriptive of the atmospheric tumult to which its station is exposed in stormy weather. Pure, bracing ventilation they must have up there, at all times, indeed: one may guess the power of the north wind, blowing over the edge, by the excessive slant of a few stunted firs at the end of the house; and by a range of gaunt thorns all stretching their limbs one way, as if craving alms of the sun. Happily, the architect had foresight to build it strong: the narrow windows are deeply set in the wall, and the corners defended with large jutting stones (I, 14).

The whole paragraph is really an opening out of the word "wuthering" as a matrix of component images whose continual recurrence and modification is to provide the staple thread in the novel's pattern, the central reality towards which all characters, events and other images are relentlessly drawn. Its components are storm and tumult, exposure (note, for example, the relation between this word and the word "anatomy" already discussed), power which stunts and produces an "excessive slant", deprivation, denial, narrowness, and a craving for warmth and health—the whole range of creative positives associated with the word "sun".

No distinction is drawn between these forces as they manifest themselves in man and in nature; the dreadful personification of the gaunt thorns as starving human beings is the first of many images which erode such distinctions. This dense pattern of coherent imagery is, as in *King Lear*, the life-blood of the drama. It is in these terms that the novel's major themes receive their most definitive statements. Edgar Linton cries to Nelly:

> "Tell her what Heathcliff is—an unreclaimed creature, without refinement, without cultivation; an arid wilderness of furze and whinstone" (X, 89).

Heathcliff's counter-attack employs the same primal image:

> "He might as well plant an oak in a flower-pot, and expect it to thrive, as imagine he can restore her to vigour in the soil of his shallow cares!" (XIV, 129).

He conceives his revenge through the stunting of Hareton in the same terms:

> "we'll see if one tree won't grow as crooked as another, with the same wind to twist it!" (XVII, 154).

But young Hareton had been born on a fine June morning during the hay-harvest, a hint that his craving for the sun will ultimately be answered.

These most striking outcrops, as it were, of the underlying imagery are often a hundred pages apart. Yet we forget none of them. The intensity of language which fixes them in the mind forces us to read the novel as also a dramatic poem—"the first in English which invites the same kind of attention that we give to *Macbeth*" (G. D. Klingopulos, Scrutiny XIV, 269).

But the reader of the paragraph we are discussing need not wait a single page for his first example. When we read that "the narrow windows are deeply set in the wall, and the corners defended with large jutting stones" we can hardly have forgotten the description of Heathcliff on the previous page, "his black eyes withdrawn so suspiciously under their brows".

I considered at one stage giving this essay the title "The Modernity of *Wuthering Heights*", or even "*Wuthering Heights, the First Modern Novel*". I suppose I could have gone further and claimed that *Wuthering Heights* is the first modern anything, since Emily Brontë antedates both the first modern poet (Whitman) and the first modern dramatist (Ibsen). But I could not have taken modernity as my central concern without committing myself to a definition of it and a discussion of its relationship with romanticism, an undertaking which, had I been capable of it at all, would have taken far more space than I could have justified in the mere introduction to an essay. As it is I need only offer a few relevant observations here, and can safely leave most of what I have to say on the subject to emerge from the detailed commentary on the novel which follows.

In any case, it would perhaps be no great advantage to have a definition of the modern which aimed at any great precision or exclusiveness. One wants a set of loosely related and vague suggestions, with, at the centre, the feeling that, when we enter this writer's imaginative world, we do not have to cross any kind of historical barrier or divide, do not have to readjust or make allowances on that score, but can respond as we would to a contemporary writer using language and forms which seem fitted to communicate directly to us of what deeply concerns us now. Partly it is a matter of attitudes, a way of looking at the world which involves stripping away the layers of appearances, conventions, complacencies, contingencies, fashions. . . . There is something characteristically raw and exposed, not so much physically, not just a morbid preoccupation with "the skull beneath the skin", but psychically.

Alienation is an inescapable word, for there is that prevailing sense that those "truths" which are offered by society or can be extracted from any study of the outside world are irreconcilable with and invalidated by the deepest inner truths which it is the business of the imagination to reveal. Arnold defined modernism in 1853 as "the dialogue of the mind with itself". The imagination seeks to express itself in metaphors of its own nature, to tap that inexhaustible fund of potent images we call the unconscious. A poem can be pure psychic drama, but in a novel or play an apparently external world is reconstructed out of these images, and offered as an alternative reality, corresponding hardly at all to the world we think we live in, but corresponding to the ultimate truths, to Nature or to God, for the "Great Outer Darkness" is "the same as the small inner darkness" (Ted Hughes). One of the finest readings of *Wuthering Heights*, by J. Hillis Miller in *The Disappearance of God* (1963) is very much in these terms; for example:

This innermost room has a window to the outdoors, and through that window, in Lockwood's dream, the ghost of Catherine Earnshaw tries to come. The otherness of nature is replaced by the more frightening otherness of a ghost, and the stormy moors are established as the expression of a supernatural as well as a natural violence. These spiritual powers are immanent in nature, and identified with its secret life.

It is self-evident that the Brontë novels are very different from those of their contemporaries and predecessors, but the terms of that difference are often badly stated. It is not simply that the Brontës were interested in the psychological, the personal and the passionate, while the rest were concerned with some form of social criticism. As Raymond Williams has pointed out, that distinction does not go very deep:

> The world we need to remember if we are to see these connections of the 1840s is the world of Blake: a world of desire and hunger, of rebellion and pallid convention: the terms of desire and fulfilment and the terms of oppression and deprivation profoundly connected in a single dimension of experience.
>
> (*The English Novel*, 1970, 60).

The essential distinction (and it sets Emily as much apart from her sisters as from the rest) is that in the other Victorian novelists their concern with deprivation and fulfilment is abruptly arrested at the point where it touches the unconscious or the non-human. The arbitrary boundaries of their concerns are those of rational humanism. It is not just that Emily Brontë goes further in her exploration of inner needs, but that she constantly relates these to the permanent realities of nature and supernature. When these perspectives are not there, when the social, civilized and rational world becomes, as it has been in most English novels from Defoe to C. P. Snow, a closed system, we have a falsification of experience which no amount of good sense, fine sensibility, or high moral purpose can redeem. Emily Brontë's contemporaries were engaged in developing a fictional mode wonderfully well fitted to the presentation and evaluation of that closed world.

But despite the strong Gothic and Byronic elements in *Wuthering Heights* and its hints of the supernatural, one brings from it a far stronger sense of psychological realism and of general modernity than from any other novel of its period. It is not so much that Emily Brontë is a better psychologist, or even that she is so much more frank and courageous (though that she certainly is); it is rather that she has created for herself a truly imaginative form of art which is able to accommodate the whole of her experience, including that large area of her own experience which she can never have brought into full consciousness. Her unconscious self speaks through the book's structure and imagery as powerfully and uninhibitedly as her conscious self. She accedes to the imperative demands of her imagination that these characters, incidents, images, must be there. And nothing goes in that has not been so demanded. At the same time she strove to reconstruct the novel in a form capable of objectifying her experience, withdrawing herself totally from the novel, leaving it as incontrovertible as a living thing.

Much good criticism has now accumulated on *Wuthering Heights*. Every theme and character has been examined, every strand of imagery, every technique of structure and characteristic of language. But it has been done almost entirely in the form of short discrete essays, each picking out its chosen strand of the pattern. It is a great tribute to the novel that so coherent an account will emerge from following through a single image or theme—wind, darkness, window, book, blood, two children. . . . But we cannot see the whole pattern simply by laying the strands end to end, as in a casebook; and the few attempts to describe it have been less satisfying than the more detailed studies. If we can keep them all in mind simultaneously, noting how the novel throws one or another into prominence or twists them together, we shall see how marvellously coherent it is, like printing when all the colours are overlaid in perfect register.

This coherence invariably disappears when the novel is adapted for any other medium. There have been many adaptations for large and small screen and for the stage. The story is indeed highly dramatic. But when that story is extracted from the novel, all we have is romantic melodrama. One of my purposes here is to indicate how much more than and other than a romantic melodrama *Wuthering Heights* is.

The essential story needs only four words to tell:

    Catherine Earnshaw, here and there varied to *Catherine Heath-cliff*, and then again to *Catherine Linton*.

The Catherine Earnshaw who wrote that was not yet Catherine Linton, and was never to be, in this world, Catherine Heathcliff. Her childish doodle was prophetic beyond the grave. She was always Catherine Earnshaw in her wild wilfulness and attachment to the Heights; always Catherine Linton from the moment she had looked through the window of Thrushcross Grange and been seduced by what she saw there; always Catherine Heathcliff, for Heathcliff, as we shall see, is but the name of her own soul. She leaves behind her another Catherine Linton who becomes, briefly, Catherine Heathcliff, and, finally, Catherine Earnshaw. The novel has come full circle, Earnshaw to Earnshaw, the Linton element assimilated, the Heathcliff element exorcised. Before he passed the threshold of Wuthering Heights, Lockwood had detected, among the mass of grotesque and "shameless" carvings, the date 1500 and the name Hareton Earnshaw. On his second visit he is to meet a living Hareton Earnshaw and mistake him for a servant. The three names of Catherine he detects scratched on the shelf which bears her library. The top book is a musty Testament, but again appearances deceive, for Catherine had used "every morsel of blank" for her own alternative testament in the form of a diary. That shelf is another threshold into the unknown, the past, which Lockwood, despite his first premonitory dream—

    a glare of white letters started from the dark, as vivid as spectres
    —the air swarmed with Catherines

confidently crosses.

He first discovers a caricature of Joseph, then the entry: "H. and I are going to rebel". The rebellion, he learns, is against the regime of Hindley (a "detestable substitute" for Mr Earnshaw) and, more directly, against Joseph (a living caricature of crazed Puritanical repressiveness) and his "awful Sunday" when he had condemned the miserable children first to a three-hour sermon, then to such "good books" as *The Helmet of Salvation* and *The Broad Way to Destruction*. The rebellion takes the form of hurling this "lumber" into the dog-kennel and subsequently breaking out of their back-kitchen prison for a scamper on the sodden moor. The next fragmentary entry gives us the aftermath—the forced

138

separation of Catherine and Heathcliff, and the threatened reduction of Heathcliff to his proper status as a "vagabond".

Emily Brontë was no doubt all too familiar with such lumber as Joseph's in her own childhood. Indeed, her mother had been closely associated with the famous Methodist preacher, the Reverend Jabez Bunting of the Halifax circuit, who seems to have furnished Emily with her Jabes Branderham. His sermon was probably suggested by this passage from James Hogg:

> It was about this time that my reverend father preached a sermon, one sentence of which affected me most disagreeably. It was to the purport that every unrepented sin was productive of a new sin with each breath that a man drew; and every one of these new sins added to the catalogue in the same manner. I was utterly confounded at the multitude of my transgressions; for I was sensible that there were great numbers of sins of which I had never been able thoroughly to repent, and these momentary ones, by moderate calculation, had, I saw, long ago, amounted to a hundred and fifty thousand in the minute, and I saw no end to the series of repentances to which I had subjected myself.
>
> (*The Private Memoirs and Confessions of a Justified Sinner*, Cresset Press 1947, p. 98)

The title of Branderham's "pious discourse": *Seventy Times Seven, and the First of the Seventy First* is the last thing Lockwood sees before he falls asleep and, appropriately enough, provides the material for his first dream, in which Joseph takes him to the chapel at Gimmerton Sough to hear Branderham preach on this very text.

> —good God—what a sermon! divided into *four hundred and ninety* parts, each fully equal to an ordinary address from the pulpit, and each discussing a separate sin! Where he searched for them, I cannot tell; he had his private manner of interpreting the phrase, and it seemed necessary the brother should sin different sins on every occasion.
>
> They were of the most curious character—odd transgressions that I never imagined previously (III, 28–9).

At last he reaches The First of the Seventy-First, and Lockwood, on a sudden inspiration, rises to "denounce Jabes Branderham as the sinner of the sin that no Christian need pardon". Jabes accuses Lockwood of the same sin and invites the congregation to belabour him with their pilgrim's staves, and in the resulting pandemonium Lockwood wakes.

The Biblical text in question is *Matthew* xviii, 21–2:

> Then came Peter unto him and said, Lord, how oft shall my brother sin against me, and I forgive him? till seven times? Jesus saith unto him, I say not unto thee, Until seven times: but, Until seventy times seven.

Christ's answer is, of course, a memorable way of saying "You must forgive every time". But Joseph's vocation, we are told, was "to be where he had plenty of wickedness to reprove", and the Buntings and Branderhams of the early nineteenth century found punishment far more attractive than forgiveness. Branderham has taken Christ literally and works his congregation up to a frenzy of anticipation as he approaches the four-hundred and ninety-first sin, which no Christian need pardon, when the cruellest punishment may be meted out with the assurance of complete righteousness. The basic Christian tenet of love is thus denied: "every man's hand was against his neighbour". Perhaps the injunction to love thy neighbour as thyself was unfortunately phrased in a world where men may hate and deny themselves with lifelong dedication. We are not told what the four-hundred and ninety-first sin is. The passage ridicules the whole idea of sin. The one really unforgivable sin of which Branderham and Lockwood are both guilty is, perhaps, intolerance.

Lockwood's intolerance, inhumanity even, is starkly revealed in the second dream:

> Terror made me cruel; and, finding it useless to attempt shaking the creature off, I pulled its wrist on to the broken pane, and rubbed it to and fro till the blood ran down and soaked the bedclothes (III, 30).

The "little ice-cold hand" belongs to Catherine Linton, a child who claims to have been a waif for twenty years. The details, "Linton": "(why did I think of Linton? I had read Earnshaw twenty times for Linton)", and "twenty years", are typical of Emily Brontë's handling of the supernatural. Rather than try to persuade us that we are dealing with a ghost, she simply leaves us to react against Lockwood's easy assumption that he has had a nightmare by giving the ghost credentials which could not be accounted for in a dream. It is in fact within a few months of twenty years (the summer of 1780) since Catherine's final separation from Heathcliff. It is only seventeen years since she married and left Wuthering Heights for Thrushcross Grange.

At several of the great crises of *Wuthering Heights*, people look through windows, open windows, or break them.[2] The window of Thrushcross Grange is large and bright. It attracts the two little outsiders to gaze through it in wonder composed partly of envy, partly of scorn, as at another world. A moment later Cathy enters that world, after being savaged by a dog. Many times she yearns to pass the other way, claims that she can see the Heights from her window, which she cannot, with earthly vision, hastens her death by throwing open the window during her illness, begs, as a ghost in Lockwood's dream, to be let into Wuthering Heights through the window and has her wrist dragged across its broken glass.

Both the broken window and the tortured child in Lockwood's dream are the first of many in the novel, and the broken window must remain for us a potent symbol of violation. A window is, as it were, a membrane which divides calm from storm, light from darkness, the known and secure from the unknown and terrifying. Inside is what Lawrence called "the extant social world", the personal world, outside the untamed, impersonal, elemental world which Lockwood would lock out. But a normal window can be opened (when the hasp is not soldered into the staple); the personal life can be brought into creative contact with "the terriffic action of unfathomed nature" (Lawrence). The open window stands for air to breathe, space to play and grow in, freedom to go where your own nature would be leading, union, intercourse, with that which is other. The fastening of a window is a denial of the need for such intercourse. The breaking of a window is the violation and pain which such deprivation brings. Perhaps we can link Lockwood's lacking a staff in the first dream and his breaking of the window-membrane in his second to take an implication of sexual inadequacy, which is one form the refusal of the other can take. The forces which Lockwood has repressed in the depths of his inner, unacknowledged, darkness, manifest themselves in dreams in gratuitous cruelty.

And what is the connection between Lockwood's two dreams?

It is revealed, I think, in the terms in which Lockwood describes his dreams to Heathcliff:

> 'If the little fiend had got in at the window, she probably would have strangled me!' I returned. 'I'm not going to endure the perse- cutions of your hospitable ancestors again. Was not the Reverend Jabes Branderham akin to you on the mother's side? And that minx, Catherine Linton, or Earnshaw, or however she was called—she must have been a changeling—wicked little soul! She told me she had been walking the earth these twenty years: a just punishment for her mortal transgressions, I've no doubt!' (III, 31–2).

What "mortal transgressions" is Catherine supposed to have com- mitted for which her torment is "a just punishment", what sin which no Christian need pardon? To call her a "creature", a "fiend" is to deny her a common humanity. We see Lockwood condemning quite irrationally what he cannot begin to under- stand, and withhold our own moral judgements.

The window is also the membrane between the living and the dead. When he hears Lockwood's story, Heathcliff, bursting into tears, wrenches open the lattice and cries out to Cathy. But the union, after the death of one (she "caught her death" at an open window) can only be achieved by the death of the other. It is this same window swinging open which draws attention to the death of Heathcliff:

> The lattice, flapping to and fro, had grazed one hand that rested on the sill; no blood trickled from the broken skin, and when I put my fingers to it, I could doubt no more—he was dead and stark! (XXXIV, 264).

His face is washed with rain driving through the open window, and Nelly cannot close his eyes.

> Is Mr. Heathcliff a man? If so, is he mad? And if not, is he a devil? (XIII, 115).

I do not know how the contemporary reader took Heathcliff. Charlotte calls him "a man's shape animated by demon life— a Ghoul—an Afreet" and scarcely thinks it can be right to create such a being. Though this is nearer than the romanticized Heath- cliff (a screen role for the young Laurence Olivier), the ideal reader must surely feel, without in the least condoning him or identifying with him, much sympathy for Heathcliff as a man who appears to have no choice but to torture himself and others. To achieve this Emily Brontë seeks to modify her readers' sympathies much more radically than any other English novelist until Hardy, and more successfully than any until Lawrence. Any attempt to "explain" Heathcliff in realistic terms seems to me futile. One of the most striking features of the novel is precisely Emily Brontë's refusal to provide any such explanations, her determination that the reader shall be unable to account for Heathcliff in purely human terms. Richard Chase has said:

> We realize that with a few readjustments of the plot he need not have entered the story as a human being at all. His part might have been played by Fate or Nature of God or the devil. He is sheer dazzling sexual and intellectual force. As Heathcliff expires at the end of the book, we feel, not so much that a man is dying as that an intolerable energy is flagging.[3]

I cannot see what Heathcliff has to do with intellect, and his sexual significance is, to say the least, oblique. But the general principle remains inescapable. Charlotte Brontë was more specific. Heathcliff, she said,

> exemplified the effects which a life of continued injustice and hard usage may produce on a naturally perverse, vindictive, and inexorable disposition. Carefully trained and kindly treated, the black gypsy-cub might possibly have been reared into a human being, but tyranny and ignorance made of him a mere demon. (Letter to W. S. Williams 14.8.1848).

Our first introduction to Heathcliff embraces "both the worlds of heaven and hell":

> "you must e'en take it as a gift of God; though it's as dark almost as if it came from the devil" (IV, 38).

For two paragraphs before we come to the naming, the child remains "it" rather than "him". Mrs Earnshaw "was ready to fling it out of doors", and during the night Nelly "put it on the landing of the stairs, hoping it might be gone on the morrow" (IV, 39). Spontaneous rejection is thus Heathcliff's first experience at Wuthering Heights, before he has done anything to deserve it.

He is rejected because, dark and dirty, of unknown origins, speaking gibberish, the child is felt to be an alien and a threat. Hindley sees him as a usurper of his privileges and his father's affections, calls him "Imp of Satan" and begins almost at once his systematic persecution. Heathcliff's origins are totally obscure. Geographically, racially and morally obscure. Being found in Liverpool he could have come from the far ends of the earth, he could be a Lascar or a gypsy, he could be a child of sin, even a bastard of Earnshaw's. Imagination is let loose in the household. Perhaps his origins were supernatural, infernal. What is made clear is that he is both a changeling and a cuckoo in the nest.

That Heathcliff should be given the name of a son who had died confirms the impression of a fairy changeling. The name itself suggests something larger than the human, permanent, indestructible. And the man fits the name. Again and again we have his face clouding, brightening, overcast, like a landscape, and Cathy, offering to tell Isabella what Heathcliff is, describes him as "an unreclaimed creature, without refinement, without cultivation; an arid wilderness of furze and whinstone" (X, 89). Heathcliff is not, at this stage, physically ugly. He can look handsome or repulsive according to his mood, as a landscape changes with the weather. Later it is his deprivation of love, nurture and education which, inevitably, affects his appearance:

> Then personal appearance sympathised with mental deterioration; he acquired a slouching gait, and ignoble look; his naturally reserved disposition was exaggerated into an almost idiotic excess of unsociable moroseness; and he took a grim pleasure, apparently, in exciting the aversion rather than the esteem of his few acquaintance (VIII, 63).

We need not assume that his cruelty and spite come naturally to him. Hatred is his anodyne, the only means by which he can relieve the pain of his constant frustration and humiliation. Hindley's treatment of him is, as Nelly says, "enough to make a fiend of a saint. And, truly, it appeared as if the lad were possessed of something diabolical at that period" (VIII, 61). Heathcliff becomes a fiend only when his life becomes a hell.

Heathcliff, it seems to me, represents the basic, elemental energies of nature (including human nature) which are both creative and destructive. But in Heathcliff we see this energy only in its destructive, demonic aspect. It manifests itself in cruelty and sadism, as blasting wind rather than fruitful sun:

> we'll see if one tree won't grow as crooked as another, with the same wind to twist it! (XVII, 154).

he says of Hareton. The destructiveness is a direct result of deprivation. Heathcliff has himself been denied even the most fundamental forms of nurture and care a child needs. It is not only Hindley who has twisted his growth. The spirit of Wuthering Heights itself seems to be generally malignant, as its name implies. The human equivalent of that malignancy is Joseph for whom everything natural is wicked. In him are concentrated all the worst excesses of nineteenth-century puritanism which Emily Brontë knew so well and knew to have contributed to her own sense of deprivation. Joseph is the only representative of Christianity in the novel and it is a mark of Emily Brontë's uncompromising fearlessness that he should be also the most evil character.

Even when she grows old enough for the question of marriage to arise, Catherine's relationship with Heathcliff remains much as it was when they were children, asexual, as of siblings. Thus Catherine is able to assume that her marriage to Edgar Linton need not in the least affect her relationship with Heathcliff, and she is later indifferent to his pursuit of Isabella. Cathy seldom uses the word love in relation to Heathcliff, though often in relation to Edgar. She clearly feels that the two relationships are different in kind. No attempt is made to indicate to the reader what qualities in Heathcliff so attract her to him. Indeed she is fully aware that he is not a rough diamond but a "fierce, pitiless, wolfish man".

It can be argued that the exigencies of publication in the mid-nineteenth century would have put difficulties in the way of an overtly sexual relationship. But the uncompromising starkness and candour of Emily Brontë's work in other respects, particularly in language and imagery, makes me strongly doubt that she would have been prepared to compromise in this respect. Another explanation which has been offered, and may have an element of truth in it, is that Emily Brontë has very much in mind her own relationship with Branwell, which she palliates in the book by making Cathy and Heathcliff unrelated.

It seems to me that the novel contains its own quite adequate explanation, an explanation which goes far to account for many of its structural features and difficulties.

I believe that *Wuthering Heights* demands to be read in such a way that Heathcliff functions simultaneously on three levels, none of which, alone, can account for him. On the surface he functions as an autonomous character in a drama whose meanings are ethical and social; first exemplifying the evil effects of cruelty, deprivation and conventional education upon the young; then as a critic of the artificial social and moral refinement of the Lintons; finally as a man destroyed by sterile passions of hate and revenge. On another level there are the meanings associated with his name and his close identification with the Heights, with what Lord David Cecil called the principle of storm. What he stands for and embodies is a permanent reality, indestructible, against which all social values are seen to be flimsy and ephemeral, all moral values relative:

> My love for Linton is like the foliage in the woods. Time will change it, I'm well aware, as winter changes the trees. My love for Heathcliff resembles the eternal rocks beneath—a source of little visible delight, but necessary (IX, 74).

When Cathy says that she dreamed the angels flung her "out into the middle of the heath on the top of Wuthering Heights" where she awoke sobbing for joy, her feelings and ours are the same as if she had said they flung her into the arms of Heathcliff, since she never distinguishes between what he has that she needs and what the heath itself offers. Both offer freedom to be herself and to feel herself part of the universe. And this brings us to the third and primary level at which Heathcliff functions (the levels being continuous, not discrete).

When Cathy says that Heathcliff is "necessary" to her, as "the eternal rocks beneath" are necessary, she is speaking quite literally. The word perfectly describes the relationship we have come to know, which is far more than either love or affinity. An oak does not resist splitting (the metaphor is Catherine's) because the two halves love each other. Cathy breaks her own heart, her integrity, then struggles to the death to regain it. She is also speaking literally when she says that she *is* Heathcliff. There is a sense in which Heathcliff does not function as an independent character at all, but as a projection of a part of Cathy's own being, "one who comprehends in his person my feelings to Edgar and myself".

> I cannot express it; but surely you and everybody have a notion that there is, or should be, an existence of yours beyond you. What were the use of my creation if I were entirely contained here? My great miseries in this world have been Heathcliff's miseries, and I watched and felt each from the beginning; my great thought in living is himself. If all else perished, and *he* remained, I should still continue to be; and if all else remained, and he were annihilated, the Universe would turn to a mighty stranger. I should not seem a part of it (IX, 73–4).

He is that within herself which is able to reach out and touch and be at one with the primary energies of nature; he is the ground of her being, her atonement. Heathcliff is the god within her breast of whom Emily Brontë says in "No Coward Soul":

> Though Earth and moon were gone,
> And suns and universes ceased to be,
> And Thou wert left alone,
> Every Existence would exist in Thee.

In choosing to marry Edgar Linton and become the lady of Thrushcross Grange, where nature has been tamed, accommodated to the values of good taste and order, Cathy has betrayed her own heart. To be separated from Heathcliff is to be cut off from part of herself, that part on which her health, sanity and capacity for fulfilment depends. In denying him she denies the life that is in her. Yet we see now why she cannot marry Heathcliff, why we as readers shy from the contemplation of such a marriage. Marriage implies a union in otherness. The union of like with like is obscene.

Thus Catherine reacts to the separation by becoming dangerously ill. She is taken to Thrushcross Grange where she promptly kills Mr and Mrs Linton (her fever proving fatal to them). The three years of Heathcliff's absence occupy some two pages. Catherine has ceased to be. Her life is in abeyance. The reunion is rendered in terms of Catherine becoming "an angel" and radiating sunshine throughout the house for several days. But her need for Heathcliff is thwarted by Edgar and again she becomes ill, almost insane. When she learns that Edgar has been reading in the library she cries:

> What in the name of all that feels, has he to do with *books*, when I am dying? (XII, 104).

When Nelly tells Heathcliff that it is only common humanity and a sense of duty which supports Edgar's concern for Cathy, he replies that it is

> quite possible that your master should have nothing but common humanity, and a sense of duty to fall back upon. . . . It is not in him to be loved like me, how can she love in him what he has not? (XIV, 125–6).

What Edgar has not is an affective life. To expect Cathy to thrive in the soil of his shallow cares is to expect an oak to thrive in a flower-pot. Heathcliff is Cathy's deepest capacity for life, and also the ground in which that capacity can flourish most freely.

In her illness, Cathy claims to have been tormented, "haunted", for three nights. Her dreams appal her. Her spirit cries to be let out of Thrushcross Grange to return to Wuthering Heights, to hear there "that wind sounding in the firs by the lattice". She is "no better than a wailing child", her face bathed in tears. This takes us back to the "haunting" of Lockwood, where the ghost claimed to have been a waif for twenty years, since her final separation from Heathcliff, that is. Now, in her dreams, she dates further back the moment when she became an exile and outcast from what had been her world, (the universe become a mighty stranger):

> the whole last seven years of my life grew a blank! I did not recall that they had been at all. I was a child; my father was just buried, and my misery arose from the separation that Hindley had ordered between me and Heathcliff. I was laid alone, for the first time (XII, 107).

Not to be separated from Heathcliff, to lie with him, merges into the desire to be "among the heather on those hills" where she can be "herself", "half savage and hardy and free". The passions

148

which should make her hardy, given the freedom of heath and cliff, denied that freedom turn back upon her and destroy her. Kenneth fears that the outcome might be "permanent *alienation* of intellect" (my italics). We see what this alienation might mean when Edgar comes to her:

> At first, she gave him no glance of recognition—he was invisible to her abstracted gaze. The delirium was not fixed, however; having weaned her eyes from contemplating the outer darkness, by degrees she centred her attention on him, and discovered who it was that held her (XII, 109).

The "outer darkness" clearly represents another reality which she is about to enter permanently, though not in madness. In that darkness there is no concern with appearances, only with being. Only there can she recover her wholeness.

I should like at this stage to suggest some parallels between the way in which Emily Brontë uses Heathcliff and D. H. Lawrence's symbolic technique. "Darkness" is one of the most heavily worked words in Lawrence's vocabulary. Ursula, in *The Rainbow*, comes to perceive that "the world in which she lived was like a circle lighted by a lamp":

> The darkness wheeled round about, with grey shadow-shapes of wild beasts, and also with dark shadow-shapes of angels, whom the light fenced out, as it fenced out the more familiar beasts of darkness (XV).

The image is applicable not only to human knowledge in relation to the vast darkness of the unknown universe, but equally to the area of the human psyche which is illuminated by the conscious mind (Edgar's world of books) in relation to the fecund darkness of the unconscious. Lawrence makes this very clear in the essay on Benjamin Franklin where he sets this creed against Franklin's:

That I am I.
That my soul is a dark forest.
That my known self will never be more than a little clearing
                                                in the forest.
That gods, strange gods, come forth from the forest into the
        clearing of my known self, and then go back.

That I must have the courage to let them come and go.
That I will never let mankind put anything over me,
> but that I will try always to recognize and submit
> to the gods in me and the gods in other men and women.[4]

Heathcliff is such a god in Cathy. These visitors from the surrounding darkness are intuitions and promptings with which the conscious mind must come to terms, from which the whole being draws its sustenance.

The work of Lawrence's which most strongly suggests itself for direct comparison is not a work of fiction at all, but the poem "Snake". The snake, like Heathcliff, functions at three levels: as fully realized snake; as psychological analogue—the poet's own deepest, most spontaneous self; and as a "living myth". The snake is a god coming out of the darkness, recognized immediately by the poet as "one of the lords of life". But another part of him, the voice of his education, his superego, does not have the courage to let the snake come and go, but, responding with irrational fear to that which is alien, attempts to kill it or maim it or at least drive it quickly back into its darkness. Thus the Christians had driven the old fertility god, Pan, underground, calling him Lucifer and evil.

The snake represents, for Lawrence, "the deep, deep life in us that has been denied, and still is denied". This life cannot be killed, only repressed, and in repressing it, its beauty and dignity is lost. St Mawr, the stallion, another Lawrencian embodiment of this life, becomes "reversed and purely evil" when his rider perversely bullies him and drags him down. Then the hooves flash viciously, and the face of a bystander is kicked in. Elsewhere this life has a human embodiment—always an outsider of some kind who experiences rejection by the "extant social world"—foreigner, gamekeeper, gypsy.[5]

Surely Heathcliff represents this deep life in Cathy, which, denied, becomes perverse, cruel, and ultimately self-destructive. At Thrushcross Grange they call Heathcliff a gypsy—"a wicked boy at all events and quite unfit for a decent house!" Isabella wants the frightful thing to be put in the cellar. What is this but the classical Freudian repression of the id? Nelly describes his eyes as "that couple of black fiends, so deeply buried, who never open their windows boldly, but lurk glinting under them, like devil's spies". Nelly challenges Heathcliff to "change the fiends to confident, innocent angels"; she encourages him to frame high notions of his birth:

> You're fit for a prince in disguise. Who knows, but your father was Emperor of China, and your mother an Indian queen (VII, 54).

The fiends were once brightest of angels. Heathcliff is a king in exile, made mad by the horrors of his prison-house.

We must beware of pushing the analogy with Lawrence too far. There is no reverence for the life of the body as such in Emily Brontë. Rather, the body is thought of as the prison-house of the tortured soul which can only find its fulfilment when totally unrestrained by limitations of any kind, social, moral or physical:

> the thing that irks me most is this shattered prison, after all. I'm tired, tired of being enclosed here. I'm wearying to escape into that glorious world, and to be always there; not seeing it dimly through tears, and yearning for it through the walls of an aching heart; but really with it, and in it (XV, 134).

When it becomes impracticable for Cathy's body to be on the hilltop, then her soul must be freed from the body. What Cathy's soul passionately desires is to inhabit a world "where life is boundless in its duration, and love in its sympathy, and joy in its fulness" (XVI, 137). Even Nelly believes that such a life is only available on the far side of the grave. Cathy challenges Heathcliff to find a way to her "not through that Kirkyard", but she herself can conceive of no other adequate reunion, and Heathcliff finally accepts that way with relish:

> 'by the time Linton gets to us, he'll not know which is which!' (XXIX, 228–9).

Where the life force is not accommodated and given expression in daily social living, it must burst that frame. But it is not entirely, in the case of Heathcliff and Cathy, a matter of deprivation, the ignorance and cruelty of others. They ask for too much in the name of fulfilment, selfhood and freedom. No human being can merge himself wholly with the life force and not go mad. That is for gods. There must be constraints and modifications out of respect for the conditions life itself imposes upon men, out of respect

for other people with their different natures, out of respect for
one's own body.

When Cathy dies the novel is only half over. Heathcliff does not
long hold the centre of the stage. There remains the second-gener-
ation story in which the whole process starts again, but without
these excessive longings, and, consequently, with a very different
outcome.

Joseph's comment on Linton Heathcliff "we've allas summut uh
orther side in us" (XXIV, 201) has frequently been taken as a
choric indication of a central concern with heredity in the second
part of the novel. I do not find this. Linton has a distorted nature,
and it is easy to explain this in terms of a combination of the
worst features of either side (an explanation underlined by his
name), the weakness and peevishness of the Lintons and the
cruelty of Heathcliff. He will undertake to torture any number
of cats provided their teeth be drawn and their claws pared. But,
whatever our reservations about the Lintons, young Heathcliff
can in no way serve as their continuing representative. It is the
contrast rather than the comparison which first strikes Nelly:

> A pale, delicate, effeminate boy, who might have been taken for
> my master's younger brother, so strong was the resemblance; but
> there was a sickly peevishness in his aspect that Edgar Linton never
> had (XIX, 163–4).

To Nelly he is like neither parent. Linton asks her if he is like his
father.

> 'Not much', I answered. Not a morsel, I thought, surveying with
> regret the white complexion and slim frame of my companion, and
> his large languid eyes—his mother's eyes, save that, unless a mor-
> bid touchiness kindled them a moment, they had not a vestige of
> her sparkling spirit (XX, 168).

Certainly Heathcliff can recognize nothing of himself in his son:

> "Thou art thy mother's child, entirely! Where is *my* share in
> thee, puling chicken?" (XX, 169).

It is necessary for the mechanism of the plot that Heathcliff
have a son who marries the heiress of Thrushcross Grange, but
does not long survive his wedding. Yet nothing in the treatment

of him seems mechanical. Emily Brontë's psychology is extraordinarily advanced (by our standards, I mean, not those of the mid-nineteenth century). A great deal of evidence accumulated in recent years indicates that inheritance is less important than was formerly supposed, and environment very much more so, in determining what we are. And environmental influence begins not at birth, but at conception. Emily Brontë offers no overt explanation of Linton Heathcliff's character, but surely the reader must feel that a fatherless child (for the first twelve years; then motherless), unwanted by anyone, born while his mother was under severe strain, is likely to be ailing and peevish whatever his genetic make-up. A good seed will only produce a good plant if it has space, soil and sunshine. The human equivalents of space, soil and sunshine are freedom, home and love. Linton dies because, denied these essentials, he never becomes a viable human being.

Hareton and Cathy, though both are motherless and vulnerable, are born of love and are not lacking in vitality. Hareton's birth is accompanied by auspicious imagery of sunshine:

> On the morning of a fine June day, my first bonny little nursling, and the last of the ancient Earnshaw stock, was born.
> We were busy with the hay in a far-away field, when the girl that usually brought our breakfasts came running, an hour too soon, across the meadow and up the lane, calling me as she ran. 'Oh, such a grand bairn!' she panted out. 'The finest lad that ever breathed!' (VII, 59).

Here is ripening sun, fertility, nourishment, and a clear indication in the phrase "bonny little nursling", that, despite the death of the mother, the child will not entirely lack maternal care. A hundred and twenty pages later the same imagery reappears:

> Still I thought I could detect in his physiognomy a mind owning better qualities than his father ever possessed. Good things lost amid a wilderness of weeds, to be sure, whose rankness far over-topped their neglected growth; yet, notwithstanding, evidence of a wealthy soil that might yield luxuriant crops, under other and favourable circumstances (XVIII, 161).

Cathy is not quite "a second edition of the mother", but very near it. She may be said to combine the best features of either side:

She was the most winning thing that ever brought sunshine into
a desolate house—a real beauty in face, with the Earnshaws' handsome dark eyes, but the Lintons' fair skin, and small features, and
yellow curling hair. Her spirit was high, though not rough, and
qualified by a heart sensitive and lively to excess in its affections.
That capacity for intense attachments reminded me of her mother;
still she did not resemble her; for she could be soft and mild as a
dove, and she had a gentle voice, and pensive expression: her anger
was never furious, her love never fierce; it was deep and tender
(XVIII, 155).

Cathy "grew like a larch", while Hareton suffered under Heathcliff's attempt to "see if one tree won't grow as crooked as another, with the same wind to twist it". It is not only the same
wind, the same deprivation which had deformed Heathcliff's life;
it is also virtually the same tree. Hareton is as much a second
edition of Heathcliff as Cathy is of Catherine, though completely
unrelated to him. Inheritance, therefore, cannot be the determining factor.

Emily Brontë clearly wishes to recapitulate the childhood of
Heathcliff and Catherine with a few small but decisive adjustments. These adjustments are partly genetic, but mainly environmental. Heathcliff probably could have made Hareton as crooked
as himself had he been able to keep up the pressure:

'I can sympathise with all his feelings, having felt them myself—
I know what he suffers now, for instance, exactly—it is merely a
beginning of what he shall suffer, though. And he'll never be able
to emerge from his bathos of coarseness, and ignorance. I've got
him faster than his scoundrel of a father secured me, and lower;
for he takes a pride in his brutishness. I've taught him to scorn
everything extra-animal as silly and weak' (XXI, 178).

What Heathcliff is denying Hareton is, in its largest sense, education. Without that, Hareton's natural intelligence becomes in-
effective, so that Cathy asks "Is he all as he should be? . . . or is
he simple—not right?" (XXI, 178). Nelly rebukes her for despis-
ing him so unjustly:

'Had you been brought up in his circumstances, would you be
less rude? He was as quick and as intelligent a child as ever you
were' (XXIV, 200).

154

Heathcliff is not the only source of the deprivation. The Heights are still exposed and wuthering. When Cathy as a child looked out from her nursery window to Penistone Crags, Nelly "explained that they were bare masses of stone, with hardly enough earth in their clefts to nourish a stunted tree". Joseph is still the malign human embodiment of the spirit of the Heights. Zillah has replaced Nelly. She acquiesces in the worst excesses of Heathcliff's regime:

> 'it was no concern of mine, either to advise or complain; and I always refused to meddle.
>
> Once or twice, after we had gone to bed, I've happened to open my door again, and seen her sitting crying, on the stairs' top; and then I've shut myself in, quick, for fear of being moved to interfere' (XXX, 232).

Yet as Nelly, on a fateful day, had groomed Heathcliff as a suitor for Catherine, so Zillah is moved to offer the same help to Hareton:

> 'I saw he meant to give her his company; and I guessed, by his way, he wanted to be presentable; so, laughing, as I durst not laugh when the master is by, I offered to help him, if he would, and joked at his confusion' (XXX, 234).

Though education means for Emily Brontë anything which fosters the healthy growth of the whole personality, she does not despise formal learning. Hareton's illiteracy is presented as perhaps the most shameful manifestation of his degradation. His reclamation is effected by a combination of love and books. Books have made several earlier appearances in the novel. The first separation of Heathcliff and Catherine resulted from an incident involving the burning of books – the lumber thrust upon the children by Joseph which made Catherine resolve that she hated a good book. But primarily we have associated books with Thrushcross Grange with its well-stocked library in which Edgar had read, unaware, during Catherine's fatal illness. As Mr McKibben[6] has pointed out, it is the distinctive misuse of the book in each household we see in the first part of the novel. At Wuthering Heights it is something to be spurned or destroyed or overwritten if it cannot be seen to contribute directly to the life of wilful passion. At the Grange it offers a refuge and a retreat, an alternative, neatly-processed version of human life and nature which prepares Cathy very badly for her exposure to the reality at the Heights.

For Catherine, home and heaven were the same thing, the moors above the Heights. We picture her at the Grange as an outcast gazing through an open lattice towards the Heights while a bitter wind rustles the pages of an unread book Edgar has left on the sill for her. Cathy's position at the Heights is exactly the contrary, exiled against her will from the Grange with its library of well-read, well-loved books, the books she has smuggled in burnt or confiscated, escaping at last through the very lattice at which her mother's ghost is to beg admittance of Lockwood. Her home is the Grange, but it is not her heaven:

> 'Mine was rocking in a rustling green tree, with a west wind blowing, and bright, white clouds flitting rapidly above; and not only larks, but throstles, and blackbirds, and linnets, and cuckoos pouring out music on every side, and the moors seen at a distance, broken into cool dusky dells, but close by, great swells of long grass undulating in waves to the breeze; and woods and sounding water, and the whole world awake and wild with joy' (XXIV, 198–9).

Home for Cathy is not a retreat, an artificially cultivated park surrounded by a high wall. It is a place to move out from to confront life in all its fullness. She is not attracted by the hot dreamy stillness and unbroken blue of Linton's heaven. In hers there is wind and cloud, but not storm. Her mother's moors are there, but "at a distance". Instead of choirs of angels, Cathy's heaven is filled with birdsong. Her list of songbirds cannot fail to remind us[7] of the birds which filled her mother's imagination shortly before her death—wild duck, pigeon, moorcock and lapwing, all birds commonly shot. The lapwing in particular dominates her thoughts, a bird with plaintive cry, feigning a broken wing to protect the young, helpless and exposed in their ground nest. Heathcliff once set a trap over such a nest so that the parents dare not come, and they found the nest "full of little skeletons" the following winter. This image of the deserted nest, the vulnerability of the young, wanton cruelty, suffering and death, contains within it the central theme of the novel.

When books, towards the end of the novel, come to play a more positive role, it is not so much their content that matters as the fact that they symbolize a human faith in communication and social intercourse. The importance of the books is established long before Hareton is able to actually read them. The first sympathetic act of co-operation towards Cathy he makes, or is allowed to make, is when he reaches down some books in the dresser which are too high for her. From her cruel mockery of Hareton's efforts to teach himself to read (stealing from her and profaning books "consecrated by other associations") she progresses gradually to the point of neatly wrapping a handsome book and tying it with riband as a peace offering, grudgingly accepted, together with the promise "if he take it, I'll come and teach him to read it right" (XXXII, 248).

Love effects a remarkable transformation:

> His honest, warm, and intelligent nature shook off rapidly the clouds of ignorance and degradation in which it had been bred; and Catherine's sincere commendations acted as a spur to his industry. His brightening mind brightened his features, and added spirit and nobility to their aspect (XXXIII, 254).

The human transformation is only the first of a series of transformations it generates. The process of the first generation where the house helped to distort its occupants is now reversed. Joseph's barbed currant bushes are displaced to make room for an importation of plants from the Grange. Lockwood, on his next visit, is greeted with "a fragrance of stocks and wall-flowers" and is amazed to find the gate unlocked and doors and lattices open. Nelly has also been "transplanted" from the Grange, and fills the house with "Fairy Annie's Wedding".

Of course this transformation is made possible only by the collapse of Heathcliff. Cathy expresses her compassion for Linton in the words:

> He'll never let his friends be at ease, and he'll never be at ease himself! (XXIV, 203).

The idea of being at ease, like the idea of being at home, is central, and particularly relevant to Heathcliff. The opposite of ease is torment. It is torment Heathcliff expects to suffer for the rest of his life after the death of Catherine. The best he can hope for is the distraction of his revenge. And it is torment with which he curses Catherine's ghost. It is the need for ease which, after eighteen years of torment, drives Heathcliff to Catherine's grave, to make preparation for their reunion in death:

> 'and I gave some ease to myself. I shall be a great deal more comfortable now; and you'll have a better chance of keeping me underground, when I get there. . . . yesternight, I was tranquil. I dreamt I was sleeping the last sleep, by that sleeper, with my heart stopped, and my cheek frozen against hers' (XXIX, 229).

Heathcliff's heaven is six feet under ground. It is wherever Catherine is.

In the final chapter each generation simultaneously reaches its heaven. Hareton and Cathy stand at the threshold of a life of rewarding fruitfulness. They are at ease with themselves, each other and the world. Their children will lack for nothing. But they feel it necessary to end the three-hundred-year Earnshaw occupation of Wuthering Heights. They must put a distance between themselves and unaccommodated nature; they commit themselves, like Shakespeare's late heroines, to a civilized living which neither capitulates to nature, nor cuts itself off from nature's sustaining sources of vitality. The Heights is left "for the use of such ghosts as choose to inhabit it" (XXXIV, 265). Joseph sees them every rainy night looking out from Heathcliff's window. They are equally at home and at ease "under t'Nab" where the shepherd boy and his sheep see them.

The demolition of conventional morality in the first part of the novel, the apparently total commitment to the imperatives of passion, is, in the second half, followed up with an amazingly mature and self-critical reconstruction of morality which is also a repudiation of romanticism. The honesty and depth of Emily Brontë's vision forces upon her the recognition that passions are not necessarily "natural" but may well have become, under adverse environmental pressures, perverse, unnatural and destructive. Yet the repudiation of passion is the repudiation of life. It follows that the greatest immorality is not murder, sadism and debauchery in adult life, but the imposition upon the helpless young of conditions which divert their natural energies and aspirations into these channels. There is also the recognition that it is natural for a human being, in his deepest humanity, to need to modify and control his passions in understanding and sympathy in order that he might experience that deepest fulfilment which depends upon fruitful human relationships and those co-operative human activities which go to make a civilization.

The resolution is like that of a Shakespearian comedy, but played by tiny actors in the shadow of their tragic predecessors, whose grandeur they altogether lack. They compromise as their unbending creator never could. Emily Brontë was a great romantic rebel and a great religious mystic, and at the same time an unsparing critic of romantic rebellion and religious mysticism. Her stage spans, like a cosmic rack, the space between the necessary and the possible.

NOTES

1. I have concentrated here, since my context is the novel, on Lawrence as the primary inheritor. In a larger context one might very profitably discuss Emily Brontë's influence on, or affinity with, Ted Hughes, born on the edge of these same moors, and with a temperament perhaps closer to hers than Lawrence. See my *The Art of Ted Hughes*, Cambridge University Press, 1975, pp. 6–7, 26–8, 53–4, 160–1.
2. For a fuller account of the window imagery see Dorothy van Ghent's splendid essay in *The English Novel, Form and Function*. It is reprinted in several of the casebooks.
3. "The Brontës: or Myth Domesticated", in *Forms of Modern Fiction* ed. W. V. O'Connor, (Minneapolis, 1948).
4. *Studies in Classic American Literature* (1924).
5. For a fuller account of the symbolism of "Snake" and *St Mawr* see my *The Art of D. H. Lawrence*, Cambridge University Press, 1966, pp. 120–6, 151–9.
6. "The image of the Book in *Wuthering Heights*, *Nineteenth Century Fiction*, XV, no. 2 (1960).
7. Cf. "The Rejection of Heathcliff" by Miriam Allott, *Essays in Criticism*, XIII, no. 1 (1958) to which I am much indebted throughout this section.

2

A New Heaven and a New Earth

by J. F. GOODRIDGE

Wuthering Heights is a love story. In recommending it for adolescents, David Holbrook is not afraid to state the obvious, and in superlative terms: ". . . *Wuthering Heights* is a perfect book in that it deals with love as it transmutes and transcends sexuality. In a sense it is a sexual book: in another it is as beyond the sexual as much as the end of *King Lear*, and renders the 'togetherness' of Catherine and Heathcliff as something triumphant over anything we call love or sex. . . . To the child of early adolescence it is a *marvellous romantic tale*, and makes implicitly the profound point that such a love, expressive of a supreme vitality, may be more important than life itself" (my italics), (*English for Maturity*, 1961, p. 169).

How, then, does it stand out from the whole stream of romantic tales that have filled library shelves since the mid-eighteenth century? And why have nearly all Emily Brontë's critics, from Charlotte[1] onwards—Swinburne, Symons, Saintsbury[2], Herbert Read,[3] among them—insisted on its isolation from the main tradition of English fiction? F. R. Leavis spoke for them all when he said, "That astonishing work seems to me a kind of sport. . . . She broke completely, and in the most challenging way, both with the Scott tradition that imposed on the novelist a romantic resolution of his themes, and with the tradition coming down from the eighteenth century that demanded a plane mirror reflecting the surface of 'real' life" (*The Great Tradition*, 1948, p. 27n.).

Leavis's word "sport" here (presumably used in the old sense of *lusus naturae*) tells us nothing about the genesis and nature of

Wuthering Heights, but dismisses it as a totally unexplained "variation". This is almost as useless as Saintsbury's absurd phrase, "one of those *ornaments* of novel history". But before we look into the real heredity of *Wuthering Heights*, we should do well to examine more closely Leavis's representative comment on the traditions that Brontë broke with.

Just as the opening chapters naturally suggest the comparison with Scott, so the final chapter provides a clear test of its relation to the eighteenth century tradition. If we were to compare Brontë's conclusion with, say, the crudely "spooky" passages in Mrs Radcliffe—or with the subtly suggestive, retrospective technique of Henry James[4]—Nelly's precise, factual narrative might seem at first (as it did to Herbert Read) to have more in common with, say, Defoe's *Mrs. Veal*. But it is quite unlike Defoe in that it bears all the traces of tense, personal excitement. Nelly does not sleep, she only "dozes into unconsciousness": she is still preoccupied with the problem of Heathcliff even when she is "half-dreaming". The actuality is as much that of a clinging nightmare as of remembered facts.

In *The Sources of 'Wuthering Heights'* (1937), F. S. Dry has claimed that the Bertram family in Scott's *Guy Mannering* were prototypes for the Earnshaws. What kind of curiosity, then, concerning the Bertrams do Scott's opening chapters arouse, and how does he proceed to satisfy it? Why is Scott not content to let us take in the essential data (as Lockwood registers the main features and persons of Wuthering Heights) through Mannering's eyes? Lockwood, who is something of a dilettante antiquarian, "would have made a few comments, and requested a short history of the place", had he not been checked by Heathcliff's "attitude at the door". Brontë does not deliberately parody Scott, but through the medium of Lockwood's gentlemanly curiosity, she shews her awareness of the kind of interest in ancient houses and decaying provincial families that a writer of historical romance was expected to satisfy. Her irony is expressed in the fact (as Mr T. Crehan has put it) that "Lockwood . . . becomes involved in what he observes by misunderstanding it" (London English Literature edition, 1973). By courting curiosities and interesting himself in old-fashioned life and manners, he becomes caught up in contradictions that demand a very different mode of family history from what he anticipated. He is, as Dorothy Van Ghent says, "a city visitor in the country, a man whose very disinterestedness and facility of feeling and attention indicate the manifold emotional economies by which city people particularly protect themselves from any disturbing note of ironic discord between civilized life and the insentient wild flux of nature in which it is islanded" (*The English Novel, Form and Function*, 1953). Scott, it is not unfair to say, wrote with half an eye on such "city people", accommodating his pictures of country life to their tastes.

The only resistant subject-matter in Scott's novels is the doom of the old heroic life, whether of Covenanters or Jacobites, Lowlanders or Highlanders, and the tenacity with which people in remote fastnesses still clung to it. The "parallels" between, say, *Redgauntlet* and *Wuthering Heights* are obvious: Lockwood, like Darsie Latimer, becomes interested, and partly involved in, a world of outlandish passions; but the kind and degree of imaginative involvement for both narrator and reader is completely different. Scott used, first, the eighteenth-century form of letters from Darsie to a friend and, later, a reported narrative based on his journal. His Darsie does not arrive at the primitive cottage, with its strange, uncouth inhabitants, until Letter IV, and then he has ample time to describe everything—fishing-spears, old-fashioned implements, trenchers, gridirons—as if they were laid out in a museum. Consider by what dramatic encounters, and how soon, Lockwood's urbane composure is destroyed, and he is drawn into the personal lives of the protagonists. Scott, in comparison, writes like a leisurely reporter. "Doubtless" wrote Charlotte in her Preface, with sublime sisterly patronage, "had her lot been cast in a town, her writings . . . would have possessed another character. Had Ellis Bell been a *lady* or a *gentleman* accustomed to what is called 'the world', her view of a remote and unreclaimed region . . . would have differed greatly from that actually taken by the home-bred country girl". The language here ("view of a . . . region") already assumes that, in her own rude way, Emily was simply trying to do the same kind of thing as Scott.

"Scott," says Mr V. S. Pritchett, "writes like a citizen. He asserts the normal man, the man who has learned to live with his evil; what his evil might have done to him if he had not learned to live with it can be guessed by the grotesque declamations of

'The Black Dwarf', the creature who cuts himself off from mankind" (*The Living Novel*, 1954). For *The Black Dwarf*, he adds,
is the only novel of Scott where he tries to represent evil as anything other than "a fatality that ensues from the nature of the
times".—And *The Black Dwarf*, too (though from the time of its
publication until now it has been regarded as the one complete
failure among the Waverley Novels) is the only novel of Scott
that impressed Emily Brontë sufficiently to leave visible traces on
Wuthering Heights—names like Scott's Earnscliff, some similari-
ties of plot, and a number of strong echoes in language and
imagery (the dwarf had a "heart of whinstone").

It is not surprising that William Blackwood read the first
hundred or more pages of this novel with a fever of enthusiasm,[5]
before finding himself let down. Beginning as a moorland novel
of revenge, it presents the Dwarf at first as a deformed misanthropist living alone on a bleak moor. As Mr Pritchett has put it,
"the black dwarf is excellent when he is seen as local recollection,
a piece of Border hearsay, and no-one could surpass Scott in portraying that tortured head, with its deep-sunken pin-point eyes,
the almost legless and hairless little body with its huge feet, and
the enormous voice that issues". But this crude force is lost as
the Dwarf's speeches degenerate into "dreary, savage, Calvinist
lectures" (*op. cit.*).

Strangely, in that part of her Preface to *Wuthering Heights*
where she is insisting on Emily's independence of all literary
influences, Charlotte Brontë seems to echo the description in *The
Black Dwarf* of Mucklestane-Moor, with its "huge column of un-
hewn granite, which raised its massy head on a knoll near the
centre of the heath". "The statuary", says Charlotte, "found a
granite block on a solitary moor; gazing thereon, he ["Ellis Bell"
or Emily] saw how from the crag might be elicited a head, savage,
swart, sinister; a form moulded with at least one element of
grandeur—power". This aptly describes the way Emily made use
of some of the crude materials she found lying in the opening
chapters of *The Black Dwarf*, a story in which "a stone legend"
(a folk-story to explain peculiar rock-formations), combined with
Scott's actual encounter with a monomaniac dwarf who claimed
evil magical powers, led to this extraordinary attempt to take up
many living elements of folk-lore and project them in a psycho-

logical picture of a man driven into seclusion and real savagery by deformity and an unfaithful betrothed. As usual in his tales of wonder, before long "rationality warns him he is misguiding himself and his public. He then becomes circumspect and faint-hearted" and "shies away from the unearthly . . . inartistically juxtaposing the real and the unreal"[6]—so that Elshender the Recluse (the dwarf) dwindles into Sir Edward Mauley, an inverted sentimentalist and humanitarian. The "romantic resolution" here amounts to a complete dissolution of the opening theme of superstition and primitive hatred. Yet Emily Brontë picks up phrases, especially images of barbaric cruelty, strips them of their gross rhetorical elaboration, and places them in a dramatic context which reveals how, with a focus much closer than "local recollection", she could retain control of her material just where Scott, as Mr Pritchett says, shews "a complete breakdown of imagination".

Heathcliff has been said to "rant" or "vociferate" in "turgid rhetoric". So it is instructive to look at a few examples of what Charlotte's "statuary" did with a few lumps of Scott:

1. *The Black Dwarf:* "Common humanity!" exclaimed the being, with a scornful laugh that sounded like a shriek, "Where got ye that catch-word—that noose for woodcocks—that common disguise for man-traps—that bait which the wretched idiot who swallows, will soon find covers a hook with barbs ten times sharper than those you lay for the animals which you murder for your luxury!"

(Compare Heathcliff's words to Nelly, in XIV, beginning "And that insipid, paltry creature attending her from duty and humanity. . . .")

2. *The Black Dwarf:* "Why should I play the compassionate Indian, and, knocking out the brains of the captive with my tomahawk, at once spoil the three days' amusement of my kindred tribe, at the very moment when the brands were lighted, the pincers heated, the caldrons boiling, the knives sharpened, to tear, to scorch, to scathe and scarify the intended victim?"

(Compare the passage in Isabella's narrative, XVII, where she says, "Pulling out the nerves with red-hot pincers requires more coolness than knocking on the head").

3. *The Black Dwarf:* "And why should other worms complain to
me when they are trodden on, since I am myself lying crushed and
writhing under the chariot wheels?"

(Compare Heathcliff, XIV, "I have no pity! I have no pity!
The more the worms writhe, the more I yearn to crush out their
entrails. . . .")

All these examples shew Brontë's power to transform the crud-
est rhetoric by her instinct for dramatic immediacy. The Black
Dwarf's shrill speeches take place in the course of lengthy dis-
putations with his noble-hearted friend Hobbie, and are unrelated
to any immediate emotional strain. Heathcliff's (and Isabella's)
violent language arise suddenly out of uncontrollable stresses of
feeling. For example, Heathcliff's reference to writhing worms,
often quoted out of context, is not shouted at Nelly, but muttered
to himself at the moment when, goaded to fury by Isabella's defiance, he has just thrust her out of the room.

Whether consciously or not, Emily Brontë has taken into her
drama just those hints of spontaneous barbarity which made
Scott's novel unacceptable. Far from being forced, her violent
language bears a relation to the kind of naïve directness sometimes found in the best dramatic work of children, when they are
too engrossed in the drama to be aware of its effect on others.
Charlotte said, more than once, that Emily was quite unaware of
the impression *Wuthering Heights* made on its readers: "If the
auditor of her work, when read in manuscript, shuddered under
the grinding influence of natures so relentless and implacable . . .
Ellis Bell would wonder what was meant, and suspect the complainant of affectation" (*op. cit.*, Preface).

From early childhood, the Brontë children first created their
"plays" by a process of spontaneous dramatization and discussion,
in which stock "romantic" figures and situations had to be brought
to life in "real" situations. It was a game they played for no
audience but themselves, uninhibited by the moral or social pressures that were bound to influence a great public figure like Scott.
Even in this context of play, Emily was as impervious to criticism
as, later, she was averse to M. Héger's formal methods of instruction (the analysis and imitation of various models of style).
Yet more than either of her sisters, she devoted her life to writing,
pursuing her art with the devotion of a celibate, and craving for

the security of Haworth Parsonage and the freedom of the moors chiefly in order to practise it.

Emily Brontë's passionate independence, which has even given rise to the legend of her as a superwoman, possessed from childhood by a dark, demoniac spirit[7] that she later embodied in Heathcliff, was no doubt nourished by her reading in the field of romantic literature. Heathcliff, the man of foreign aspect whom she planted in the actuality of a Yorkshire moor, cannot be considered without some reference to the long succession of "fatal men" (including The Black Dwarf) derived in part from Milton's Satan, with his "baleful eyes", who appear in many disguises in romantic fiction.[8] This type was best known to Emily through Byron's *Lara, Corsair, Gaiour* and *Manfred*, and Scott's *Marmion*—though she may well have been familiar, too, with Mrs Radcliffe's Schedoni and Ambrosio, Matthew Gregory Lewis's Abellino, John Moore's Zeluco and many more. Similarly, the character of Catherine bears some relation to the stock figure of the *femme fatale*, for which Cleopatra may be regarded as the prototype—though, superficially, Catherine has more in common with Katharina in *The Taming of the Shrew*; and young Cathy, as well as Isabella (of whom Heathcliff says "No brutality disgusted her: I suppose she has an innate admiration of it") may be related to the regular type of the "persecuted woman" that appears in all Mrs Radcliffe's "tales of terror".

The qualities which recur insistently, according to Mario Praz, in the Fatal Men of the Romantics are "Mysterious (but conjectured to be exalted) origin, traces of burnt-out passions, suspicion of a ghastly guilt, melancholy habits, pale face, unforgettable eyes". They are men of fallen splendour who retain an immense pride and severe reserve and, having experienced all the storms of passion, ruin the happiness of others by their cruelty. Yet they exercise a demoniac power and fascination, that lurks chiefly in their flashing eyes; and, like Heathcliff, they are all in some sense haunted men.

Once we begin looking for such connections as these, they start up on all sides: some interpreters of Brontë have been tempted to link her prose and verse with a wider tradition of European romanticism, finding likenesses between her vision of life and that of authors as widely separated as Richardson, Rousseau, Chateaubriand, de Laclos, Edgar Allan Poe, Hoffmann, Novalis, Nietzsche, Dostoevsky and D. H. Lawrence. To take one example, Mr T. Crehan states: "The notion of a demon-man who dies because he is haunted by a ghost-woman is the kind of fantasy one would expect from a specialist in grotesquerie like Hoffmann, whose German tales Emily had read" (*op. cit.*). (What evidence is there of this?). And Philip Henderson, who also believes that she was influenced by Hoffmann, says "She was evidently familiar with the idea of the *doppelgänger*, the early nineteenth-century formulation of the dual personality in which the conscious and unconscious minds pull in different directions".[9]

All such theories, in so far as they may tempt us to impose on *Wuthering Heights* a doctrinaire interpretation, should be treated with extreme caution; not because they open up too many possibilities, but rather because they tend to *limit* our appreciation of the novel's range of meaning and narrow its terms of reference; for *Wuthering Heights* is indeed deeply rooted in traditions of Indo-European mythology—but ones that are not confined to nineteenth-century romanticism. The qualities of feeling that we respond to in Emily Brontë are in fact universal, and we should naturally expect to find counterparts to them in all kinds of literature, especially in the writings of those German romantic poets and story-tellers who shared her passion for legend, folklore and myth, and her rare capacity for "mystical" insight and experience. But it is essential to draw a distinction between "influences" that may have meant much to her personally, as revealed in her poems and Gondal writings, and those (if any) which are directly relevant to the texture of *Wuthering Heights*.

To make clear the gulf that separates Heathcliff from the typical Byronic hero, one has only to read Byron's idealized self-portrait in the three famous stanzas of *Lara* (Canto I, xvii-xix), and see what happens when we apply this "character" directly to Heathcliff. Byron's grandiloquent tone, building up slowly to an attitude of awed reverence as if to silence all belittling criticism, strikes one as singularly inappropriate the moment we remember Heathcliff's hanging of Isabella's puppy, or Nelly's sturdy common sense ("Mr. Heathcliff," said I, "this is the talk of a madman . . .").

The constant controls which *Wuthering Heights* exercises over a reader inclined to extravagance—the harsh realism that makes it

167

resist every attempt to see it as a manifestation of that decadent, "frenetic romanticism" documented by Praz—are more significant than the superficial resemblances of theme.

For example, Edgar Allan Poe remarked, in his *Philosophy of Composition*, that "the death of a beautiful woman is, unquestionably, the most poetical topic in the world". If one examines the chapters dealing with the illness and death of Catherine in the light of this statement, one finds that, though Nelly betrays a "touching interest" in the beauty of "one doomed to decay", and Edgar (who lies all night by her corpse) seems to share something of the romantic tendency to necrophilia, Heathcliff betrays no such morbid interest—"I plainly saw that he could hardly bear, for downright agony, to look into her face! "[10]

We might consider, too, in the light of the typical romantic fascination for death and corruption, Heathcliff's three attempts to come near Catherine's dead body. Do they shew a gloating, morbid fascination? Are they closer to Poe's *Berenice, Morella, Eleonora* and the rest, or to a ballad like *The Unquiet Grave*? Catherine's body is strangely preserved from corruption by the peaty soil. Heathcliff's matter-of-fact words to Nelly (XXIX) about his reaction to seeing her face eighteen years after her death show his *inability* to understand her conventional response to the supposedly gruesome and macabre.

The nineteenth century romantics were also fascinated by consumptive ladies. Yet Nelly passes over the death of Frances with a ruthlessness which allows no time even for sympathy. It is only Hindley (who "had room in his heart only for two idols—his wife and himself") who betrays, in his self-indulgent love and frantic grief, an element of weakness and morbidity.

Are the "persecuted women" of *Wuthering Heights* held up to us as specimens of that "Beauty of the Medusa" which so fascinated Shelley? Lockwood (who *is* something of a "romantic") betrays in his description of young Cathy (II) his disappointment that she is not pathetic in quite the way he expects—her look of scorn and desperation prevents his "susceptible heart" from feeling for her as he thinks he should. And at the time of her greatest misery when she is in effect married to a corpse in a locked bedroom, her story is told by the hostile, unsympathetic Zillah.

These are only a few of the ways in which *Wuthering Heights* cauterizes sentimental feeling in the reader where a poet like Byron would deploy all his rhetoric to enlist sympathy, especially for Heathcliff. Even Shakespeare's Richard III ("There is no creature loves me; / And if I die, no soul shall pity me") has something of the attraction of self-pity. One could compare, in its context, the effect of Cathy's words to Heathcliff: "*Nobody* loves you—*nobody* will cry for you when you die!" (XXIX).

Yet in their "infernal world" of fantasy, the Brontës lived within the romantic tradition with extraordinary intensity. Charlotte said of her dream-kingdom, Angria, that it "takes up my spirit and engrosses all my living feelings" and implied, too, that she attributed Emily's chronic homesickness to the same cause. From earliest childhood they created myths in which they tried to dramatize and explore every extreme of passionate feeling. Emily's heroine, Augusta Geraldine Almeda, was the perfect type of the *femme fatale*, passionate, irresistible, changeable and cruel, and much of the Gondal poetry concerns her love adventures, which prove disastrous for all the men concerned.

It is impossible to guess the quality of Emily's prose sagas, since not a fragment of them has survived. The atmosphere of the poems that take their inspiration solely from Gondal is that of sham Scott or Byron, suggesting, as Derek Stanford has said, a "ham Ruritanian world" of "cardboard sublime" and "wire-pulled puppets".[11] Whether or not this was true of the prose, there is little to justify the idea that the Gondal writings, reconstructed, might provide essential clues for the interpretation of Wuthering Heights—as if Catherine, Heathcliff and Cathy were simply Gondalians in a Yorkshire setting. The example of Walpole's *Castle of Otranto* is sufficient to shew that the intensity with which a fantasy is experienced in no way ensures that it will be convincing as a work of fiction.

The important fact is that Emily had developed, with her sisters, an extraordinary capacity for what they called "making out"— envisaging and dramatizing imaginary situations without the aid of wide experience or observation. This made it possible for her, in maturity, to transform the stock romantic situations, transplant them into a world of local tradition and, retaining whatever was most vital in the romantic vision of childhood, cast away the Byronic trappings and create something new.

Wuthering Heights is not a "romance", though elements of myth and fairy-tale lie hidden beneath its surface, affecting us unconsciously rather than by conscious suggestion. So, for example, Nelly's hint to Heathcliff that he might be of high birth comes out so naturally in its context of idle chatter, washing and hair-combing (VII) that one might read the whole dialogue without noting how fraught it is with hints, half-ironic, of a romantic, fairy-tale interpretation of Heathcliff's origin and destiny. If we search Emily's poems for the innumerable clues they provide to these underlying motifs, we may not notice the irony, and we may be tempted to interpret the novel in terms of pure myth. Dorothy Van Ghent's brilliant treatment (*op. cit.*), based on the poems, of the "two children" figure in *Wuthering Heights* provides a good example of the advantages, and the dangers, of this method of interpretation.

For this reason it is better to leave aside the poems until the novel has been fully assimilated on its own level, and to make use of them as much for purposes of critical comparison as for direct interpretation. If we compare, for example, the great "mystical" stanzas of *Julian M. and A. G. Rochelle* with Catherine's words in XV: "And," she added musingly, "the thing that irks me most is this shattered prison . . ."—the poem seems to convey, and actually describe through its rhythm, a personal, mystical experience. Catherine's words do nothing of the kind; but in their dramatic context (notice the unexpected pause in her struggle with Heathcliff, the "prolonged gaze" that precedes her sudden change of tone, and the significance of "musingly"—her temporary abstraction from the violence of the scene), they leave us in no doubt of the reality of her longing for death and her faith in an unseen "glorious world", so putting a question in our minds which modifies our view of all that happens after, though the novel can never finally resolve it. A novel may so present the raw elements of life as to convince us of the possibility of spiritual realities: it cannot distil for us the essence of mystical experience.[12]

A reading of Emily's great poem "Death, that struck when I was most confiding", which has been well analyzed by Mr Derek Stanford (*op. cit.*) may help us to see how, behind her preoccupation with the fate of the dead, lies an immense faith in life and a resilience in the face of guilt, loss and destruction. For in this poem the sense of fulness and fruition, stretching beyond death and pain, is wholly convincing. This abounding energy and trust in Nature's economy, persisting after experience has confirmed a tragic view of life, is perhaps the one primary quality of feeling common to her few major poems and *Wuthering Heights*, which gives the novel its commanding unity of tone.

It is the sureness and suppleness of rhythm in Emily's best poems that defines their emphatic and individual quality of dramatized feeling. If we were to analyse "Death, that struck" purely in terms of language, we should find that it is loaded with stock "poetic diction" ("fervent heat", "winged grief", etc.). Only very occasionally does the language of common speech, or of ballads and folk-songs, break through.

But in the prose of *Wuthering Heights*, her sure sense of rhythm relies on the stark directness of common speech—not a crude simplicity or insistent use of colloquialisms, for Nelly's speech, as Lockwood remarks, is quite cultivated. But the style is never laboured, like Hardy's; it is always close enough to every-day speech to make us feel the presence of a speaking voice. Emily's father and brother, talented raconteurs, and the family servant, Tabby, a great retailer of local gossip, were perhaps more important "sources" for *Wuthering Heights* than either Scott or Byron. The strength of her style springs from her relying on her natural "ear" for the language of story-telling, which is close to that of the ballads:

"And dreary, and chill, and dismal, that morrow did creep over".

"It's yon flaysome, graceless quean, that's witched our lad, wi' her bold een".

"His eyes met mine so keen and fierce, I started; and then he seemed to smile".

"Hareton, with a streaming face, dug green sods, and laid them over the brown mould himself".

"There's Heathcliff and a woman, yonder, under t'nab".

Apart from the rather garbled reference to the ballad *Fair Annie* (XXXII), we are given one odd specimen of Nelly's "nursery lore" (IX):

"It was far in the night, and the bairnies grat,
The mither beneath the mools heard that—"

I have traced this to the ballad "The Ghaist's Warning", which Emily almost certainly found in the Notes to Scott's *Lady of the Lake*.[13] Both this, and *Fair Annie* and other related ballads like *Sweet William's Ghost*,[14] belong to the most primitive Danish sources, embodying pre-Christian beliefs. With this important source in mind, we should also remember Charlotte's emphatic statement in her Preface that, though Emily never associated much with the people around Haworth, "yet she knew them: knew their ways, their language, their family histories; she could hear of them with interest, and talk of them with detail, minute, graphic and accurate".

So, beginning with a place she knew well and combining this with scraps of family history, ballad folk-lore, half legendary gossip and superstition, Emily's imagination recreated the living drama of which these were the surviving remnants. At the end of *Wuthering Heights*, the story of Catherine and Heathcliff has already become a local superstition, though a very active and palpable one—"But the country folk, if you ask them, would swear on the Bible that he *walks*. . . . Idle tales, you'll say, and so say I".

Barely hidden beneath the surface of Nelly's guarded scepticism, Christian sentiment and "nursery lore", and Joseph's Calvinistic pharisaism, there lies a whole world of country superstition[15]— a world inhabited by ghosts, fairies, witches, ghouls, goblins and vampires, inextricably confused with the language of hell-fire sermons and Victorian fairy tales. The final chapter of the novel alone provides plenty of evidence, for anyone who cares to look. Lockwood may wonder "how anyone could imagine unquiet slumbers for the sleepers in that quiet earth". But Emily Brontë did not need to look far for the evidence of such imaginings. The very language in which the narrators express their scepticism is fraught with suggestions of the supernatural. The universality of the beliefs expressed by Heathcliff is attested by the many versions of ballads like *The Unquiet Grave* (the belief that "excessive grief on the part of the living disturbs the peace of the dead") or *Sweet William's Ghost*, with their dialogues between living and dead lovers that come to life above the grave, whose breath is mingled with the cold air and drops of rain. The traces of this belief in life after death as an extension of this life are to be found in every place where the Christian Heaven which Heathcliff repudiates (and which "did not seem to be Catherine's home") had not taken full hold on the popular imagination.

Brontë's dating of her story, which separates it by fifty years from the Yorkshire of her own day, is important in this connection. She had no interest in the social changes brought about in the intervening years, but resurrects the kind of intense life, lived (as Lockwood put it) "more in earnest . . . less in surface change", which she knew to have existed high up among the dales not so very long before her time.

All that we need to know of this local background is described in the Introduction and first two chapters of Mrs Gaskell's *Life of Charlotte Brontë* (1857). First, she notes the extraordinary contrast between the rich soil and vegetation of the valleys, with their "becks" flowing through rich meadows, and the bareness of the higher ground, where only stunted trees and shrubs will grow.[16] Describing her first walk with Charlotte on these moors, Mrs Gaskell tells us: "Here and there in the gloom of the distant hollows she pointed out a dark, gray dwelling . . . and told me such wild tales of the ungovernable families who lived or had lived therein that *Wuthering Heights* even seemed tame comparatively".

She explains, too, how in such houses crimes might be committed almost unknown, and describes precisely the type of house and family, the remains of the old yeomanry, then becoming extinct, which we may suppose the Earnshaws to have been. "Still there are those remaining of this class—even at the present day, who sufficiently indicate what strange eccentricity—what wild strength of will—nay, even what unnatural power of crime was fostered by a mode of living in which a man seldom met his fellows. (Compare Lockwood's picture of a "homely northern farmer"!)

Mrs Gaskell's account of the religious life of the district is also of some relevance: "But after his [the evangelical parson, Mr Grimshaw] time, I fear there was a falling back into the wild rough heathen ways . . . only fifty years ago, their religion did not work down into their lives. Half that length of time back, the

173

code of morals *seemed to be formed upon that of their Norse ancestors*. Revenge was handed down from father to son as an hereditary duty" (my italics). So Heathcliff, for all his mysterious origins, is more a native of Yorkshire than he is of Byron's orient or Emily's Gondal.

But Emily comprehended realities much deeper than those described by Mrs Gaskell: she dug down beneath the level of local history to the elements of that heathen folk-lore which still survived in country districts and is embodied in the English and Scottish ballads. Heathcliff's beliefs, and to some extent Catherine's, are simply the universal ballad-beliefs personified and fully dramatized.

"The Ballads," says Mr M. J. C. Hodgart, "are typically amoral and tragic". The "ballad universe" is peopled "with fairies and witches and with ghosts who return from the grave. There is no clear line of demarcation between such creatures and ordinary mortals. The supernatural is treated in a matter-of-fact and unsensational way" (*The Ballads*, 1950). Nor, in some of the ballads, is there any essential difference between men and animals.

The "ghosts" of the ballads "are not disembodied spirits in the accepted sense, for in most cases *the 'ghost' is the actual corpse* . . . 'Ghosts' is the wrong word for these corporeal beings who rise from their unquiet graves: revenants, returners would be a better description. They are described in material and human terms. . . . They return sometimes because the tears of the living will not let them rest" (my italics).

Again, L. C. Wimberley[17] tells us: "The conception that the Otherworld does not extend beyond the grave-mound or barrow is found side by side with the belief in a general realm beyond the tomb". (Does not Catherine, in her delirious ravings and elsewhere, express both these beliefs?) "In some ballads", says Mr Hodgart, "future life is associated only with the grave 'where the channering worm doth chide'."

We might go much further and consider, in connection with Lockwood's nightmare, the terrible significance in the ballads of the drawing of life-blood, or the magic of "dead-naming" which might have power to bring the dead to life. Or it may not be far-fetched to think of the oak-closet. Catherine's coffin-like bed, in terms of the "object-soul" which the dead still seek to inhabit.

Certainly these ideas are all relevant for an understanding of Heathcliff's frenzied, literal mind—"And when I slept in her chamber—I was beaten out of that. I couldn't lie there; for the moment I closed my eyes, she was either outside the window, or sliding back the panels, or entering the room, or even resting her darling head as she did when a child" (XXX).

But the clearest example of reincarnation in the ballads, says Mr Hodgart, "is that of lovers' souls going into plants which grow from their graves". This motif is repeated in a number of ballads, such as Earl Brand, *as a fitting end to a tragic love-story*".

The ballads "present love and violence in the same matter-of-fact way as the supernatural". The only virtue they recognize, apart from prowess in war, is loyalty, particularly to the beloved. The necessity for revenge is taken for granted.

These ballad-beliefs are, of course, only one strand in a novel that preserves them, intact, as part of a much more complex pattern. But the ballad mood and outlook is, I believe, one important key to a novel which, for this very reason, stands so far outside the main stream of English prose fiction. It stands outside, because it belongs essentially to a deeper stream, that which Coleridge and Wordsworth sought to make use of in their lyrical ballads. Brontë's art is like that of Coleridge—that of "interesting the affections by the *dramatic* truth of such emotions as would naturally accompany such situations, supposing them real". In her intense inner life, Emily must have responded with a sensitiveness only equalled, perhaps, by that of Coleridge and Shakespeare, to all that she was able to seize on or divine of "romantic" legend, folklore, myth and mystical insight. *Wuthering Heights*, like *The Ancient Mariner* or *Macbeth*, is a unique crystallization of human experiences—a novel in the full, Jamesian sense, yet steeped in myths far deeper than the shallow lakes of Byronic romance. She seemed to *know*, instinctively, so much more of the dialectic of passion than her life and circumstances would seem to make possible. She was capable of receiving, as it were from afar, the vibrations and rhythms of ancient belief and experience as clearly as the impressions of her own locality. The closer she comes to the inner working of human passion, the surer her rhythms become. Catherine's "I cannot express it, but surely you and everybody

175

have a notion . . ." leads directly into what must be the most convincing attempt to give "it" utterance in the English language.

She knew, perhaps better than Novalis, how "the lover is alone with all that he loves"—better even than her great contemporary Wagner, whose *Tristan und Isolde* (based partly on Schöpenhauer's idea that the "will" only reaches its full development when the "will to live" is abandoned) is the richest embodiment of the "myth" of romantic love in European art. Several years before Wagner began work on it, Brontë, more in touch perhaps with everyday reality than he, was discovering its wild roots on a Yorkshire moor.

The love of Catherine and Heathcliff stands, like an ancient rock, very near the centre of the stream of Western romantic tradition as it is embodied, less in the novel than in the greatest poetry, drama and music. Denis de Rougemont, in her book, *Passion and Society* (1940), has boldly attempted to trace this stream from its source to the present day. The nearer one gets to the primitive sources, as opposed to the sophisticated meanderings of later date, the closer one seems to be to Catherine and Heathcliff. A brief summary of a few points about the myth will illustrate this.

A myth is a fable that both embodies, and masks, certain constant aspects of human experience: in the case of *Tristan and Isolde*, that aspect of the passion of love which links it, inseparably, with death. Myths have their origin in religious experience, and the ideal of romantic love may be derived, partly from Platonism, and partly from the primitive Celtic religion that sprang to new life in the dualistic heresies, Manichaeism and Catharism, which spread like wildfire through Western Europe in the Dark and Middle Ages. These religions recognized two principles, Light and Darkness: terrestrial matter was properly the sphere of darkness, reigned over by the Devil. But the soul is angelic, imprisoned in the body. It longs, like Catherine, to escape from this "shattered prison" which is its earthly Hell.

Christianity does not regard the flesh as a shattered prison, yet to a romantic lover *it* might seem to be a dualistic religion, since it consigns the soul after death either to Heaven or Hell. The dualistic religions, on the other hand, might seem ultimately monistic, since they believe in a heaven which will reconcile all contradictions and transcend both good and evil. Catherine's "glorious world" and Nelly's "shadowless hereafter" represent this popular, ineradicable belief in the possibility of such a transcendence; and all Heathcliff's words in his final conversation with Nelly express a direct apprehension of the dualism of soul and body—"My soul's bliss kills my body, but does not satisfy itself".

Christianity also put *agape* in the place of passion or *eros*, thus bringing forth the idea of our *neighbour*. This, sayes de Rougemont, meant "the death of the solitary human being". But as Lockwood learnt in his nightmare, *Wuthering Heights* represents a world without neighbours, "where every man's hand is *against* his neighbour".

The other important factor is Platonism. "It is impossible to tell," said Ortega y Gasset in his book on Love, "to what deep levels of the Western mind Platonic notions have penetrated. The simplest sort of person regularly employs expressions and betrays views which are derived from Plato."

For Plato (*Phaedrus* and *Symposium*) love could transform desire into "enthusiasm" or limitless aspiration. A lover with his beloved may become "as if in heaven". Love is a way that ascends by degrees of ecstasy to the source of existence, remote from all that divides one self from another. But such a unity is a negation of the present human being: when man rises to be a god, there is no return. (But the Celts believed in an after-life which was a continuation of this life, though freed from pain, and allowed some of their heroes to return to earth).

Thus in European mythology and the literature of courtly love, passion is dreamed of as an ideal and its fatal character is welcomed. It is a kind of fate, stronger and more real than happiness, society or morality. The lovers seek a complete identity with one another: they imagine they have been ravished into an absolute beyond good and evil, more real than the world. Their love is selfish: they need one another in order to keep passion aflame ("I *cannot* live without my life", etc.): and (perhaps unconsciously) they create obstructions to its earthly fulfilment.

Such passion means suffering, usually death, as in *Romeo and Juliet*. It is regarded as an *askesis* (exercise or training) for an ultimate bliss of union which transcends, and is opposed to,

177

earthly life as we know it. Therefore it has no place for marriage. The lover will gladly endure any pain to attain his goal. "For me, however", wrote the Arab poet Ibn al Fariah, "death through love is life".[18] And Cleopatra:

> 'I am fire, and air: my other elements
> I give to baser life. So; have you done?'
> (*Anthony and Cleopatra*, V., ii)

Where it is not regulated by a civilized code of courtly love, passion may lead to lawless violence, and the lover may even seek to be avenged for what he has suffered (Emily had read *Ossian* with enthusiasm). But in nineteenth-century Germany, Goethe, Hölderlin and Novalis, as well as Wagner, revived the myth in its undiluted form, subjectivizing it and stripping it of both courtly formality and popular violence. Emily Brontë, on the other hand, made it struggle for its life, a hardy perennial, amidst all manner of opposed forces, both brutish and over-civilized. Though this opposition gives rise to terrible violence, the myth frees itself and triumphantly survives on the extreme edge of civilization.

"Surely you and everybody have a notion that there is or should be an existence of yours beyond you. What were the use of my creation, if I were entirely contained here?" (IX)—Catherine's personal brand of Platonism is at one with that of all the great romantics in identifying her "other existence" with her lover, Heathcliff, and *not* expecting much earthly pleasure from it: "A source of little visible delight, but necessary." Necessary, that is, in order to keep her soul aflame with the passion to identify herself with something beyond ("That is not *my* Heathcliff. I shall love mine yet; and take him with me: he's in my soul"). In her case, this beyond means the whole cosmos beyond the pale of civilization, which he, the "unreclaimed creature", represents. "If all else perished, and *he* remained, *I* should still continue to be; and if he were annihilated, the universe would turn to a mighty stranger: I should not seem a part of it" (IX).

The love of Catherine and Heathcliff does indeed begin as a childhood "togetherness"—a "heaven" of the kind that only children who are thrown together in a natural environment, deprived of all other love, can fully experience. Once Cathy is loved by others and her pride is affected, she truly takes on something

of the characteristics of the *femme fatale* in her ambiguous relation with Heathcliff. All the inherent contradictions of "romantic
love" are present in the rhythms and counter-rhythms of her dialogue with Nelly—"Every Linton on the face of the earth might
melt into nothing, before I could consent to forsake Heathcliff.
Oh, that's not what I intend—that's not what I mean!" (IX).
She must retain her love for Heathcliff as a consuming passion—
keep him as a power within her soul ("the eternal rocks beneath")
—not degrade herself by turning him into a husband. This is not
solely a matter of an awakened class-consciousness.

Since Heathcliff cannot understand this contradictory passion
in her, he turns all his energy into the negative path of revenge—
he becomes a Sadist, in the original sense: using cruelty as an
escape from suffering ("While I'm thinking of that I don't feel
pain"); for, as de Rougemont has put it in speaking of the Mar-
quis de Sade, "The mind proceeds to invent in the guise of acts
of cruelty the sufferings it has forbidden the heart to undergo".
(This is where Heathcliff may have most in common with Byronic
heroes, turning suffering into a kind of megalomania or will to
power; but Brontë does not hold this up to admiration). Only
at the end, through influences which we may, if we like, interpret
as the result of Catherine's still devouring need of him, is he
driven to take the path of all the great lovers, and seek his happiness through the consummation of death.

But there is one further strand woven into the web of Brontë's
thought, that links her treatment of the myth with the scientific
awareness of "nature" that was characteristic of her own time—
and bridges any gulf we may feel between Heathcliff's natural
violence as an unfeeling child of nature,[19] and the unbreakable belief in a transcendent world which the novel dramatizes. The five
essays written in French[20] for her Belgian teacher, M. Héger, throw
interesting sidelights on her poetic and fictional treatment of the
theme of the transcendence or transfiguration. In "The Butterfly",
after first arguing that all living creatures, including man, prey on
one another and "life exists on a principle of destruction", she uses
the image of the butterfly springing forth from the caterpillar to
illustrate how the soul is liberated by death into an eternal realm
of happiness and glory: "Just as the ugly caterpillar is the beginning of the splendid butterfly, this globe is the embryo of a new

heaven and of a new earth whose meagrest beauty surpasses mortal imagination".

NOTES

1. See the Preface to her 1850 edition: ". . . hewn in a wild workshop, with simple tools, out of homely materials".
2. "*Wuthering Heights* is one of those isolated books which . . . are rather ornaments than essential parts in novel history" ("Three mid-century novelists" in *Corrected Impressions*, 1895).
3. In comparing Nelly's account of Heathcliff's death with Jane Austen's treatment, in *Persuasion*, of Louisa's fall from the Cobb, Read says that Brontës "emotional intensity . . . compels the expression to economy, directness, and speed". This "new vitality" and "stricter realism" of the Brontë's was "a return to Swift and Defoe, or rather . . . the Bible", which was "the most considerable literary influence on Emily Brontë's life" ("Charlotte and Emily Brontë" in *Reason and Romanticism*, 1926).
4. For example in *The Turn of the Screw*, ch. 3, the paragraph beginning "It produced in me, this figure in the clear twilight . . . " .
5. "Its [*The Black Dwarf's*] first 192 pages threw William Blackwood into such a fever of of enthusiasm . . . that he was unable to go to sleep" (Edgar Johnson: *Sir Walter Scott, the Great Unknown*, 1970, p. 553).
6. Coleman O. Parsons: *Witchcraft and Demonology in Scott's Fiction* (1964).
7. See for example Romer Wilson: *All Alone: the Life and Private History of Emily Jane Brontë* (1928).
8. See Mario Praz: *The Romantic Agony* (1933) II, "The Metamorphosis of Satan".
9. Preface to his *Selected Poems of Emily Brontë* (1951).
10. How far could we apply to Catherine and Heathcliff D. H. Lawrence's remark about Poe's *Ligeia*: "It is a tale of love pushed over a verge. And love pushed to extreme is a battle of wills between the lovers . . . which shall first destroy the other"? (*Studies in Classic American Literature*, 1924).
11. In Muriel Spark and Derek Stanford: *Emily Brontë, Her Life and Work* (1953).
12. Further tests of this statement might be: 1. To compare "No Coward Soul is Mine" with Catherine's "If all else perished, and *he* remained, *I* would still continue to be . . ." etc. (IX). 2. To consider the various resonances given in many of the poems to the words "heaven" and "hell", "wind" and "heath", and compare these with their charged dramatic contexts in the novel.
13. Canto IV, stanza XII, Note VI.

14. Here, the lover returns from the grave without arms because
    "By worms they're eaten, in mools they're rotten
    Behold, Margaret, and see."
15. "I see in you, Nelly, . . . an aged woman—you have grey hair, and bent shoulders. This bed is the fairy cave under Penistone Crag, and you are gathering elf-bolts to hurt our heifers . . ." etc. (XII).
16. She writes: "All around the horizon there is this same line of sinuous, wave-like hills, the scoops into which they fall revealing other hills beyond, of similar colour and shape, crowned with bleak, wild moors".
17. Quoted in Hodgart, *op. cit.*
18. Quoted by de Rougemont, *op. cit.*
19. ". . . the bird was not shot—we saw its nest in the winter, full of little skeletons. Heathcliff set a trap over it. . . . Did he shoot my lapwings, Nelly? Are they red, any of them?" (XII).
20. *Five Essays Written in French by Emily Jane Brontë*, translated by L. W. Nagel, edited by F. E. Ratchford (University of Texas, 1948).

3

"Divided Sources"

by PHILIPPA TRISTRAM

> "I saw a Spirit standing, Man,
> Where thou dost stand—an hour ago;
> And round his feet, three rivers ran
> Of equal depth and equal flow—
>
> "A Golden stream, and one like blood,
> And one like Sapphire, seemed to be,
> But where they joined their triple flood
> It tumbled in an inky sea.
>
> "The Spirit bent his dazzling gaze
> Down on that Ocean's gloomy night,
> Then—kindling all with sudden blaze,
> The glad deep sparkled wide and bright—
> White as the sun; far, far more fair
> Than the divided sources were! "[1]

In the diary paper written on her twenty-seventh birthday, Emily Brontë records "our first long journey by ourselves together", which she and Anne had made the previous month.[2] This excursion, of barely three days' duration, extending only to York, was heightened for the older sister by its parallel in an imaginary Gondal expedition: "we were Ronald Macalgin, Henry Angora, Juliet Augusteena, Rosabella Esmalden, Ella and Julian Egremont, Catharine Navarre, and Cordelia Fitzaphnold, escaping from the palaces of instruction to join the Royalists who are hard driven at present by the victorious Republicans". For Emily Brontë, only three years before her death, "The Gondals still flourish bright as ever. . . . We intend sticking firm by the rascals as long as they delight us, which I am glad to say they do at present".[3] But for her younger sister Anne, the conviction of that childhood game has gone; in her paper of the same date she notes: "The Gondals are at present in a sad state".

In the following year, when the manuscripts of *Wuthering Heights* and *Agnes Grey* set out in search of a publisher, their text made it evident that Anne, unlike her sister, had learnt to view childhood with the jaundiced eye of the governess. Amongst the Bloomfield children, "First Lessons in the Art of Instruction" are bitterly disillusioning: Tom tortures birds, Mary Ann is "incorrigible" in her "insensate stubbornness", whilst even the supposedly gentle Fanny proves to be an "intractable little creature, given up to falsehood and deception".[4] In contrast (despite her experience as a teacher at Law Hill and in Brussels) Emily Brontë's portrayal of childhood in *Wuthering Heights*, though conducted from the nurse's point of view, identifies chiefly with the children. "Falsehood and deception" are the characteristics of "sober disenchanted maturity" (XXXIII, 254),[5] whilst that intractability and stubbornness, which may seem to a Nelly Dean "insensate", marks a fidelity to early convictions, fiercely sustained in despite of time and change.

To suggest that Emily Brontë's enigmatic genius drew much of its strength from the tenacity of her childhood experience,[6] may have its dangers if it seems to imply nostalgia or immaturity, neither of which do justice to her novel or the best of her poems. Even the Gondal game is not romantically escapist in any usual sense, for it is as real to her imagination as her cogently prosaic perception of the actual: "The Gondals are discovering the interior of Gaaldine Sally Mosley is washing in the back kitchen".[7] *The Songs of Innocence and Experience* provide an analogy corrective to any derogatory impression, for Blake too is convinced that the innocent vision of childhood has a validity which the harsh rigours of experience do not displace: the two are co-existent, if paradoxical, necessities.[8] Both writers moreover glimpse, at least as vision, some further state of innocence in which those contraries are reconciled: the final state of Lyca, the little girl lost, and that condition beyond death which Catherine and Heathcliff seek, mark the same union of "divided sources". Nostalgia for a past perception of corn as "orient and immortal wheat" is familiar enough in English literature; but the retrospect of Vaughan's

183

"Retreate" or Wordsworth's "Recollections" is as absent from Emily Brontë as from Blake. Her writing does not only retain but actually maintains the intensity of an unimpeded vision into the iron inurement of adult experience. The exposure of innocence to experience is as radical and damaging in *Wuthering Heights* as it is in the *Songs*; but whilst Catherine's and Heathcliff's obdurate refusal to acknowledge their division through the agency of time and change is a direct cause of catastrophe throughout the novel, their ultimate union places the temporal harmonies, achieved by a more pliant generation, in a perspective which diminishes them.

Before examining those paradigms of early experience expressed in the two generations, it may be helpful to suggest the unobtrusive ways in which the childhood state, though directly described with relative brevity, is nonetheless kept continually before the reader. The narrative mode, apparently so straightforward, though on inspection so intricate, is a major resource. It is, for example, easily forgotten that five of the eight figures central to the two households are dead before the tale begins; yet Catherine, whose life is briefer than all but Linton's, is undoubtedly the novel's most vital figure. Moreover, the actual narration of the story belongs, for the most part, to the winter of 1801–2, a date irrelevant to virtually all those concerned in it; thus the novel's "present" is of tenuous substance, and even the events of 1802, which occupy the three final chapters, are reported that September, not directly witnessed. For a substantial part of the narrative, Nelly's memory is the effective "present"—although her recollections, with astonishing precision, extend back some thirty years.[9] It is surprisingly difficult to reconstruct an exact chronology,[10] although, as one reads the novel, it seems idle to ask the year, when Nelly gives us the season, day and hour with such exactitude. Cathy is, for example, born "about twelve o'clock, that night" (XVI, 137), the night of Sunday, the fourth day after Nelly's visit to the newly-married Isabella (XV, 130), five days before the "summer" weather is broken by a return to sleet and snow (XVII, 140). Yet this "date", once reconstructed as the Spring of 1784, precedes the narration by some seventeen years; the effect of Nelly's precision is to make of the past a "here and now" more vividly present than the winter fireside of 1801, where she entertains the convalescent Lockwood. Heathcliff's occasional reports, or those of Zillah, Isabella's letter and direct account of her escape, the scrap of Catherine's own childhood diary, intensify this impression. Their immediacy—"last night", "yester-evening", "I have got the time on with writing for twenty minutes"—makes the past more urgent than the novel's current events.

By these unobtrusive means, Emily Brontë disengages her readers, not only from conventional notions of past and present, but from expectations of development and maturity. Those vital years of transition from childhood to adulthood are virtually eradicated, in both generations, from the novel. When Catherine and Heathcliff first glimpse the Lintons through the brilliant windows of Thrushcross Grange, all four are children, Isabella "eleven, a year younger than Cathy" (VI, 47). Yet the summer following, Catherine, courted by Edgar, is given the more probable age of fifteen (VIII, 61), whilst on his proposal to her only a few pages later Nelly remarks of her "catechism": "for a girl of twenty-two, it was not injudicious" (IX, 70).[11] The narrative flow has suggested a lapse of months, from the weeks before Christmas in one year to the latter months of the next; but ten years, at this point, appear to have elapsed, and a further three must pass before she marries Edgar. Yet Catherine, dying at Thrushcross Grange in the year following her marriage, dreams that she is a child of twelve again, " 'the whole last seven years of my life grew a blank!' " (XII, 107). Time accelerates or contracts in accordance with the novel's need to omit those years which span the transition from childhood to maturity.

Other such omissions may indeed be quite overt: we see nothing of Catherine from the illness which follows Heathcliff's departure to that day, more than three years later, when Edgar "led her to Gimmerton chapel" (IX, 79). The period in which she alters from child to bride, transforms Heathcliff (quite without explanation) from a "ploughboy" to a gentleman, whose "countenance was much older in expression and decision of feature than Mr Linton's" (X, 84). Edgar indeed looks "quite slender and youthlike beside him", yet Heathcliff, at this point is barely twenty.[12] Similar omissions occur, though more explicably, in the second generation; Cathy is only seventeen and a widow when Lockwood comes to Thrushcross Grange, whilst Hareton's illiteracy gives him, at twenty-two, a childlike aspect. Since Isabella is last seen "in the girlish dress she commonly wore, befitting her age more than her position" (XVII, 141), whilst her son dies when barely seventeen, only Hindley, Edgar and Heathcliff have time to mature. Like Heathcliff, Hindley is absent in the years which precede his marriage, and on his return passes rapidly from infatuation to raving. Heathcliff himself, although the narrative centre until the age of forty, seems only to harden as the "iron man" he becomes in absence. Edgar alone, in the years that follow Catherine's death, achieves a state one might justly describe as "mature".

Where Heathcliff is unchanged by the years, the other characters, preserved by death, absence or the novel's end, sustain a youthful image. Even Edgar, on his deathbed, looks "very young . . . though his actual age was thirty-nine, one would have thought him ten years younger, at least" (XXVIII, 224). For the two main parts of the story, broken by the twelve year lapse that follows Catherine's death, the characters are much of an age, ranging from childhood into their early twenties. Only Heathcliff actively spans the generations, and when, on the evening following Edgar's funeral, he enters the library at Thrushcross Grange, the emphasis lies on time's arrest, not its passage:

> It was the same room into which he had been ushered, as a guest, eighteen years before: the same moon shone through the window; and the same autumn landscape lay outside. We had not yet lighted a candle, but all the apartment was visible, even to the portraits on the wall—the splendid head of Mrs Linton and the graceful one of her husband.
>
> Heathcliff advanced to the hearth. Time had little altered his person either. There was the same man; his dark face rather sallower, and more composed, his frame a stone or two heavier, perhaps, and no other difference (XXIX, 227).

That portrait of the newly-wedded Catherine, the "graceful" head of a younger Edgar, the Heathcliff of "eighteen years before", are the images which dominate the novel. Heathcliff exclaims of the painting: " 'I shall have that home! Not because I need it, but—' " (XXIX, 228). His sentence is completed when, some time later, he comments on Hareton's resemblance to Catherine: " 'That, however, which you may suppose the most potent to arrest my imagination, is actually the least, for what is not connected with her to me? and what does not recall her?' " (XXXIII, 255). For the reader of the novel, equally, the features of all three are indelibly traced in its detail as those of Catherine are, for Heathcliff " 'shaped on the flags! In every cloud, in every tree—filling the air at night, and caught by glimpses in every object, by day I am surrounded with her image!' " In the three children of the second generation, both the features and situations of the first are perpetually recalled, yet, as in their names, confusingly interwoven.

Hareton, the child of Hindley and his short-lived wife, whose origins are as mysterious as Heathcliff's own ("What she was, and where she was born, he [Hindley] never informed us"), is more vividly reminiscent of Catherine and Heathcliff than either of their own children. Cathy's "handsome dark eyes" alone reflect her Earnshaw descent; her "fair skin and small features, and yellow curling hair" are Linton characteristics. Her "capacity for intense attachments" certainly recalls her mother to Nelly: "still she did not resemble her . . . her anger was never furious, her love never fierce" (XVIII, 155). Linton manifests his Grange origins even more exclusively, for he bears no trace of Heathcliff's "rock": "A pale, delicate, effeminate boy, who might have been taken for my master's younger brother, so strong was the resemblance" (XIX, 163).

These genetic traits are as haunting in their absence as in their presence; the direct descendants of Catherine and Heathcliff revitalize the gentle Lintons, but reveal little trace of the Earnshaw fire, much less of Heathcliff's gipsy durability. Hareton, similarly, bears little resemblance to his father and none to his mother; Nelly describes him objectively as "a well-made, athletic youth, good looking in features", but in these she perceives more difference from his father than affinity: "I thought I could detect in his physiognomy a mind owning better qualities than his father ever possessed" (XVIII, 161). As Heathcliff comments, Hindley's son " 'is gold put to the use of paving stones' ", where his own " 'is tin polished to ape a service of silver' " (XXI, 178). In Hareton's situation, the young Heathcliff lives again; in his physiognomy, Catherine is reincarnated. He bears more resemblance to his aunt than Cathy to her mother; the eyes of Cathy and Hareton "are precisely similar, and they are those of Catherine Earnshaw", but

Cathy "has no other likeness to her, except a breadth of forehead, and a certain arch of the nostril", where in Hareton "the resemblance . . . is singular at all times" (XXXIII, 254). Whilst for Heathcliff " 'his startling likeness to Catherine connect[s] him fearfully with her' ", Hareton's repetition of his own boyhood situation is even more disturbing, for it makes him seem " ' a personification of my youth, not a human being' ":

> "Hareton's aspect was the ghost of my immortal love, of my wild endeavours to hold my right, my degradation, my pride, my happiness, and my anguish—" (XXXIII, 255).

"One might doubt in seasons of cold reflection" (as Nelly comments of Catherine's salvation), whether the ingenuity with which Emily Brontë enables that early relationship to dominate the book, in despite of the normal processes of time and change, does not evade some taxing scrutinies. The poet's reply to the sceptic's "Never again"—"Never again? Why not again? / Memory has power as real as thine"[13]—is one kind of answer, authenticated by the life of the past in Nelly's recollections. It must also be acknowledged that most of the narrative is entrusted, not to the convinced, but to the sceptical, not to passionate youth, but to an adulthood "sober" enough in the case of Nelly, "disenchanted" in Lockwood's view with which the novel begins and ends.

Certainly Lockwood, for whom Emily Brontë shows some disdain, is more justly described as "disenchanted" than "mature". He belongs to "the noisy crowd" from which the poet retreats to "barren hills / Where winter howls," or to that other "clime",

> Where tongues familiar music speak
> In accents dear to memory.[14]

As a member of "the busy world", Lockwood is not only fated, but eager, to return to "its arms" (XXV, 205). He understands neither the "barren hills", nor the enduring purchase of early affections. "A situation so completely removed from the stir of society" is to him "a perfect misanthropist's heaven" (I, 13); one which he so readily forgets in the course of a few months—"my residence in that locality had already grown dim and dreamy"— that it takes the chance comment of an hostler to remind him that he is still legal tenant of Thrushcross Grange (XXXII, 241).

If he recognizes certain values in those who inhabit this solitude, the tone of his comment is flippantly urban:

> "They *do* live more in earnest, more in themselves, and less in surface change, and frivolous external things. I could fancy a love for life here almost possible; and I was a fixed unbeliever in any love of a year's standing" (VII, 58).

His own somewhat shabby seacoast flirtation confirms the impression that Lockwood's own emotions are far from profound; nor do they develop, since, near the story's end, he is still capable of such incomprehending vanity as this:

> "What a realization of something more romantic than a fairy tale it would have been for Mrs. Linton Heathcliff, had she and I struck up an attachment, as her good nurse desired, and migrated together into the stirring atmosphere of the town!" (XXXI, 240–1).

Those whose formative years are not spent at Wuthering Heights —Hindley's wife and Linton, as well as Lockwood—cannot survive its rigours, either physically or spiritually. It is perhaps important that a stranger should introduce its world, but much more so that the "good nurse", a true inhabitant, should reveal it. Nelly is not only a child of the moor; she is a participant in its childhood experience, and her fidelity to the Earnshaw family is rooted in a relationship which eclipses any direct mention of her own kin. She is "born in one year" with Hindley (XVII, 153), his "foster sister" moreover; she thus excuses "his behaviour more readily than a stranger would" (VIII, 61). A memory of that sibling relationship, recalling a time previous even to her tale's beginning or Catherine's birth,[15] comes upon Nelly with "a gush of child's sensations" as she passes a signpost on the Gimmerton road (XI, 94). A hole at its base is still stored with the snail-shells and pebbles which she and Hindley, as six-year-old play-mates, hid there "twenty years before". So vivid is that moment that Nelly, who later doubts the shepherd boy's claim to have seen Catherine and Heathcliff—"he probably raised the phantoms from thinking"—here sees an apparition herself:

> as fresh as reality, it appeared that I beheld my early playmate seated on the withered turf, his dark, square head bent forward, and his little hand scooping out the earth with a piece of slate.

"Poor Hindley!" I exclaimed, involuntarily.

I started—my bodily eye was cheated into a momentary belief that the child lifted its face and stared straight into mine! It vanished in a twinkling; but, immediately, I felt an irresistible yearning to be at the Heights (XI, 94).

This retrospect, however, provides the only glimpse of Nelly as child; from the moment of Heathcliff's arrival, with which her story opens, she assumes the role of nurse, of foster-mother rather than foster-sister: "Mr. Earnshaw told me to wash it, and give it clean things, and let it sleep with the children" (IV, 39). Some two years later, following Mrs Earnshaw's death, "the children" fall ill with measles, and Nelly, who has "to tend them", takes on "the cares of a woman" (V, 40). Her perspectives on the three then change; hitherto she has sided with Hindley against Heathcliff, but the latter now proves "the quietest child that ever nurse watched over. The difference between him and the others forced me to be less partial". When Hareton is born and his mother dies, he becomes Nelly's "first bonny little nursling" (VIII, 59)— "more than all the world to her" as she laments, when forced by Catherine's marriage to leave him five years later (IX, 80). His place, however, is speedily taken by the motherless Cathy, and Nelly, the nurse of the first generation, becomes effective mother to the second.

Throughout her narrative, her attitudes to her variously recalcitrant charges accords with her role. Thus, although her identification with the families gives her criticisms much more weight than Lockwood's, they are, on the one hand, limited by the perspectives appropriate to her position, and become, on the other, a further means of perpetuating the childhood image. Like any nurse, Nelly responds most warmly to those charges who reciprocate her affection and comply with her wishes. She is, for example, well aware that "hardness not gentleness" makes Heathcliff "give little trouble" as her patient; but for this reason, and because "he would have me constantly by his pillow", she "softened towards the being" whose recovery earned her commendation (IV, 40). On the same occasion, Catherine's contrasting behaviour correspondingly alienates her; she remains ever after to Nelly the wilful child, who "put us all past our patience fifty times and oftener in a day" (V, 42). Nelly's attitude to her is never softened by the devotion she consistently shows to her daughter, whose "perverse will" is modified by charm, tenderness and affection.

There is, for example, little distinction between that comment on Catherine, and Nelly's attitude to Mrs Linton, mistress of Thrushcross Grange:

> She rung the bell till it broke with a twang: I entered leisurely. It was enough to try the temper of a saint, such senseless, wicked rages! (XI, 102).

To the nurse, this mortal fury is merely a childish tantrum, to be dealt with accordingly. " 'There is nothing in the world the matter' ", she whispers to Edgar; "I did not want him to yield . . . I told him how she had resolved, previous to his coming, on exhibiting a fit of frenzy". Despite a tremor—"I could not help being afraid in my heart"—she remains confident through the early stages of Catherine's fatal illness that her mistress is merely seeking to win her way through sustained, childish display. When, after a three-day fast, Catherine declares she believes she is dying, Nelly sets it down "as a speech meant for Edgar's ears; I believed no such thing, so I kept it to myself" (XII, 103). When Catherine, in delirium, finds "childish diversion" in pulling the feathers from her pillow, Nelly drags it away with the sharp injunction: " 'Give over with that baby-work!' " (XII, 105). When Edgar reproves her for "heartless" negligence she justifies herself in the tones of Agnes Grey to Mrs Bloomfield:[16] " 'I knew Mrs Linton's nature to be headstrong and domineering . . . but I didn't know that you wished to foster her wicked temper' " (XII, 109–10).

Agnes Grey trusts to time, "for a child of nine or ten as frantic and ungovernable as these at six or seven would be a maniac"; since Catherine is nineteen, Nelly's attitude to her "maniac's fury" has its justification. But where a child in a tantrum, though frightening, may be reasonably expected to recover, the cold truth is that the adult Catherine is dying. Even to Heathcliff at forty, also within days of his death, Nelly remains the prosaic nanny who offers him her "bit of admonition" (XXXIV, 257):

> "And supposing you persevered in your obstinate fast, and died by that means, and they refused to bury you in the precincts of the Kirk? . . . How would you like it?" (XXXIV, 263).

191

She still reacts as Aunt Branwell probably did when the Brontë children persisted in their hunger-strike, until they secured the reinstatement of their beloved old servant, Tabby.[17] Nelly can only understand her vicarious families as the children who were once her charges, in whose two households she remains as a "human fixture". She cannot comprehend that "childish" responses, perpetuated into adulthood, have a significance quite different and much more formidable. Whilst her comments justly criticize the evident immaturity of their self-tormenting behaviour, they do not begin to ask, much less to answer, the poet's own painful and crucial question:

> Why dost thou hold the treasure fast
> Of youth's delight, when youth is past
> And thou art near thy prime?[18]

" 'I wish I were a girl again' ", exclaims the dying Catherine, " 'half savage, and hardy, and free; and laughing at injuries, not maddening under them! Why am I so changed? why does my blood rush into a hell of tumult at a few words? I'm sure I should be myself were I once among the heather on those hills' " (XII, 107). For Catherine and Heathcliff both, as for the voice in Emily Brontë's poems, maturity is synonymous with imprisonment, torment and loss; in holding fast to "the treasure of youth's delight", they purchase a perpetual "hell of tumult". To the "smiling child" the future seems:

> "A sea beneath a cloudless sun;
> A mighty, glorious, dazzling sea
> Stretching into infinity."[19]

But with the years the "ardent boy", "too heavenly now", becomes the "iron man", one "doomed to be / Hell-like in heart and misery".[20] The limitless freedoms of that "dazzling sea" prove illusory, and only "shadowy gleams of infancy" can "draw his tired gaze from futurity".[21]

Catherine's question, " 'Why am I so changed?' " is in one sense answered by that other enquiry: "Why dost thou hold the treasure fast / Of youth's delight?" The refusal to acknowledge change does not mean that she, much less the world around her, remains unchanged: when Heathcliff returns after his three-year absence, they both, but she especially, ignore the transformations those years have produced, and persist in believing that their relationship, "half savage, and hardy, and free", can continue uninterruptedly. But the gossamer threads of Linton refinement, which in child-hood they disprized as too frail for challenge, are now binding upon them; in the context of a social maturity to which they refuse to adapt, the mores of their youth harden into destructive posture.

The violence of children is acceptable as adult violence, at least amongst "civilized" people, cannot be. When Heathcliff demands Hindley's pony, his own having fallen lame, the true son first throws an iron weight at the "changeling", then knocks him under the horse's hooves. Nelly "was surprised to witness how coolly the child gathered himself up, and went on with his intention, exchanging saddles and all, and then sitting down on a bundle of hay to overcome the qualm which the violent blow occasioned" (IV, 41). One can comprehend the young Hindley's reaction to a demand that is, after all, outrageous, and simultaneously admire Heathcliff's stoicism in gaining his point. A related scene in Chapter XVII, where the two are adults, has, however, a very different effect. Heathcliff, in disarming Hindley, pulls his knife "away by main force, slitting up the flesh as it passed on" (XVII, 147). When Hindley falls to the floor, "senseless with ex-cessive pain", Heathcliff "kicked and trampled on him, and dashed his head repeatedly against the flags. . . . He exerted preter-human self-denial in abstaining from finishing him completely." Heathcliff is fulfilling a resolution formed at fifteen:

> "I'm trying to settle how I shall pay Hindley back. I don't care how long I wait, if I can only do it, at last. I hope he will not die before I do!" (VII, 57).

The boy's determination is not surprising; its persistence into manhood, even to the very mode of retaliation, certainly is—the more so when one remembers that it is to endure for two further decades, visited on Hindley's son.

Yet, as children, the hardy, half savage resolution of Catherine and Heathcliff seems clearly preferable to the peevish Linton frailty. It exemplifies, significantly, Emily Brontë's own salient virtue, as characteristic of her in maturity as childhood;[22] which perhaps explains her indifference to her auditor's criticism of

"such fearful and vivid scenes": "Ellis Bell would wonder what
was meant, and suspect the complainant of affectation."[23] Not only
in the initial scene at Thrushcross Grange, but during their Christmas visit to Wuthering Heights, the children of the dale compare
poorly with those of the moor. Doused by Heathcliff with hot
apple sauce in response to some Olympian insults, Edgar bursts
into tears whilst Isabella, in sympathy, "began weeping to go
home" (VII, 55–56). " 'Don't cry! . . . You're not killed,' " Catherine remarks contemptuously. " 'Give over, Isabella! Has anybody
hurt *you*!' " Even as a lover, courting his impetuous mistress,
Edgar has his ears boxed and retreats "pale and with a quivering
lip" (VIII, 65). Nelly herself despises the "good children" of
Thrushcross Grange as "soft" and "petted" things; she tells
Heathcliff he shows "a poor spirit" in wishing to be a boy who
" 'cried for mamma, at every turn . . . and trembled if a country
lad heaved his fist against you, and sat at home all day for a
shower of rain' " (VII, 54).

It is the less surprising that Catherine, with "her wondrous
constancy to old attachments", should perceive no threat, but
only a source of delightfully "frivolous external things" in the
world Edgar opens to her. Nelly is more perceptive, in discerning
a predator in the "soft thing", Edgar: "he possessed the power to
depart [from Catherine], as much as a cat possesses the power to
leave a mouse half killed, or a bird half eaten" (VIII, 66). Even
Joseph describes him as "yon cat uh Linton" (IX, 77), but Catherine's failure to recognize the threat he presents is actively promoted
by the "essential" quality of her relationship with Heathcliff.
The search for Heathcliff's origins in literature (in the Byronic
hero, the *döppelganger*, the fairy-tale changeling or illegitimate
son),[24] has left them as hypothetical as they are in the novel. No
doubt he is a compound of many elements, but Emily Brontë
may well have encountered him before the age of literacy in the
Glasstown Chronicles and stories of Angria produced by Branwell and Charlotte. The Ashantee orphan, Quashia Quamina, who
turns savagely upon his benefactor, not only recalls the "gipsy
brat" of *Wuthering Heights*;[25] his development into the "iron
man" of Gondal, whose "altered, hardened spirit" seems wholly
to have lost "Remembrance of his early home",[26] suggests how he
may have become for Emily Brontë the perfect imagined playmate

of early life, whose loss, in her poems, is so bitterly regretted. Catherine's total identification with Heathcliff—" 'he's more myself than I am' " (IX, 72)—and the significance, belatedly recognized, of her "poor fancy" for the "frivolous external things" of the adult world, are both an externalization of that process traced in the poems, whereby the ranging delight of the child's imagination is atrophied by years which bring no compensations in "maturity".

Beyond the unexpected three-year transition, Catherine remains convinced that she still inhabits (or at least has the right to inhabit) that earlier world. Edgar and Isabella are to her still the soft and petted children of Thrushcross Grange whom she expects to dominate as formerly. " 'I yield like a foolish mother' ", she declares to Nelly, " 'they are spoiled children, and fancy the world was made for their accommodation' " (X, 86). She complains that Edgar whines for trifles and melts into tears (X, 86). Catherine's own "passionate temper verging, when kindled, on frenzy" (XI, 101), and her "deliberate turning of her fits of passion to account" (XI, 101), do indeed reduce Edgar to tears (X, 86), and, when abetted by Heathcliff's taunts and threats, to "a nervous trembling" which unmans him completely (XI, 99). But from these confrontations, so reminiscent, on both sides, of their childhood encounters, Edgar, faced with his wife's fatal illness and final death, acquires a mature and controlled tenderness which his opponents never master and never seek to. "In his anxiety for her" Edgar forgets "her hated friend" (XV, 136); after her death he avoids him totally. No longer exposed to their "high flights of passion" (XI, 99) he acquires mastery over himself and over his household. Nelly, comparing him at this later stage with Hindley is perplexed "to explain satisfactorily, why their conduct was so opposite in similar circumstances" (XVII, 152). Hindley "when his ship struck, . . . abandoned his post"; Edgar "on the contrary, displayed the true courage of a loyal and faithful soul".

Unlike Catherine and Heathcliff, Edgar has, however, none of that "treasure of youth's delight" to hold fast to; the twelve years that follow his wife's death are for him, as for Nelly, "the happiest of [his] life" (XVIII, 155); "Time brought resignation, and a melancholy sweeter than common joy" (XVII, 151). Time, for Heathcliff and Catherine, brings only an intensified sense of loss. Where she, in her prison, seeks liberation in death—" 'I'm tired, tired of being enclosed here. I'm wearying to escape into that glorious world' " (XV, 134)—he, as an "iron man", endures a further twenty years of torment, a "baited tiger" whom "men and laws have tortured".[27] Heathcliff justly reproaches her for yielding, of her "own will", to "the poor fancy" she felt for Linton, for in so doing she has parted them as " 'misery, and degradation, and death, and nothing that God or Satan could inflict would have parted us' " (XV, 135). "Men and laws" have indeed divided them, because Catherine so little understood the social world as to ignore her inability to leave Thrushcross Grange, and Edgar's right to exclude Heathcliff from his home.

The sexuality or asexuality of *Wuthering Heights* has, like its morality or amorality, exercised many readers. There is no avoiding a word like "passion" in describing its central relationship; yet, whilst it certainly has the connotations Nelly gives it in "fits of passion", or Catherine herself in "passionate temper verging on frenzy", it is hard, in the other direction, to extend it into adult sexuality, or even to recognize that "pang of [sexual?] envy" which reduces Edgar to tears (X, 86). Q. D. Leavis claims the term (along with moral) in her sustained analogy between Catherine and the Kate of *Jules et Jim*. She argues that, despite "the Victorian novelist's limitations in dealing with sex", Heathcliff's return "shocks Catherine into awareness of a gulf between her husband and herself . . . which undercuts their happily consummated physical love"; Emily Brontë is criticizing the failure in "the wife" to become "integrated or truly mature".[28] But "the Victorian novelist's limitations in dealing with sex" are certainly not conspicuous in George Eliot; explicit comment could not inform us more fully of the nature of Dorothea's sexual relation to Casaubon, of Gwendolen's to Grandcourt, or Mrs Transome's to the lawyer Jermyn. More relevantly, perhaps, we are in no doubt of the sexual nature of those longings which torment Charlotte Brontë's heroines, even the tense and "spiritual" child, Paulina, in her relations with her father and "Doctor John". In *Wuthering Heights* sexuality of this (familiar) kind is conspicuously absent from its major relationships.[29]

A.G.A., a heroine of Gondal, speaks of the love of a "childhood's mate" in these lines:

"Listen; I've known a burning heart
To which my own was given;
Nay, not in passion; do not start—
Our love was love from heaven;
At least, if heavenly love be born
In the pure light of childhood's morn—
Long ere the poison-tainted air
From this world's plague-fen rises there."[30]

The poet's statement, as so often, lacks the novelist's strength, but it does express a similar relationship succinctly. That interdependence and identification, which to Catherine, in childhood, seems as necessary, and as inevitable, an essential of life as air, becomes, by its removal in adulthood, a source of mortal suffocation. Thus Heathcliff exclaims: " 'O, Cathy; Oh, my life! how can I bear it? . . . I could as soon forget you as my existence! . . . What kind of living will it be when you—oh, God! would *you* like to live with your soul in the grave?' " (XV, 132–5). Certainly this relationship has its own child's morality; notions of possession are, for example, as alien to it in adulthood as in childhood. " 'When would you catch me wishing to have what Catherine wanted?' " Heathcliff asks as a child (VI, 48). As an adult, he assures Nelly that, in Edgar's place, " 'though I hated him with a hatred that turned my life to gall, . . . I never would have banished him from her society, as long as she desired his' " (XIV, 125). Exposure of the Lintons to emotions of such primitive intensity is destruction: " 'I'd as soon put that little canary into the park on a winter's day' ", Catherine remarks of Isabella (X, 89). But where the canary trills happily within the social confines of Thrushcross Grange, Catherine is " 'an oak in a flower-pot' " whom " ' the soil of [Edgar's] shallow cares' " cannot restore to vigour (XIV, 129). Because Catherine has no sense whatever of the significance of marriage, or the tenacity of social ties, she under-estimates fatally the power of the flower-pot to enclose them both; and the price of her mistake for the one, is "death", for the other, "hell".

The second generation, with the exception of Linton, is allowed a happier outcome within the temporal span. All three act out the parts taken by their forbears, Cathy and Hareton those of Catherine and Heathcliff, Linton that of his uncle. But although, on this occasion too, the bride is won by the "soft" and "petted" child of the social world, the canary is exposed in the park and dies there. The oak, on the other hand, is not confined to the flower-pot; nurtured, in contrast with her mother, at Thrushcross Grange, and confined at Wuthering Heights, Cathy survives that transplanting and thus enables Hareton to take what he chooses of "civilization's" offerings. The two are last seen at the end of a reading lesson, "about to issue out and have a walk on the moors" (XXXII, 243); last heard as "ramblers returning" when Lockwood grumbles, " *They* are afraid of nothing' " (XXXIV, 265). In the future, they will inhabit Thrushcross Grange, but of their own free choice.

To some extent the problems of this generation are simplified because the three are not childhood playmates; apart from some earlier brief encounters, they inhabit the same household only when Linton is sixteen, Catherine seventeen and Hareton twenty-three. Nevertheless, at those ages, all three are seen as children, who explore belatedly those frictions and pleasures to which the first generation are introduced much earlier. Only a year before Lockwood meets the young widow at Wuthering Heights, Cathy describes to Nelly the way she spends her time with the "man" who is to be her husband but a few months later:

"I looked at the great room with its smooth, uncarpeted floor, and thought how nice it would be to play in, if we removed the table; and I asked Linton to call Zillah in to help us, and we'd have a game at blind-man's buff—she should try to catch us; you used to, you know, Ellen. He wouldn't; there was no pleasure in it, he said, but he consented to play at ball with me. We found two in a cupboard, among a heap of old toys: tops, and hoops, and battledores, and shuttlecocks. One was marked C., and the other H.; I wished to have the C., because that stood for Catherine, and the H. might be for Heathcliff, his name; but the bran came out of H., and Linton didn't like it.

I beat him constantly; and he got cross again, and coughed, and returned to his chair. That night, though, he easily recovered his good humour; he was charmed with two or three pretty songs —*your* songs, Ellen" (XXIV, 199).

Not only are these two reviving the long-forgotten games of that earlier household; they are ones, learnt by Catherine from Nelly, which seem more appropriate to childhood than the adolescents they are, much less the young people, on the verge of marriage, which they are forced to be. Hareton at twenty-one, conning his alphabet but still ignorant of numbers (XXIV, 200), "blubbering" with fright at Catherine's threat to "tell papa" (XXIV, 202), presents an image even more clearly childlike.

Relationships in the second generation are worked out even more ruthlessly than are those of the first. The spoiled and peevish Linton receives even shorter shrift from Nelly than his mother and uncle, despite the cruel vulnerability of his position. When he is brought to Thrushcross Grange, an eleven-year-old child whose mother has just died, Nelly instantly deduces that, despite his striking resemblance to his uncle, "there was a sickly peevishness in his aspect, that Edgar Linton never had" (XIX, 163–4), whilst "his mother's eyes . . . had not a vestige of her sparkling spirit" (XX, 168). In order to persuade him to Wuthering Heights, she meets his bewildered and terrified appeals with "delusive assurances", which sharply contrast with the brutal truth exercised by children amongst themselves. Whilst at sixteen she regards him as "a dying child" (XXVI, 207), she has as little patience with him as his "tyrannic" and "wicked" father: he is "an indulged plague of a child, determined to be as grievous and harrassing as it can" (XXIII, 193), " 'the worst-tempered bit of a sickly slip that ever struggled into his teens! Happily . . . he'll not win twenty!' " (XXIII, 195) But although she now claims, " 'lucky it is for us that his father took him' " (XXIII, 195), Edgar earlier comments, " 'he'll do very well . . . if we can keep him' " (IX, 165). Had he stayed at Thrushcross Grange Linton might well have matured into the man his uncle becomes; yet although Nelly is well aware that his decay in temper is his fault only in part, she excludes him from her affection nonetheless: "I divined . . . that utter lack of sympathy had rendered young Heathcliff selfish and disagreeable, if he were not so originally; and my interest in him, consequently, decayed" (XXI, 172).

One possibility for the "iron man" of the poems lies in the restoration of innocence through the agency of his own children: "And did he never smile to see / Himself restored to infancy?"[31] But this solution is impossible for Heathcliff; Hareton, the child that he and Catherine should have had, is not only no kin to him, but also his avowed enemy. This outcome is reserved for Nelly; the vigorous tempers of her own two hardy nurslings never alienate her, and she cherishes their belated childhood with maternal satisfaction:

> Well, I reflected, there was never a pleasanter, or more harmless sight; and it will be a burning shame to scold them. The red fire-light glowed on their two bonny heads, and revealed their faces, animated with the eager interest of children; for, though he was twenty-three, and she eighteen, each had so much of novelty to feel and learn, that neither experienced nor evinced the sentiments of sober disenchanted maturity (XXIII, 254).

Cathy and Hareton "inherit the kingdom" in many senses; they not only succeed to the legal inheritance of Wuthering Heights and Thrushcross Grange, but there is nothing to suggest that "shades of the prison house" need ever close on them. No one and nothing threatens to divide the two "playmates"; even the pressure of time is removed by the novel's method. If they leave Wuthering Heights to Heathcliff and Catherine, it is not because they fear to stay, but because Thrushcross Grange holds no perils for them; they can enter freely the "heaven" that "splendid place" once seemed, glimpsed through its windows, to the half-savage Heathcliff and Catherine. There is no danger of that imprisonment and division which the young Heathcliff fears as, from without, he watches Catherine within: " 'if Catherine had wished to return, I intended shattering their great glass panes to a million fragments, unless they let her out' " (VI, 49).

But if the second generation stops short of that "hell of tumult" which adulthood involves for the first, their forbears win through that experience, of death itself, to a new form of recovered innocence. What *Wuthering Heights* externalizes in the three persons of Catherine, Heathcliff and Edgar, the poem, from which my epigraph is taken, sees as a warfare internal to the self:

> —So said I, and still say the same;
> —still to my Death will say—
> Three Gods within this little frame
> Are warring night and day.

The three rivers of gold, blood and sapphire may represent to the divided self something like that joy or vitality (gold), which may, on the one hand, dissolve itself in blood, those instinctual

energies to which it gives expression; or, on the other, marry
with reason, the cold blue gleam of Sapphire, a union calmer,
more outward and social, than that other inward and essential
mingling. But if the three "join their triple flood", they "tumble
in an inky sea" of incessant warfare. These rivers, externalized in
the novel, may correspond, respectively, to the vital Catherine
whose "spirits were always at high-water mark" (V, 42); to the
"lightening" and "fire" of the instinctual Heathcliff, "a dark
skinned gypsy, in aspect" (I, 15); and to the "moonbeam" and
"frost" of the blue-eyed Edgar Linton (IX, 72). In their descendants, this warfare is resolved because the river of sapphire is
eliminated; its distinctive virtue, in any case, runs in the veins of
Cathy, and is transmitted by her to Hareton. No such armistice
can be reached, in time, by the first generation; only the visionary
"Spirit" of the poem can mingle those three colours in one glad
white, and a lifetime's search cannot discover his presence:

> —And even for that Spirit, Seer,
> I've watched and sought my lifetime long;
> Sought Him in Heaven, Hell, Earth and Air,
> An endless search—and always wrong!
>
> Had I but seen his glorious eye
> *Once* light the clouds that 'wilder me,
> I ne'er had raised this coward cry
> To cease to think and cease to be—

For Catherine and Heathcliff, if not for Edgar, the orthodox haven
of Christianity provides no consolation: "No promised Heaven,
these wild Desires / Could all or half fulfil." Neither, as adult
has the least wish to enter there, although, as children, they
picture it "beautifully . . . in their innocent talk" (V, 44);
" 'heaven did not seem to be my home' " Catherine observes, in
describing her dream (IX, 72); she feels she has " 'no more business' " to inhabit it than to marry Edgar, whilst Heathcliff claims
that it " 'is altogether unvalued, and uncoveted' " by him (XXXIV,
263). Edgar, "aspiring to the better world" (XVII, 151), dies
"blissfully", anticipating with certainty his reunion with Catherine and, ultimately, with his daughter (XXVIII, 225); in conventional temporal perception that warfare ends with the three head-

stones in Gimmerton churchyard, whose distinctions the creeping
turf and moss will eventually bury in heath:

> "*O for the time when I shall sleep*
> *Without identity,*
> *And never care how rain may steep*
> *Or snow may cover me!*"

It is appropriate that Edgar, who can accept the normal world,
should find consolation in its normal solutions. It is also appropriate that Catherine and Heathcliff should seem to attain a distinctive heaven of their own, in which, when the weather is stormy,
they wander, as they once did when children, in the wide freedom
of the open moor. The novel does not, like the Spirit, transform
the "inky sea" into one "glad deep"; but then, no more does the
poem. Again like Blake, Emily Brontë seems only to glimpse that
recovered innocence beyond experience; it is the object of her
search because it is a necessity, not because it is a certainty—she
would be the lesser artist if it were.

NOTES

1. *The Complete Poems of Emily Brontë*, ed. C. W. Hatfield, New York
   1941, (1967); no. 181.
2. *Ibid.*; both papers are quoted p. 234.
3. After *WH* was written, and within months of her death, Emily Brontë
   continued to inhabit Gondal; cf. Fannie E. Ratchford, *Gondal's Queen*,
   Austin, Texas 1955 (McGraw-Hill Paperback edition, 1964); pp. 25 and
   32.
4. See *Agnes Grey*, chaps. II–V.
5. Many instances of "falsehood and deception" occur, for example, in
   Nelly's expedient treatment of the child Linton in chap. XX.
6. This suggestion is made, in passing, by a number of critics, notably
   Michael Black, who makes some sensitive comments in chap. XI, "*WH*,
   romantic self-commitment", of *The Literature of Fidelity*, 1975. The
   theme is treated as central in my article, "The Challenge to Maturity in
   WH", *Melbourne Critical Review*, no. 5, 1962, and in Irving H. Buchen's
   "Emily Brontë and the Metaphysics of Childhood", *Nineteenth Century
   Fiction*, vol. 22, no. 1, June 1967; pp. 63–70.
7. Quoted from her diary paper of 1834 by Winifred Gérin, *Emily Brontë*,
   1971, p. 39. It seems that, from a very early date, Emily Brontë, in

contrast to Charlotte, could assimilate the prosaic to her imagined worlds; cf. Ratchford, *op. cit.*, pp. 13–15.

8. There is no direct evidence that Emily Brontë had read Blake; cf. Gérin, *op. cit.*, p. 103.

9. When Nelly's narrative opens, with the arrival of the waif Heathcliff, Catherine is "hardly six years old", whilst Hindley is fourteen (IV, 38 and 39). It is much less easy to discover their dates of birth; however . . . Since Hareton is born in 1778 (VII–VIII, 59) and is nearly five years old when Catherine and Edgar marry (IX, 79) that marriage must occur in 1783. The following year, 1784, at winter's close, (see Edgar's remark, " 'Last spring at this time, I was longing to have you under this roof' " (XIII, 114)) Catherine is fatally ill and already pregnant (XIII, 115). Since the child is born and her mother dies at a time of "primroses and crocuses" (XVII, 140), both events must occur in Spring 1784. Hindley dies "scarcely six months" after his sister, aged "barely twenty-seven" (XVII, 153). Since this must be the Autumn of 1784, his date of birth must be 1757, and Catherine's eight years later in 1765. These dates agree with most (though not all) other indications of chronology, and Nelly's narrative of 1801 must open in 1771. Cf. David Daiches' introduction to the Penguin edition (1965) pp. 16–17.

10. As the contortions of note 9 working from the one firm date of 1778, make evident. Significantly the date of the narrative, 1801, with which the novel opens, would only yield that chronology at the novel's end, again by way of Hareton's age.

11. In accordance with the chronology worked out in note 9, Catherine is indeed thirteen when Hareton is born, so that two years elapse between VIII, 60 and 61. Given the history of the novel's publication, Nelly's mention of "twenty-two" on IX, 70 may simply be a mistake. Alternatively, it may apply to Nelly herself, and not to Catherine. It is significant, nonetheless, that few readers notice its ambiguities.

12. Nelly conjectures in VIII, 62 that Heathcliff is sixteen, a year older than Catherine, who is fifteen on VIII, 61; yet Lockwood in 1801 thinks him "about forty"—some four years older.

13. Hatfield, 45.

14. *Ibid.*, no. 92. Charlotte remarks: "Ellis, I imagine, would soon turn aside from that spectacle [of the great world] in disgust." "He" sees no point in studying mankind, "at least not the artificial man of cities". Quoted by Gérin from a letter, *op. cit.*, p. 229.

15. Since Nelly is recalling a period "twenty years before", and since Hindley dies the following year aged twenty-seven, they must both have been then only six; whereas Hindley is fourteen when her story begins, and Catherine eight years younger.

16. Cf. *Agnes Grey*, chap. III:
    "Mary Ann is a naughty girl, ma'am."
    "But what are these shocking screams?"
    "She is screaming in a passion."
    "I never heard such a dreadful noise! You might be killing her."

17. Cf. Gérin, *op. cit.*, p. 62.

18. Hatfield, 188.

19. *Ibid.*, no. 3.

20. *Ibid.*, nos. 99 and 112.

21. *Ibid.*, no. 114.

22. For example, Catherine's stoic endurance of Skulker, and the stone thrust by Heathcliff between the dog's jaws (VI, 48) recalls her own treatment of Tartar and Keeper, and her self-cauterization with red-hot iron when bitten by a mad dog. Cf. Gérin, *op. cit.*, pp. 109–10, 146–7, 155.

23. Charlotte Brontë's preface to the 1850 edition, reprinted in the Norton Critical Edition of *WH*, p. 11.

24. Cf. Q. D. Leavis, "A Fresh Approach to *WH*", pp. 84–152 of *Lectures in America,* 1969. Also Gérin, *op. cit.*, pp. 217–21.

25. See Gérin, *op. cit.*, p. 23.

26. Hatfield, 120 and 99.

27. *Ibid.*, no. 143.

28. *Op. cit.*, p. 126.

29. Isabella's infatuation with Heathcliff, or Hindley's with his wife, come closest to the passionate longings of Charlotte Brontë's heroines; but the fate of those affairs in Emily Brontë's hands, suggest the contempt with which she regards such "normal" tendencies.

30. Hatfield, 143. Significantly, this mate, "my all-sufficing light" is female, and her memory (and betrayal) is used by the adult A.G.A. as a weapon with which to reject a male suitor.

31. Hatfield, 154.

4

Romanticism and Romantic Love in *Wuthering Heights*

by T. E. APTER

A Romantic conception of romantic love can easily wilt and stew in a sickening sweet decay. When it supposes itself to be poignantly in bloom it may be stifled by an escapist's self-massaging imagination. This is the fate of Goethe's Werther who luxuriates in his pain, crying his heart out among gnarled oaks until he shoots himself in the hope that he will eventually be united with his love in the world to come. This is also the fate of Goethe's Ottilie and Eduard in *Elective Affinities* who expire through unfulfillable love (Ottilie, like Heathcliff, starves herself to death) and join one another in the grave. Goethe saw both these loves as irrational passions which could not be satisfied within the moral world and the idea of unity in death was an attempt to reconcile the passion with morality. These attempts to portray romantic passion in the language of Romanticism fail to make either the tragedy or the love convincing. Inadvertently the passion is portrayed as a weak thing, nourished for the sake of anguished ornamentation. Pain is valued because it supposedly measures intense emotion, but because the emphasis is on the self-reflecting pain, the love has no real intensity. The inclination for torment and the idea that there is depth in pain mistake themselves for the substance of tragic love. *Wuthering Heights* is a study of romantic love undertaken by a Romantic imagination, but it contains a serious study of the destructive elements within the magnetism of anguish and passion alongside a potent expression of their value and projects a far more original and useful resolution of irrational passion and morality than death while nonetheless expressing sympathy with that old Romantic solution.

The elements in the Catherine/Heathcliff theme which place it clearly within a Romantic tradition include an involvement with nature so intense, so mystical that it contains a death wish, or, more specifically, a desire to return to the mindless unity of nature, to mend the separation from nature effected by society and sophistication; also included are a love which longs for a soul unity with the beloved, a love which grows viciously single-minded when thwarted, and circumstances which prohibit the earthly satisfaction of love. But it is part of Emily Brontë's complete lack of sentimentality that she shows the prohibitive circumstances to stem from the characters' own destructive and self-destructive impulses; for although every Romantic knows that passion involves suffering, he does not often admit that the characters who enjoy the intensity of passion also enjoy, and are willing to generate, the suffering from which the intensity issues, and that it is the impulse to destroy, or rather, the capacity to value something only in its absence, or through torturous trials, that gives rise to the Romantic tragedy of love. Usually the relishing of pain takes place in the artist's imagination, spinning tales of doom and destruction which innocent characters must then enact, but Emily Brontë carries this problem of the Romantic imagination into the tale itself, and thus the meaning of that typical suffering is given a new depth and a new criticism.

The emphasis in *Wuthering Heights* is on the reality of passion. The novel insists that passion is a force with its own laws, a cosmic, inhuman thing that cannot be denied or treated lightly, and if the people who have passion disregard it, they will be divided against themselves and destroyed by their defiance. But not everyone is subject to its laws, for not everyone is able to enter the sphere in which passion is a reality. The book opens with a mistaken conception of deep feeling and deep suffering. Lockwood supposes himself to be within the world of Romantic disappointment and isolation. At first he identifies Heathcliff as a fellow member of this clan. He is in fact correct to see Heathcliff as an intriguing Romantic figure, but this correctness is ironic because Lockwood's own conception of the Romantic cult is so mistaken. When Heathcliff shouts rudely at the lovely young

Cathy, Lockwood supposes his initial impression of Heathcliff to be wrong because he now sees Heathcliff as a thoroughly hard, unsentimental man; but Lockwood is mistaken in thinking that a Romantically isolated, anguished figure must have essentially a kind heart, that isolation and anguish are only surface wounds covering a good, normal nature. In short, Lockwood makes the mistake that many would-be Romantic artists make; he supposes suffering on passion's account to be a good excuse for poignant ornamentation.

Again, Lockwood is right to see Heathcliff as a misanthrope, but he is ridiculous in supposing that he shares Heathcliff's attitudes, for he does not know what it means to be misanthropic. For Lockwood misanthropy is merely an attractive posture. There is real anger directed towards Lockwood by the author not merely because he is shallow but because he is shallow and considers himself to be deep. In this anger a jealousy of depth is felt: only those who truly suffer emotional intensity have a right to claim its glamour. Though Lockwood has an impulse to destroy love— he once fancied himself in love but grew cold when he saw that his attraction was returned, and he toys with the idea of winning young Cathy's love, but decides against it in case her temper should turn out to be as bad as her mother's—his self defeat comes from a source far inferior to the source of Catherine's or Heathcliff's destructive impulses. In Lockwood's case fear of emotion rather than emotional greed or bitter vengefulness leads him to believe he is a highly emotional person; because he tries to avoid emotional contact he assumes that his problem stems from the overwhelming intensity of his feelings; but there is no doubt in the author's mind that however horrendous Heathcliff's soul is, it is more significant than Lockwood's soul. This hierarchy of values underlines a Romantic pride in the strength of emotion, be the strength good or ill.

The good and ill, however, are not irrelevant. Early critics of the novel complained that the work was without moral design, but it is difficult to believe they actually meant that. There are numerous references to the devil and heaven and hell: Heathcliff is nearly as dark as if he came from the devil; he is prepared to defy the devil in order to protect Catherine from the Linton's dog; Hindley calls him an "imp of Satan"; in her diary the young

Catherine writes that "Joseph asseverated 'owd Nick' would fetch us sure as we were living", and the sober Nelly also expresses her puzzlement as to what sort of creature Heathcliff is, implying that he might be some kind of demon. Although such references need not have a moral focus—they could be used simply for eerie effect, as in a ghost story—Emily Brontë uses them to emphasize the inhuman and demonic aspects of passion, and undoubtedly the early critics' real complaint lay not with a lack of moral design but with the particular moral design. The novel continually questions where in the human and extra-human world passion lies; and though its value is never undermined, passion is not seen to be a warm, tender thing, full of the goodness of life or neatly tied to compassionate, considerate feelings.

It is primarily the pontificating Joseph, self-righteously using religious vindictiveness as an excuse for his own sadism, and Hindley, who is afraid of his position vis-à-vis Heathcliff, who express belief in this goblin-like wickedness; but other characters, too, through fear and incomprehension, share this sense of a demon in Heathcliff. Isabella asks in her desperate letter to Nelly, written after her marriage, "What kind of man is he?" and in his last meeting with Catherine Nelly says "I did not feel as if I were in the company of a creature of my own species; it appeared that he would not understand, though I spoke to him; so I stood off, and held my tongue, in great perplexity" (XV, 134). Heathcliff, as the embodiment of relentlessly single-minded passion, does not even speak the same language as ordinary, sociable humans. People do not fear him simply because he is cruel, but because he is unbelievably cruel while following his own moral law—passion's law. As he is dying Nelly suggests he make his peace with God, but he replies that he has done nothing wrong, and Catherine, when she is dying, admits that he has done nothing wrong. The lovers are not concerned with humanity's law, they are concerned with passion's law, and this law is shown to be startlingly different from the laws in which Joseph and Hindley and Nelly and Lockwood believe. Ordinarily love is thought to redeem destructive impulses, but in Heathcliff's case it is his love for Catherine which motivates his cruelty. He would not have minded Hindley's degradation if Catherine had stood by him; but because that degradation led to Catherine's rejection, he must destroy Hindley. He would not have bothered with Edgar Linton and his family had Catherine not married Edgar. His revenge is of primary importance and must overcome his affection for Hareton; as Hindley's child Hareton must be the object of revenge. Indeed, Heathcliff's savagery is not without sentimentality, for it is thoroughly unredeemed, indulgently consistent, and this exaggeration puts it out of focus. The more interesting factor is the love which is its cause.

What kind of love demands such destruction? Though the love between Catherine and Heathcliff is seen as a terrible and valuable force, there is no divinity or even nobility in it, no embodiment of human ideals. It is a rigidly personal, specific connection, forged by habit, without illusion, without respect, but a connection so strong that it defies the notion of separation. The dying Catherine recalls how painful it was when, at the age of twelve, Hindley prevented her and Heathcliff from sharing the same bed. Their clothes, as children, are often mingled: Catherine fastens her and Heathcliff's pinafores together to form a curtain round them, and they want a woman's cloak—one cloak—to shelter them on a scamper across the moor. Unlike Goethe's novels of love and death there is no sense here that this love would not live up to expectation. In *Wuthering Heights* the union desired in death is not an easy assertion of a nice but not quite believable connection; the union in death is seen as a point towards which inexorable forces are moving. Catherine's speech about her love for Heathcliff resembling "the eternal rocks beneath—a source of little visible delight, but necessary" (IX, 74) has a ring of sentimentality, but the support it gets from the rest of the novel absorbs the false tone. Her language is self-indulgent, but she is fighting to understand the depth of her attachment to Heathcliff at the very moment she has tried, by promising to marry Edgar, to deny that attachment; she is not simply enjoying a Romantic pose.

Their attachment defines their world and provides their own morality. Together they can settle down comfortably to await the advent of "owd Nick" threatened by Joseph because the hell of others has no meaning to them as long as they are together. Furthermore, the heaven of others is rejected by Catherine; she dreams that she finds herself in heaven and weeps because she is separated from the Heights, and the angels, angry with her blasphemous dissatisfaction, throw her from heaven, and she awakes on the Heights, sobbing for joy. When Nelly advises Heathcliff to prepare for death he answers that he has nearly attained his heaven—and his heaven is death, and union with Catherine. No laws other than those which pertain to their attachment are binding upon them. When Isabella declares her love for Heathcliff, Catherine tells her that he is "a fierce, pitiless, wolfish man". She never says to him "let this or that enemy alone, because it would be ungenerous or cruel to harm them, I say—'Let them alone because I should hate them to be wronged'," (X, 90). And Heathcliff spurns the idea of Edgar looking after the altered, ailing Catherine on grounds of Christian charity and duty. To him such bonds are paltry things in contrast to the love which would bind him to her.

Their love, however, does go wrong; but even in the thwarting of their attachment only the laws of passion are relevant; they are not separated by an outside force—no outside force would be strong enough to eclipse their emotions. The crux of the tensions which both bind them together and tear them apart can be seen in the episode in which Catherine, having returned to the Heights after her first visit to the Lintons, is anxious to return her new friends' hospitality and quarrels with Heathcliff because he is too dirty to receive her guests. He sulks for a while, but then asks Nelly to make him look decent. She replies:

> 'High time, Heathcliff,' I said, 'you *have* grieved Catherine; she's sorry she ever came home, I dare say! It looks as if you envied her, because she is more thought of than you.'
>
> The notion of *envying* Catherine was incomprehensible to him, but the notion of grieving her he understood clearly enough.
>
> 'Did she say she was grieved?' he inquired, looking very serious.
>
> 'She cried when I told her you were off again this morning.'
>
> 'Well, I cried last night,' he returned, 'and I had more reason to cry than she' (VII, 53).

The incomprehensibility of envy comes from a complete identification of interests, and is combined with a fierce protectiveness of the other's interests. When Heathcliff watches Catherine through the window of Thrushcross Grange as the Lintons, having thrown him out, comb Catherine's hair and wash her wounded foot, his purpose is to determine whether she wants to be rescued. If she does, then he will smash the window to save her; but when he sees that she is content, he leaves. The reader is clearly aware of his loneliness, but Heathcliff does not sulk over his exclusion. He waited by the window, not to savour his unhappiness, but simply to determine whether Catherine needed him.

This lack of envy is tied to his lack of common jealousy. When Edgar becomes Catherine's husband Heathcliff refrains from killing him because he is afraid that Catherine would suffer from this loss, and he claims that he would never banish Edgar from her society as long as she desired his. But the staunch protectiveness and identification of interests implied in his inability to understand the notion of envying Catherine, is cancelled by the full meaning of "but the notion of grieving her he understood clearly enough". Nelly is remarkably insensitive to Heathcliff's attitude when she says to him, "if you be ashamed of your touchiness, you must ask pardon, mind, when she comes in", for his concern about her grief is not a straightforward concern lest she be grieved. The notion of grieving her is important to him because through the extent of her grief he can measure her attachment to him and by grieving her he can remind her of that attachment when she tries to deny it. "Well, I cried last night, and I had more reason to cry than she",—this is not a simple childish competition; it is a means of punishment and reassurance, pride's refuge when their union seems threatened. How can he sympathize with her pain when her pain stems from her attempt to deny him? And, in turn, Catherine is angry with him because his grief at her insults hurts her, and it is wrong for him to hurt her. Sometimes the spiral is controlled. Sometimes others wound Heathcliff more than Catherine has done, and so it is not out of place for her to comfort him; she does not have to admit herself in the wrong to do so. But the tension of their grieving one another is explosive when it survives the comparative safety of childhood behaviour. Here is Catherine at her last earthly meeting with Heathcliff:

'. . . and should a word of mine distress you hereafter, think I feel the same distress underground, and for my own sake, forgive me! . . . Nay, if you nurse anger, that will be worse to remember than my harsh words!
. . . Oh, you see, Nelly! he would not relent a moment, to keep me out of the grave! *That* is how I am loved! '(XV, 133–4).

Heathcliff's anger will be worse to remember than her harsh words, but it was caused by her harsh words and she would have been furious if Heathcliff did not get angry with her (as she is furious with her husband when he does not get angry with her). She taunts Heathcliff with the image of himself visiting her grave with wife and children by his side, whom he will love more than he now loves her, and he groans at this picture, he feels how strongly it denies his love for her; yet still she is not satisfied with his love; nor is there any way he could satisfy her emotional greed.

Their naturally forged union has been broken by Catherine's marriage and now they must struggle for possession of one another. This struggle is a desperate attack; they cannot be gentle with one another; they must be ruthless in their attempt to maintain their hold upon one another:

> 'I wish I could hold you,' she continued, bitterly, 'till we were both dead! I shouldn't care what you suffered. I care nothing for your sufferings. Why shouldn't you suffer? I do! Will you forget me—will you be happy when I am in the earth? . . .'
> 'Don't torture me till I'm as mad as yourself,' cried he, wrenching his head free, and grinding his teeth.
> . . . Her present countenance had a wild vindictiveness in its white cheek, and a bloodless lip, and scintillating eye; and she retained in her closed fingers, a portion of the locks she had been grasping. As to her companion, while raising himself with one hand, he had taken her arm with the other; and so inadequate was his stock of gentleness to the requirements of her condition, that on his letting go, I saw four distinct impressions left blue in the colourless skin (XV, 133).

Catherine's assertion that she cares nothing for Heathcliff's sufferings does not mean that she is actually indifferent to them. She wants him to suffer; only through his suffering will she be assured of his love for her after she is dead. The "wild vindictiveness" she expresses here is not the hatred and revulsion seen in the love and death struggle between Gudrun and Gerald in *Women in Love*; it is important that Heathcliff's and Catherine's love is not ambivalent as the possessive loves Lawrence portrays; this love becomes a lurid struggle for possession because its intensity and singleness, i.e., its lack of ambivalence, has been ignored by Catherine. But their anger towards one another is never hatred, and the physical pain they inflict upon one another at this meeting is a straightforward expression of love.

This vicious struggle for possession undermines Catherine's assertion that she *is* Heathcliff; but, because she believes this herself, she thinks it safe for her to marry Edgar Linton: Heathcliff is within her soul, therefore nothing can dislodge him. Nonetheless, it is clear from the way they wound one another that each is in continual need of reassurance—something that occurs only between two separate people. Catherine thinks only of her reassurance of her own feelings. She does not consider Heathcliff's need for proof of those feelings. She does not believe she needs to behave in accordance with her feelings, and so, blind to the meaning of her action, she marries Edgar. Heathcliff demands of her:

> '*Why* did you betray your own heart, Cathy? I have not one word of comfort. You deserve this. You have killed yourself . . . You loved me—then what *right* had you to leave me? . . . Because misery, and degradation, and death, and nothing that God or Satan could inflict would have parted us, *you*, of your own will, did it. I have not broken your heart—*you* have broken it—and in breaking it, you have broken mine.' (XV, 134–5).

"What *right* had you to leave me?" is the cry of outraged passion. Catherine thought she could slip beneath passion's net and take the offer of Edgar's pleasant love, but she is destroyed by her defiance. Her own emotional greed is drawn like a noose round Heathcliff's neck, but she thought he would be satisfied by her own inward assurance that they were one person. Her passion was so real that marriage to her had no reality.

The success of the Catherine/Heathcliff theme depends upon the felt potency of their love, and Mrs Leavis in her classic essay on *Wuthering Heights* complains that Emily Brontë does not show their shared interests, and wonders what they conversed about during their adult companionship;[1] but it is difficult to believe that such knowledge is actually necessary to understanding their attachment. Their shared interests are one another and one another's company. They fought and played and walked much as they had done as children. But it is true that the development and continuation of their attachment is taken for granted. The strength of their attachment is expressed not in dramatic episodes but in extremely effective Romantic rhetoric. The author achieves this rare success partly through oblique presentation of the lovers' outbursts; thus, a direct request for sympathy never embarrasses the reader. Heathcliff's first Tristanesque cry is presented through Lockwood's eyes, and at first the emphasis seems to be on the horror of Heathcliff's fascination with the spectre Lockwood has seen in a dream and which has so terrified him that the apparently ordinary man behaves towards the spectral waif with vicious cruelty. The keen sympathy then forced from the reader comes as a surprise:

> 'Come in! come in!' he sobbed. 'Cathy, do come. Oh, do—*once* more! Oh, my heart's darling, hear me *this* time—Catherine, at last!' (III, 33).

This cry is heard only once in the novel, yet it carries the force of a relentless repetition. "Hear me *this* time," shows how many times Heathcliff has called to her. Even before the story is known (for at this point Lockwood is ignorant of his landlord's history) the hopeless longing and deadly despair are clear. And when, in Werther fashion, Heathcliff beats his head upon the knotted oak in rage and grief at Catherine's death, sentimentality is just about overcome by Nelly's response: "It hardly moved my compassion—it appalled me". The Romantic exaggeration is effective because its point is not to pull heart strings but to lay bare the inexorable strength of grief and passion.

Catherine's outbursts, on the other hand, do not belong to the Romantic tradition of *Angst*. Always her emotional fits are fits of temper and are undercut by Nelly's impatience. Of Catherine as a child Nelly says, "She beat Hareton, or any child at a good fit of passionate crying". (Imagine an old nurse of Werther's saying "He always did go on a bit much about things". In Goethe's novel passionate fits are valued for their own sake; they are signs of emotional intensity and therefore are good. It is part of the effective Romanticism in *Wuthering Heights* that intensity is seen as a harsh necessity for some natures, not as a decorative thing, and when intensity is indulgently cultivated, it is shown to be so.) And as an adult, angry with Edgar's insistence that she see no more of Heathcliff, Catherine is no more, Nelly says, than a wailing, spoiled child who works herself up to the point of illness.

Indeed, Catherine's despair stems from having broken with her childhood; her childish wailing expresses a longing to return to the time when she was able to be at one with her passion. Her illness and frustration stem from the inability to absorb the deepest part of herself within her adult life:

> 'But, supposing at twelve years old, I had been wrenched from the Heights, and every early association, and my all in all, as Heathcliff was at that time, and been converted at a stroke into Mrs Linton, the lady of Thrushcross Grange, and the wife of a stranger; an exile and outcast, thenceforth, from what had been my world—' (XII, 107).

This fantasy evokes impatience rather than compassion, for Catherine herself is responsible for this harsh transformation; *she* has wrenched herself from the Heights and from Heathcliff. Nonetheless her longing and frustration have an hypnotic pathos:

> 'Oh, I'm burning! I wish I were out of doors—I wish I were a girl again, half savage, and hardy, and free; and laughing at injuries, not maddening under them!' (XII, 107).

The hot, closed room at Thrushcross Grange becomes a prison. Repeatedly she begs Nelly to open a window. Her sense of being stifled by illness and emotional conflict, her vision of the Heights as she leans out of the window, set her within a world impossibly out of contact with the world in which she must live. Her longing rips up reality and fires her dreams with a deathly life; but Catherine's escapism is not the author's, and though the longing is startlingly vivid, there is no suggestion that the author shares it.

Though Emily Brontë does not straightforwardly endorse a scheme of value based upon emotional intensity alone, Catherine and Heathcliff do. When Edgar, as Catherine's husband, wants to know whether she will continue her friendship with Heathcliff even after he has eloped with Isabella and threatened violence to himself, she dismisses his morality of family loyalty and asserts her own:

> 'Oh, for mercy's sake,' interrupted the mistress, stamping her foot, 'for mercy's sake, let us hear no more of it now! Your cold blood cannot be worked into a fever; your veins are full of icewater, but mine are boiling, and the sight of such chillness makes them dance' (XI, 101).

Edgar's arguments have no point because they are not expressed with passion. Her argument against him is simply that she is passionate. Heathcliff, too, continually asserts his rights on the grounds that his feelings are the stronger. He insists, when Edgar banishes him from Catherine's company, that his own emotions are finer:

> 'and there you see the distinction between our feelings. Had he been in my place, and I in his, though I hated him with a hatred that turned my life to gall, I never would have raised a hand against him. You may look incredulous, if you please! I never would have banished him from her society, as long as she desired his' (XIV, 125).

He despises Edgar for the character of his concern for Catherine and believes that the lower grade of her husband's feelings gives him the right to claim her:

> 'But do you imagine that I shall leave Catherine to his *duty* and *humanity*? and can you compare my feelings respecting Catherine, to his?' (XIV, 125).

Isabella, too, tries to play their Romantic game. When Catherine is incredulous at her declaration of love for Heathcliff, she replies, "I love him more than you ever loved Edgar". But Isabella does not really understand this Romantic universe. Like Lockwood, she merely fancies herself to be among the passionate ones. Like Lockwood, she believes that suffering for the sake of one's emotions is an attractive, glamorous thing. Her misunderstanding of passion's and cruelty's reality, destroys her.

In ordinary terms Catherine and Heathcliff are unfair in their assessment of Edgar's feelings, for he certainly does love Catherine; but at no time do his feelings rise to the Romantic standard. After Catherine's death Nelly says of him:

> 'But he was too good to be thoroughly unhappy long. *He* didn't pray for Catherine's soul to haunt him. Time brought resignation, and a melancholy sweeter than common joy. He recalled her memory with ardent, tender love, and hopeful aspiring to the better world, where, he doubted not, she was gone' (XVII, 151).

How Catherine would have despised his *resignation* and *hopeful aspiring* and *melancholy sweeter than common joy*. She has, after all, said, "If I were only sure it would kill him, . . . I'd kill myself directly!'" (XII, 104). From her point of view Edgar's return to life would be a betrayal. She would feel that Edgar had no right to live because she had suffered and died. Even Heathcliff, who gives her everything, has difficulty in giving her enough. While she is dying she taunts Heathcliff with his strength and asks how many years he intends to live after she is dead. He demands of her:

> 'Is it not sufficient for your infernal selfishness, that while you are at peace I shall writhe in the torments of hell?'
> 'I shall not be at peace,' moaned Catherine. . . . (XV, 133).

Catherine believes that others should die because she has to die, and she accuses both Edgar and Heathcliff of killing her; but once she has passed childhood, and her inability to integrate her emotions into her behaviour shows its poisoning effects, she actually longs for her own death. The desire to return to childhood, the wish for regression and stagnation, is a wish for death, and in her adult life this death wish becomes integrally connected with her love for Heathcliff:

> 'And,' added she, musingly, 'the thing that irks me most is this shattered prison, after all. I'm tired, tired of being enclosed here. I'm wearying to escape into that glorious world, and to be always there; not seeing it dimly through tears, and yearning for it through the walls of an aching heart; but really with it, and in it' (XV, 134).

She is proud of this wish to escape into death, into the glorious world of her imagination. She believes herself to be better than other people because she desires this, and because the desire will soon be fulfilled:

> 'Nelly, you think you are better and more fortunate than I, in full health and strength. You are sorry for me—very soon that will be altered. I shall be sorry for *you*. I shall be incomparably beyond and above you all' (XV, 134).

Her death is the means by which she can satisfy her love for Heathcliff—and it is not even the adult Heathcliff she loves, for the real Heathcliff can be so tormented by her emotional greed and accusations that he turns lividly away from her. When the real Heathcliff hurts her because she sees how much she has hurt him, she says, "Never mind, that is not my Heathcliff. I shall have mine yet". Her love is not a longing for anything in this world; it is a longing for an impossible freedom from emotional conflict and her own excessive demands. Heathcliff shares her desire for death, but he does not want to die simply to regain a lost glorious world; he wants to die because Catherine is dying; he wants to join her in death. "Do I want to live?" he demands of her. "What kind of living will it be when you—oh, God! would *you* like to live with your soul in the grave?" (XV, 135). Catherine does not give a straightforward answer. "Let me alone, let me alone", she sobs; for the perplexing truth is that she does want to live with her soul in the grave. With her soul in the grave she will not be encumbered by her own nature; she will be free to identify with passion alone. In death she feels that the best and deepest part of herself will come alive.

Though Catherine can in part be blamed for the thwarted love between herself and Heathcliff, there is here, as in all cases of Romantic longing, a sense of the impossibility of fulfilment *no matter what*. The intensity of the desire involves an excitement which is far from the pleasure and contentment implied in *happiness*. When Heathcliff returns after his long mysterious absence,

> Catherine flew upstairs, breathless and wild, too excited to show gladness; indeed, by her face, you would rather have surmised an awful calamity (X, 83).

The excited joy has to battle to find a place in reality; it seems impossible to sustain it in the ordinary world. Catherine "kept her gaze fixed on him as if she feared he would vanish were she to remove it" (X, 84). The inability to trust the reality stems from a nervous intensity which is never resolved. The satisfaction of her longing would be explosive, annihilating. Only death is deep and dark enough to absorb the shock of fulfilment and bring the continuing peace which must follow that fulfilment.

Towards the end of his life Heathcliff becomes a Tristanesque figure, longing for the union with Catherine which will be his death. When he feels close to the realization of his desire he calls himself happy, but it is clear that he is tormented by a mingling of excitement and pain. The young Cathy describes to Hareton how he appeared:

'Why almost bright and cheerful—No, almost nothing—*very much* excited, and wild and glad!' (XXIV, 257).

While Heathcliff stands at the open window, watching for Catherine, he is pale, he trembles, there is a "strange joyful glitter in his eyes", and he breathes "as fast as a cat". The description is of one possessed, demonic, but not of someone who is *happy*. The anticipation is unbearable, and he must struggle towards death. He says to Nelly:

'. . . you might as well bid a man struggling in the water, rest within arms-length of the shore! I must reach it first, and then I'll rest . . . I'm too happy, and yet I'm not happy enough. My soul's bliss kills my body, but does not satisfy itself' (XXXIV, 262).

The metaphor is ironic, for Heathcliff is swimming towards death, not to a life-sustaining shore; but the irony underlines an essential element of Romanticism—the notion of death as a freer, finer form of life, the notion that death alone can sustain the exultation whose intensity and continuation are thwarted and deflected in life. Death provides for that impossible Romantic combination: ecstasy and peace. Heathcliff's longing has grown to such a pitch that only in death can he rest. His longing makes life an impossible torment. The world, without Catherine, has become a hell: her ghost fills all material objects with her image, other people mock him with their resemblance to her, the entire world is "a dreadful collection of memoranda that she did exist, and that I have lost her!" (XXXIII, 255). Soon his "one universal idea" of joining himself with her in death triumphs; the anticipation carries a bliss of soul which kills his body; only in death is there satisfaction for this devouring Romantic passion.

The destructive, unsatisfiable, death-ridden elements of Romantic love are harshly underlined. There is no sweet nostalgic sense that the lovers might have been happy if only the world had been a bit kinder to them. This love, generated within a Romantic vision, is suffering love. But the harsh facts of such love are not related with a simple moralising tongue, and the main power of the novel does lie in the magnetism of Catherine's and Heathcliff's bond. However, Emily Brontë effectively and convincingly portrays an alternative to that destructive, Romantic love, keeping much of the vitality of the first love, but transforming it into something which can survive in this life.

Young Cathy Linton's nature is similar to that of her mother: she is lively, agile (she delights in swinging from tree branches twenty feet from the ground), pert, affectionate but not always gentle (she awakens Nelly by pulling her hair), proud of her strong emotions and healthy spirits; but the important difference between Cathy and her mother is Cathy's ability to care about hurting people in the sense of not wanting to hurt them, and her ability to suffer at the hands of others without feeling the need for revenge. When her father is ill she promises Nelly that she will not vex him:

> 'I love him better than myself, Ellen; and I know it by this: I pray every night that I may live after him, because I would rather be miserable than that he should be—that proves I love him better than myself' (XXII, 187).

This shows a complete reversal of her mother's feelings, for Catherine felt that others should suffer at the very least as much as herself. When young Cathy does cause a friend pain she is able to sustain a true regret. In her anger with Linton Heathcliff for insisting that her mother hated her father, she pushes his chair, and he is seized by a suffocating cough. Nelly says that Cathy then "wept with all her might, aghast at the mischief she had done" (XXIII, 192). Nor does she subsequently, as Catherine would have done, grow angry with Linton for upsetting her with the pain she has caused him. Her mother's proud spirit is apparent, but without the vindictiveness:

> 'I'm sorry I hurt you Linton!' she said at length, racked beyond endurance. 'But I couldn't have been hurt by that little push; and I had no idea that you could, either—you're not much, are you, Linton? Don't let me go home thinking I've done you harm! answer, speak to me' (XXIII, 193).

Even when faced with Linton's reply, which is a pathetic version of Catherine's morality ("you've hurt me so, that I shall lie awake all night, choking with this cough! . . . but you'll be comfortably asleep, while I'm in agony") she presses forward kindly and regretfully, though she fully understands his game:

'He's good and patient, now. He's beginning to think I shall have far greater misery than he will to-night, if I believe he is the worse for my visit' (XXIII, 194).

Only when she is treated with sustained cruelty, when she is separated from those who love her and is tormented by the thought that they are worrying about her, does she become cold, aloof, unhelpful. However, even during her captivity at the Heights, her hostility towards her companions does not completely separate her from them. Nelly says that she complained of loneliness and "preferred quarrelling with Joseph in the kitchen to sitting at peace in her solitude" (XXII, 245). Cathy can work out her hostility through quarrelling whereas her mother could only work herself up. Cathy is able to notice what is happening to other people as she quarrels with them whereas Catherine's mind was devoured by rage and she could only see that people were hurting her. When Hareton is confined to the house on account of an arm injury Catherine is able to understand his pain at their mutual insults and they become friends. Her belief that people should be nice to her because it will make her happy, that they should forgive her unkindnesses because she demands it of them, has more warmth and playfulness, less "infernal selfishness" than similar demands made by her mother. Cathy is able to show gratitude rather than righteousness in the face of forgiveness; she is also able to be patient, and to forgive before forgiveness is granted her:

> 'Say you forgive me, Hareton, do! You can make me so happy, by speaking that little word.'
> He muttered something inaudible.
> 'And you'll be my friend?' added Catherine, interrogatively.
> 'Nay! You'll be ashamed of me every day of your life . . .'
> 'So, you won't be my friend?' she said, smiling as sweet as honey, and creeping close up (XXXII, 248–9).

The love between Cathy and Hareton, like that between Catherine and Heathcliff, is forged by habit, without illusion, without ideal. It is also nearly incestuous—they are actually cousins, and Nelly says that they were both really her children—but the close attachment will not confuse and destroy them as it did Catherine and Heathcliff. The strength of their feelings can be expressed in

H   221

a playfulness which is connected to childhood play but is not simply childish. Catherine and Heathcliff destroyed the possibility of continuing such natural and easy expression of their love, and so the strength of their emotion turned into a Romantic death-ridden passion. It was not simply intense feeling which issued in this darkness; it was intense feeling which demanded to be measured in suffering, and Emily Brontë's diagnosis thus denies the debilitating aspect of the conventional Romantic picture, i.e. that intense feeling cannot survive in this world. For it is only a certain way of measuring emotion, not emotion itself, which explodes into death; it is only a certain way of demanding proof of intense attachment, not the attachment itself, which is destructive. Emily Brontë's assertion of the full-blooded reality and possible survival of emotion gives strength both to the Romantic tragedy of Catherine and Heathcliff and to the happiness of Cathy and Hareton; neither the former couple's suffering nor the latter couple's fulfilment is undercut by a conventionally benign Romanticism. Having shown the harshness and potency of Romantic passion, Brontë concludes by portraying a love which knows its measure without reference to tension and pain.

NOTE

1. F. R. Leavis and Q. D. Leavis, *Lectures in America* (1969), p. 96.

5

A Personal Response to
Wuthering Heights

by COLIN WILSON

In 1900, George Smith, of the firm of Smith Elder, published in the *Cornhill Magazine* his own account of the discovery of *Jane Eyre*, and of the subsequent visit to London of the two sisters "Ellis and Currer Bell". It might have been written with one eye on Hollywood. "After breakfast on Sunday morning I took the MS. of *Jane Eyre* to my little study and began to read it. The story quickly took me captive. Before twelve o'clock my horse came to the door, but I could not put the book down. I scribbled two or three lines to my friend, saying I was very sorry that circumstances had arisen to prevent my meeting him, sent the note off by my groom, and went on reading the MS. Presently the servant came to tell me that luncheon was ready; I asked him to bring me a sandwich and a glass of wine, and still went on with *Jane Eyre*. Dinner came; for me the meal was a very hasty one, and before I went to bed that night I had finished reading the manuscript." Which, in the best Hollywood tradition, went on to become a best seller. Then came the Saturday morning when Mr Smith was told that two ladies wished to see him and declined to give their names. "Two rather quaintly dressed little ladies, pale-faced and anxious-looking walked into the room," and one of them presented him with his own recent letter to 'Currer Bell'." He asked sharply how she came by a private letter to one of his authors; to which, of course, she replied that *she* was "Currer Bell Esq". Astonishment, excitement, invitations to dinner and the theatre . . . to all of which the little ladies responded with embarrassment and alarm.

And our chief regret, of course, is that it was Anne, and not Emily who accompanied Charlotte to London. (She was presumably too ill to travel). That "mysterious genius", who has inspired such extravagant cults since her death, is as much a mystery now as she was a century ago. George Smith could scarcely have described her as a "little" lady; she was taller than her sisters. Branwell's paintings of her seem to suggest that she was the best-looking of the three—almost pretty in her mild, introspective way. Smith said of Anne's manner that it was "curiously expressive of a wish for protection and encouragement". It is doubtful whether he could have said the same of Emily; she emerges from Charlotte's descriptions as stubborn, determined and rather formidable. But unfortunately, that is about all we *do* know of Emily. As Margaret Lane remarks: "The experiences which formed her unique personality are out of our reach; we can never know what they were, or what it was that so early turned her imagination inwards and caused her to refuse the ordinary demands of life". A comment I shall presently dispute.

When I recently read *Wuthering Heights* for the third time, it was mainly with the intention of noting Emily's use of "the occult". And certainly, it could be argued that the supernatural element is vital to the book's total effect. What would it be, without those closing pages about the ghosts who walk the moor, and can be seen from the chamber window on rainy nights? The only comparable effect I can call to mind is the appearance of the ghosts of Rafi and Pirvaneh in the last pages of Flecker's *Hassan*. "This music is successful with a dying fall", Eliot remarks, "now that we talk of dying. . . ." Yet my final impression—and it is only an impression—is that Emily did not believe in ghosts. She made use of them, in her strange, detached way; but the intellect remained cool and sceptical. She would have regarded belief in ghosts as some kind of excuse for self-pity. And one of the most salient features of her character is her rejection of self-pity. It was her almost morbid loathing of self-pity that made her decline to see a doctor when she was dying.

Yes, one speculates what would have happened if it had been *Wuthering Heights* that absorbed George Smith from breakfast to bedtime, and that had become the success of the London season. . . . But then, it wouldn't have been. As Mrs Gaskell remarks, *Wuthering Heights* "revolted many readers by the power with which wicked and exceptional characters are depicted", and one old schoolfriend who read *Jane Eyre, Agnes Grey* and *Wuthering Heights* one after the other concluded that the latter had been written to deliberately shock a certain class of reader. The critics found it a nasty, repellant book, and many of them thought it to be a piece of juvenilia by the author of *Jane Eyre*. And we, of course, condemn the critics as idiots who couldn't recognize a work of genius when it stared them in the face. Or make patronizing remarks about change of taste, implying that no modern reader could be so obtuse.

And yet I have to admit that, as I re-read the book a few weeks ago, I found myself sympathizing with those critics. And it struck me as a matter of some interest to realize how much my attitude had changed over the years since I first read it. That was some time during the war, and I must have been about twelve. My mother was reading it, in that poky little Reader's Library edition. with its tiny print on cheap paper—I think she had seen the film with Olivier—and she told me the plot as she went along. I remember being rather shaken by the cruelty of the scene in which Lockwood sees the ghost of Cathy, and rubs her wrist against the broken glass to force her to let go of his hand. My mother found the whole thing totally absorbing, and I think I can understand why. She often said that she liked books about "real life"; in practice, this meant books with a fair quantity of unhappiness; *Sons and Lovers* and Cronin's *Hatter's Castle* came high on her list. Life in a provincial town can be dull for a working class housewife with three children, particularly when food and clothes and coal are rationed. But at least we weren't as poor as the Morells; and if my father was bad tempered, he was never as tyrannical as Cronin's Mr Brodie. Reading these books made her feel life wasn't so bad after all. As to *Wuthering Heights*, I doubt whether the romantic interest held her as much as the general bleakness and emotional harshness.

I read through most of the book, although I found it hard going. It struck me as cruel and frightening and wholly real. A few years later, when I was about seventeen, I bought the World Classic edition and read it again. At this time I was reading *Paradise Lost*, and I could appreciate Heathcliff as a sort of Lucifer figure. The complicated family relationships no longer bewildered me. And the last pages, with the quiet graves blowing in the wind, produced "an effect like music", so that it suddenly seemed to me one of the most tremendous novels ever written. And this was how I remembered it for some three decades.

In between 1948 and 1975, I have written a dozen novels myself, which at least places me in a good position to appreciate literary skill. When I came back to *Wuthering Heights*, the first thing that struck me was the technical achievement. It seems astonishing that a young girl brought up on the novels of Scott and the epic poems of Southey should write with this kind of economy and terseness:

> We came to the chapel. I have passed it really in my walks, twice or thrice; it lies in a hollow, between two hills—an elevated hollow, near a swamp, whose peaty moisture is said to answer all the purposes of embalming on the few corpses deposited there (III, 28).

Here even the punctuation, the semi-colon and the dash, give the impression that she knows exactly where she is going and what she means to say. And although she is never "clever", there is an epigrammatic quality worthy of Jane Austen: of the detestable Joseph: "He was, and is yet, most likely, the wearisomest, self-righteous pharisee that ever ransacked a Bible to rake the promises to himself, and fling the curses on his neighbours" (V, 42).

But from the technical point of view, perhaps the most impressive thing about it is the way she has somehow brought a credibility to a narrative method that sounds—in theory—hopelessly implausible. We are asked to believe that Nelly Dean can remember long conversations word for word—including the expressions on everybody's faces—and repeat speeches that sometimes last for a page and a half. We are also asked to believe that the narrator Lockwood recalls every word of Nelly's story. A more accomplished novelist would have used the device of letters and manuscripts found in drawers—and spoiled the whole effect. For in fact, it is not at all difficult to believe that a gossipy and lonely old servant *would* enjoy dwelling on the past and embellish her memories with all kind of invented detail. And once Lockwood has also become established as a kind of irritating busybody, like one of those tirelessly curious narrators in Henry James, you find it easy enough to believe that he would add his own embellishments when re-creating Nelly's monologue. The nett result is that the authoress manages to side-step the blame for the implausibilities—which is essential if the reader is to place himself entirely in her hands. All this seems to have been accomplished by a combination of luck and literary instinct—although, since *Wuthering Heights* was her only novel, it seems probable that instinct played the smaller part. I think that most writers are inclined to believe that some god of literature occasionally makes a direct intervention, using the author as a mere amanuensis; *Wuthering Heights* seems to be a plausible example.

Having said which, I must state that I did not enjoy my third reading of *Wuthering Heights*. Like its original critics, I found it repellant, morbid and rather sadistic. The first fit of revulsion came in the scene where Heathcliff throws the tureen of hot apple sauce in Edgar's face. A page later, Heathcliff tells Nelly he is trying to decide how to pay back Hindley for the beating: "I don't care how long I wait. I hope he will not die before I do!" And when Nelly points out that punishment is God's business, he answers: "No, God won't have the satisfaction that I shall . . . while I'm thinking of that, I don't feel pain" (VII, 57). And suddenly you are back in an older and crueller world, where tyrants have men skinned alive, or force them to eat the hearts of their own children. It would be melodramatic to call it a breath of hell. It is a breath of sheer stupidity and childishness. Joyce Cary's Gulley Jimson remarked that no one ever really gets his own back, because when you get it, it's not yours any more; it's moved on. It seems odd that Emily Brontë, with all her intelligence and sensitivity, never found this out. For there can be no doubt whatsoever that the basic emotion underlying her novel is a kind of vengefulness. "Life being what it is, one dreams of revenge", said Gauguin—a remark that Graham Greene has often quoted with approval. It is the kind of sentiment you might expect from a painter of genius whose work is ignored, or from a novelist obsessed by Original Sin. But it is unusual to find it pervading the work of a young girl who has spent most of her life as a member of an affectionate and closely-knit family. One feels like paraphrasing Gosse's remark about Thomas Hardy, and asking what Providence has done to Emily Brontë that she should shake her fist so furiously in its face?

It is, of course, always dangerous to assume that a writer is expressing his, or her, convictions through the mouths of the characters. But in the case of *Wuthering Heights*, I would have thought there was little room for doubt. Heathcliff may be "black browed" and insulting, but it is fairly clear that Emily Brontë admires him. He is her equivalent of Byron's Childe Harold or Manfred. Lockwood is a fop who treats seduction as a game; Heathcliff is a "real man", rough, strong, brutal—but honest, and totally unswerving in his affections, a "true heart", as the Victorians put it.

Yet when one looks at him objectively, declining to accept him at Emily's evaluation, he is pathetically stupid. Anyone can daydream of sweet revenge; if daydreams could kill, most traffic wardens would die fifty times a day. But what kind of a man would actually go to such dreary and nasty lengths to soothe his wounded ego? Victorian alienists sometimes used the phrase "morally insane", and there is no better instance in literature than Heathcliff. To deliberately ruin Hindley is perhaps comprehensible; Hindley is male, and a childhood rival. But Isabella Linton is neither. There is more than a touch of De Sade in the elopment scene, where Heathcliff hangs her dog.

Yet Emily Brontë obviously continues to find him rather magnificent. She makes no attempt to "cover up" his nastiness. And this in itself is curious. Byron announces that Childe Harold is weighted down by his sins, but you never actually *see* him doing anything that would shock you. On the contrary, he remains consistently pale and sensitive and noble. This is even true of Dostoevesky's Byronic villain Stavrogin in *The Devils*; in the suppressed chapter we see him sexually assaulting a ten year old girl (although apparently with her co-operation) and stealing money from a poverty-stricken clerk; but Dostoevsky leaves us in no doubt that these actions are a cry of desperation, a frantic groping after meaning. Heathcliff is driven by sheer childishness, and his actions have the predictable effect of ruining his life and everyone else's. He spends two hundred and fifty pages cutting off his nose to spite his face.

My capacity for gloating on self-inflicted torture is limited. After the dog-hanging scene, I gave it up, and turned to Daphne du Maurier's book about Branwell. That raised the interesting possibility that *Wuthering Heights* might have been a collaboration between Branwell and Emily. Which would certainly go far towards solving some of the mysteries. *Wuthering Heights* is a half-masculine, half-feminine book. In most novels written by males, you can sense the writer's attraction to the heroine; in novels written by women, the hero exudes more than his fair share of maleness. In *Wuthering Heights*, the author seems to be equally attracted to Cathy and Heathcliff. On the other hand, there is absolutely no evidence that Branwell had a hand in the book—even in its planning. And the few things we know about Emily suggest that she had a touch of masculinity in her character. When her father asked her what he ought to do with Branwell when he was naughty, she answered: "Reason with him, and when he won't listen to reason, whip him." Charlotte's friend Ellen Nussey described Emily, "half reclining on a slab of stone", and how she "played . . . with the tadpoles in the water, making them swim about, and then fell to moralising on the strong and the weak, the brave and the cowardly, as she chased them with her hand. . . ." Am I, perhaps, allowing my imagination to run away with me in supplying a Nietzschean discourse on survival of the fittest? Perhaps Nietzschean is the wrong word in this context, for it evokes images of the superman. But the young Nietzsche was very much a stoic; he once set a pile of matches alight on his hand to prove he could bear pain like Mucius Scaevola. *He* could well have written a poem beginning: "No coward soul is mine." (Neither do I find it difficult to imagine Heathcliff uttering the famous sentiment: "Are you going to woman? Don't forget your whip.") There *is* a Nietzschean touch in Emily.

And when I finally turned back to *Wuthering Heights*, armed with a bundle of theories and speculations gleaned from Daphne du Maurier, Margaret Lane and Mrs Gaskell, I found the moral revulsion had vanished, pushed aside by the purely psychological interest of the problem presented by Emily's creative drive. It is not, I think, a question of "the experiences that formed her unique personality"—in Margaret Lane's phrase—so much as the personality itself. There is one very obvious difference between

229

Wuthering Heights, Jane Eyre and *The Tenant of Wildfell Hall.* In the novels of Anne and Charlotte, there is the predictable element of wish-fulfilment that you might expect in novels by intelligent but inexperienced young ladies. You could go on to draw interesting parallels with the novels of Jane Austen or Daphne du Maurier. Modest and sensitive young girl meets dominant male; after two hundred pages of complications, they are united and live happily ever after. . . . But Emily is not one to daydream by the open window. She knows the kind of man she would find physically attractive, and he is not necessarily the romantic lover. And, for some reason, her fantasies are filled with resentment: "Life being what it is, one dreams of revenge."

In a book about the American psychologist Abraham Maslow, I mentioned his researches into the question of dominance in women. After several years of study, Maslow came to the conclusion that women—and men too—fell into three clear groups, which he labelled high dominance, medium dominance and low dominance. High dominance women were an extremely small percentage. Sexually speaking, they were inclined to promiscuity and experimentalism; many of them had tried Lesbian experiences. They liked dominant males—unsentimental men who would make love violently. Medium dominance women were "romantics", inclined to settle with one man, although they might experiment under propitious circumstances. They liked the kind of male who would bring them bunches of flowers and take them to restaurants with soft lights. Low dominance women were scared of men in general; they thought sex was rather nasty, strictly for the purpose of producing children; they liked the kind of man who would admire them from a distance for years without daring to make an advance. All women, in all the dominance groups, preferred the male to be slightly more dominant than themselves, but not too much so. Medium dominance women were scared stiff of the kind of male who appealed to high dominance women.

I apologize for dragging in the subject of experimental psychology, and promise that I do not intend to try to explain Emily in terms of her sexual inhibitions or repressed guilt feelings. Maslow's findings strike me as basically sound, and my own observation seems to confirm them. On the basis of their novels, it is fairly clear that Emily was high dominance, Charlotte medium-to-high, and Anne medium-to-low. And so, as you would expect, the hero of *Wuthering Heights* is a brutal roughneck; of *Jane Eyre*, a gloomy, temperamental man who actually turns out to be a faithful lover and ideal husband; of *The Tenant of Wildfell Hall* and *Agnes Grey*, a fairly conventional suitor with no obvious drawbacks. (Margaret Lane speculates that the hero of *Agnes Grey* was based on Patrick Brontë's kindly curate, William Weightman).

A common theme of the three major novels is the ill-treatment of the heroine; but here the first major difference emerges. Helen Huntingdon, the tenant of Wildfell Hall, is treated with indifference by her drunken husband; Jane Eyre is bullied by everybody; Catherine Earnshaw is bullied by Joseph and Hindley. But on the whole, Cathy emerges unscathed; she is definitely an "alpha" (the term Maslow often used for highly dominant individuals). It is Heathcliff who takes the real brunt of the cruelty in *Wuthering Heights*, and who repays it all with interest. Unlike her sisters, Emily had little self-pity in her nature, and what there was she firmly suppressed. Jane Eyre overcomes the injustice of fate with her gentleness; Emily's male alter-ego fights back murderously, and drinks his revenge to the last drop. This also means that Emily can shift the blame for the moral stupidity involved. She was too bright not to know that Heathcliff's whole outlook is self-destructive, and that a world full of Heathcliffs would be a nightmarish place. But since the authoress of a novel is expected to identify with the heroine, that is hardly her affair. . . .

"Her view of mankind was, for some reason that we shall never know, profoundly pessimistic", says Margaret Lane; and again, it seems to me that Maslow can answer the implied question. Maslow rejected the notion that human beings are driven by purely biological or sexual—or even personal—drives. Of course, these drives are among the basic motivations of all human beings. If you are born in a poor country where you suffer permanent malnutrition, the craving for food will remain a basic preoccupation—until it is satisfied. This is, of course, a simple "deficiency need". If such a child were asked to write a school essay, it would almost certainly be about food. And—to extend the speculation—if an intelligent adolescent in such a situation took it into his head to write novels, their ultimate "value" would be food. The hero would live happily ever after in a land where sausage rolls grow on trees and the rivers flow with double cream. But readers who had never known hunger would find it curiously pointless; and they would be right. Our novelist himself would change his point of view if the book brought him enough money to get used to eating in good restaurants.

There is obviously a level at which the desire for sex and love, for security—a roof over one's head—or for the respect and admiration of one's neighbours, can all be deficiency needs that motivate a human being to the exclusion of everything else. But on the whole, we are inclined to agree that such deficiency needs should *not* play a central role in a work of art—for example, a novel. The artist should attempt to *transcend* the need and move towards some wider horizon. *Romeo and Juliet* and the latest trashy romantic novel are "about" the same deficiency need; but Shakespeare's play is about so much more. According to Maslow, the basic human desire is not merely to satisfy needs, but to transcend them, to move beyond the personal towards the impersonal. The craving for beauty, harmony, goodness, knowledge, is just as "basic" as the need for food or sex; but it cannot operate freely until the need for food or sex has ceased to be a deficiency need.

Towards the end of his life, Maslow had to acknowledge sadly that his picture of a "hierarchy of needs" was not as universal as he had at first assumed. Some people satisfy the need for security, sex and self-esteem, and then stop short. There seems to be no evidence whatever of a need for beauty, harmony, knowledge. Conversely, in other people, the need for beauty, harmony and knowledge is so powerful that it can override the need for sex or security, or even food. He never had time to explore these inconsistencies. But one might have thought that they are not too difficult to understand. Surely dominance fits into the picture somewhere? I do not know whether the kind of people who "stop short" are non-dominant. But I *am* reasonably certain that the kind of person who grinds on, refusing to be deflected by deficiency needs—even trampling them underfoot—is highly dominant. In short, when you combine "self-actualization" with a high degree of dominance, you have a dangerously explosive mixture. Such a person is violently impatient of his "deficiency needs" and human frailties. In the Middle Ages, he might have become a monk and gone in for self-flagellation. In the nineteenth century, with no obvious role to play in a materialistic civilization, he became an "outsider", a misfit who detested society and probably detested himself. Most of the great tragic artists of the nineteenth century, from Coleridge and Schiller to Nietzsche and Rimbaud, were dominant and frustrated self-actualizers. For Emily Brontë the problem was further complicated by the fact that she possessed a female body.

But in speaking of Emily Brontë, there is another important factor to take into account. The year 1740 was a turning point in the history of civilization; it was in that year that the first volume of Samuel Richardson's *Pamela* appeared. There *had* been novels before *Pamela*, including *Don Quixote* and *Robinson Crusoe*; but they were mainly about *events*, about "things happening". In *Pamela*, nearly everything that happens takes place *inside* the heroine. The plot is slight: a rich landowner tries to seduce a virtuous servant girl and ends by marrying her. But Richardson's contemporaries discovered that they could be absorbed by Pamela's thoughts and feelings in a way they had never been absorbed by the adventures of Moll Flanders or Gil Blas. In short, they could "identify". It was a kind of do-it-yourself play, in which the reader became the chief actor.

I would contend that the change that took place as a result of *Pamela* was wider and deeper than historians have realized. European man—and woman—learnt the use of imagination. They learned how to forget their own lives, to enter an imaginary world and stay there for hours.

To grasp the magnitude of the change, we have to imagine that contemporary scientists stumble upon some new variety of plant that can grow under any conditions, and that can provide unlimited quantities of highly nutritious food to the world's starving millions. This is a precise parallel; for before Richardson, imaginative people had to make do with gossip, sermons, broadsheets about crime, and an occasional visit to the theatre. (This explains the central role of the preacher in the age of Dr Johnson; for millions of people, the Sunday morning sermon was their only "escape" from material reality.) The novel provided easy, cheap and nutritious food for the imagination. You could commit adultery with Rousseau, die of unrequited passion with young Werther, explore Hell with "Monk" Lewis, visit the past in Scott's time machine. . . .

If Emily Brontë had been born in 1718 instead of 1818, the outward circumstances of her life might have been much the same —the lot of the country parson remained fairly constant over the centuries. But she would probably have remained as emotionally undeveloped as Richardson's Pamela. As it was, she absorbed Scott, Byron, Wordsworth, Southey, and probably Rousseau, Mrs Radcliffe, Maria Edgeworth, Jane Porter and Charles Maturin. From *Wuthering Heights*, it is clear that her imagination was drawn to ghosts, goblins and horrors. (The editor of the present volume was kind enough to send me a list of references to the supernatural in *Wuthering Heights*; it ran to sixteen typed pages, with an average of a dozen references per page.) By the 1820s, there were hundreds of Gothic romances—from Walpole's *Castle of Otranto* to Maturin's *Melmoth the Wanderer*—that would have been easily available, even to the daughter of a Yorkshire parson.

À propos this taste in horrors, I am indebted to Mr Patric Dickinson for pointing out to me the following quotation from Baudelaire: "As for the ardour with which Poe often treats horrifying material, I have observed in a number of men that this was often the result of a large fund of unused vital energy, sometimes the result of an unyielding chastity and of vital feelings kept repressed." In short, of frustrated vitality and sexual frustration. I have argued the view at some length in *The Strength to Dream* (1962), citing "Monk" Lewis, Hoffmann, Poe, Gogol, Le Fanu, M. R. James and others. This seems to me to explain Emily Brontë's Poe-like absorption in death and corruption. If Maslow is correct about dominant women, then Emily's interest in Byronic males was not purely emotional and romantic; she herself probably recognized a strong physical component—and was shocked by it. (Half a century later, we can recognize this same almost demonic chastity in Nietzsche.) Is this not the explanation of the curiously chaste relations between Cathy and Heathcliff? Unlike most young lovers, they do not kiss and hold hands. In actuality, a couple like Cathy and Heathcliff *would* have become lovers—even in 1830. Emily Brontë does not even hint at such a thing; one feels she would have rejected the idea with disgust. The closest they come to normal sexual contact is when Heathcliff holds her in his arms as she lies dying in bed. The novel is permeated with sexual passion. It crackles in the air like electricity. Yet the thunderstorm never breaks. Emily cannot even imagine a sexual relation between Heathcliff and Isabella without a shudder of disgust; it has to be transformed into bitterness and sadism.

There seems to be one curiously paradoxical element in Emily's character: her capacity for contentment. Ellen Nussey commented on her buoyancy and happiness as a child; and even in the last years, when she was dying, she often seemed to be the most contented member of the family. Margaret Lane sees the answer in her "mysticism"; but I am inclined to feel that is putting the cart before the horse. All self-actualizers have what Maslow calls "peak experiences", moments of deep contentment, a feeling of being undeservedly lucky. On a quiet evening, the frustrations suddenly die down; the soul becomes still, as if a wind has dropped; and then an enormous peace seems to spread upwards, bringing a deep inner certainty that all is well. I doubt whether it brings us any closer to the nature of such experiences to call them "mystical". On the contrary, it makes them sound unearthly, when in fact they are no more abnormal than a sexual orgasm or the pleasure of drinking when you are thirsty. In short, they are a perfectly natural part of the self-actualization process. Emily writes:

'But first a hush of peace, a soundless calm descends;
The struggle of distress and fierce impatience ends;
Mute music soothes my breast—unuttered harmony
That I could never dream till earth was lost to me.'

This certainly *sounds* like "mysticism", particularly when she goes on: "Then dawns the Invisible, the unseen its truth reveals...." And in the next stanza she writes:

'Oh dreadful is the check—intense the agony
When the ear begins to hear and the eye begins to see;
When the pulse begins to throb, the brain to think again,
The soul to feel the flesh and the flesh to feel the chain!'
(Hatfield, 190)

At this point, if there was space, I could insert a lengthy comparison with T. E. Lawrence: with his hatred of his own body, his dislike of the "thought riddled nature", his feeling that his personality was his "gaoler", his admiration of the Arabs with their mystical love of freedom and longing for the abstract. Yet I doubt whether any reader of *Seven Pillars of Wisdom* would describe Lawrence as a mystic. Like Emily Brontë, he was a highly frustrated self-actualizer, who never succeeded in clearing away the obstacles that lay between himself and self-expression. Recent biographical researches have revealed that Lawrence was a masochist who was morbidly ashamed of his craving to be flogged by vigorous young men. This guilt presented the greatest obstacle to self-realization. But as far as we know, Emily Brontë had no perverse desires. The sadism in *Wuthering Heights* is emotional, not physical, an inverted expression of the masochism that springs from self-disgust. Which suggests that if Emily had ever met her Heathcliff, the relationship would have been healthily sensual, and the ghosts and goblins would have ceased to haunt her imagination. (In fact, I suspect she would have found a real-life Heathcliff intolerable, although she might have been head over heels in love for a few weeks; she was too self-disciplined to approve of a man who was a slave to his emotions. I am inclined to believe that her ideal would have been closer to George Henry Lewes, the man George Eliot settled down with: intelligent, kindly, and capable of making her feel like a normal human being.)

In *The Outsider* (1956), I commented in a footnote on the relative scarcity of female "Outsiders", particularly in fiction. Until the editor of this volume provoked me into re-reading *Wuthering Heights*, it had never struck me that Emily Brontë is an almost archetypal female outsider, and that Catherine Earnshaw represents the same thing in fiction. Catherine is not intended as an autobiographical self-portrait—or if she was, Emily's indirect method of narration made it impossible for her to realize her intention. This is a pity. In Emily Brontë, I see the fundamental drama of the dominant self-actualizer, placed in an unsympathetic environment, wracked by frustration, inclined to wonder if the fate that placed her in the world is entirely malevolent—or at least, possessed of a sardonic sense of humour. She fought with astonishing courage, and never realized how close she came to winning her battle—for I believe that if she had held out for another year or so, the tide would have turned in her favour.

Yet I have to admit that my own final judgement on *Wuthering Heights* is that it is not a great novel. Perhaps my critical faculties are being warped by my distaste for Heathcliff; but it seems to me that *Wuthering Heights* should be classified with *Le Grand Meaulnes*, as a piece of brilliant juvenilia. Curiously haunting, perhaps, but only a rough sketch for the masterpiece that should have followed. I suspect that it is so often taken for a great novel because it makes one feel clearly that Emily Brontë could have *been* a great novelist—her powers are so obviously extraordinary. But even this could be an illusion. Great novelists—like Scott, Balzac, Dickens—are interested in people, and they have a certain attitude of indulgence towards people. Emily Brontë, like Nietzsche, found the majority of people "all too human". Like Nietzsche, she believed that lack of pity is a virtue. And she may not have been entirely wrong. The only trouble is that lack of pity ceases to be a useful virtue when it is directed against oneself. Particularly if it kills you off at the age of thirty.

Contributors

T. E. APTER is a graduate of Edinburgh University and Newnham College, Cambridge. She is the author of various articles on music and literary criticism, and has contributed to such journals as *Tempo, Musical Opinion, Forum for Modern Language Studies,* and *The Human World.* Her first novel, *Silken Lines and Silver Hooks,* was published by Heinemann (1976), and a second novel, *Adonis's Garden,* is to be published in 1977. She is currently engaged in a study of Thomas Mann.

F. T. GOODRIDGE is a Senior Lecturer in English at the University of Lancaster. He translated *Piers Plowman* for Penguin (1959; revised 1966), is the author of a study of *Wuthering Heights* in Arnold's *Studies in English Literature* series, and has written articles on educational and literary topics for various journals and reviews, as well as publishing poetry from time to time.

ROBIN GROVE is a Senior Lecturer in English at the University of Melbourne. First trained as a musician, he was awarded the A.B.C. Orchestral Composition Prize in 1957 before entering Melbourne University to study literature and philosophy. Since 1963 he has been a frequent contributor to *The Critical Review* and other periodicals on subjects as diverse as Greek drama, Romantic poetry, opera and ballet. His work in theatre and music continues, and he is a Director of the State company, Ballet Victoria. A monograph on 'The Rape of the Lock, 1712–1736' will be published next year in *Pope: Four Monographs* (Vision Critical Studies).

BARBARA HARDY is Chairman of the Department of English at Birkbeck College, University of London, and present occupant of its Chair of Literature. She is the author of *The Novels of George Eliot, The Moral Art of Dickens, The Exposure of Luxury: Radical Themes in Thackeray, Tellers and Listeners: The Narrative Imagination, A Reading of Jane Austen,* and the editor of *Middlemarch: Critical Approaches to the Novel, Critical Essays on George Eliot* and *The Advantage of Lyric: Essays on Feeling in Poetry.*

239

ROSALIND MILES is a graduate of St Hilda's, Oxford, and of the Shakespeare Institute of Birmingham University, and lectures in English at Lanchester Polytechnic, Coventry. Her publications include an eighteenth-century acting edition of *Measure for Measure* (1971), *The Fiction of Sex* (1974), and *The Problem of 'Measure for Measure'* (1976), as well as various articles and reviews.

KEITH SAGAR is Senior Staff Tutor in Literature in the Extra-Mural Department of Manchester University. He is the author of *The Art of D. H. Lawrence* (1966), *Hamlet* (1969) and *The Art of Ted Hughes* (1975), and has contributed widely to various critical journals. He is currently writing a new critical study and a new biography of Lawrence, and editing volume 7 of Lawrence's letters.

ANNE SMITH edits the Vision Critical Studies series. She is a graduate of Edinburgh University, and the author of several articles on Dickens, a number of reviews, and a play, *A Vision of Angels* (performed and published, Edinburgh, 1974). She is currently writing a book on social realism.

PHILIPPA TRISTRAM is a graduate of Lady Margaret Hall, Oxford, and lectures in medieval English literature at the University of York. She is the author of various articles, and has published studies of *A Passage to India* and *Lord of the Flies* in Macmillan's series of *Critical Commentaries*. Her book *Figures of Life and Death in Medieval Literature* is to be published by Elek this year.

COLIN WILSON is the author of more than forty books, including fourteen novels. His most recent publication is *The Craft of the Novel* (Gollancz, 1975).

Index

241

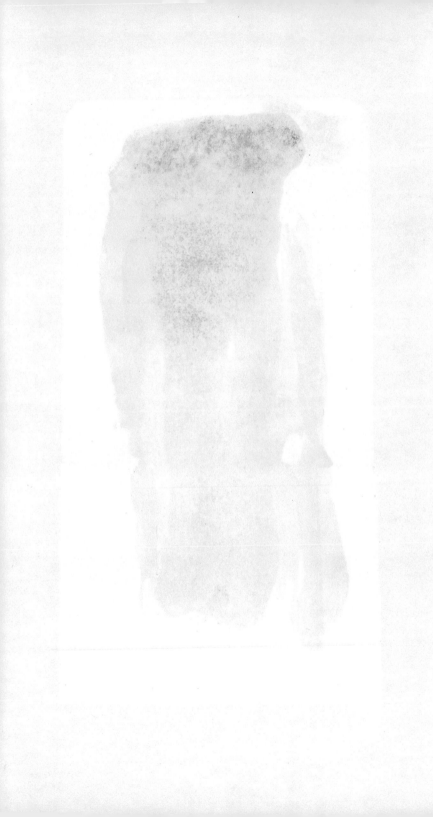